ROBERT GRAVES

Goodbye to All That

PENGUIN BOOKS

PENGUIN BOOKS

Published by the Penguin Group
Penguin Books Ltd, 27 Wrights Lane, London W8 5TZ, England
Penguin Books USA Inc., 375 Hudson Street, New York, New York 10014, USA
Penguin Books Australia Ltd, Ringwood, Victoria, Australia
Penguin Books Canada Ltd, 10 Alcorn Avenue, Toronto, Ontario, Canada M4V 3B2
Penguin Books (NZ) Ltd, 182–190 Wairau Road, Auckland 10, New Zealand

Penguin Books Ltd, Registered Offices: Harmondsworth, Middlesex, England

First published by Jonathan Cape 1929
Revised edition, with new Prologue and Epilogue, published by Cassel 1957
Published in Penguin Books 1960
33 35 37 39 40 38 36 34

Printed in England by Clays Ltd, St Ives plc
Set in Monotype Bembo

GOODBYE TO ALL THAT

Perceval Graves, the Irish writer, a[...] [...] from school to the First World War, w[...] [...] a captain in the Royal Welch Fusiliers. His principal calling was poetry, and his *Selected Poems* have also been published in the Penguin Twentieth-Century Classics series. Apart from a year as Professor of English Literature at Cairo University in 1926 he earned his living by writing, mostly historical novels which include: *I, Claudius*; *Claudius the God*; *Count Belisarius*; *Wife to Mr Milton*; *Sergeant Lamb of the Ninth*; *Proceed, Sergeant Lamb*; *The Golden Fleece*; *They Hanged My Saintly Billy*; and *The Isles of Unwisdom*. He wrote his autobiography, *Goodbye to All That*, in 1929, and it rapidly established itself as a modern classic. *The Times Literary Supplement* acclaimed it as 'one of the most candid self-portraits of a poet, warts and all, ever painted', as well as being of exceptional value as a war document. His two most discussed non-fiction books are *The White Goddess*, which presents a new view of the poetic impulse, and *The Nazarine Gospel Restored* (with Joshua Podro), a re-examination of primitive Christianity. He translated Apuleius, Lucan, and Suetonius for the Penguin Classics, and compiled the first modern dictionary of Greek Mythology, *The Greek Myths*. His translation of *The Rubáiyát of Omar Khayyám* (with Omar Ali-Shah) is also published in Penguin. He was elected Professor of Poetry at Oxford in 1961, and made an Honorary Fellow of St John's College, Oxford, in 1971.

Robert Graves died on 7 December 1985 in Majorca, his home since 1929. On his death *The Times* wrote of him, 'He will be remembered for his achievements as a prose stylist, historical novelist and memorist, but above all as the great paradigm of the dedicated poet, "the greatest love poet in English since Donne".'

LIST OF ILLUSTRATIONS

PROLOGUE

I partly wrote, partly dictated, this book twenty-eight years ago during a complicated domestic crisis, and with very little time for revision. It was my bitter leave-taking of England where I had recently broken a good many conventions; quarrelled with, or been disowned by, most of my friends; been grilled by the police on a suspicion of attempted murder; and ceased to care what anyone thought of me.

Reading Goodbye to All That *over again, for the first time since 1929, I wonder how my publishers escaped a libel action.*

Domestic crises are always expensive, but the book sold well enough in England and the United States, despite the Depression which had just set in, to pay my debts and leave me free to live and write in Majorca without immediate anxiety for the future. The title became a catch-word, and my sole contribution to Bartlett's Dictionary of Familiar Quotations.

A good many changes have been made in the text – omission of many dull or foolish patches; restoration of a few suppressed anecdotes; replacement of the T. E. Lawrence chapter by a longer one written five years later; correction of factual misstatements; and a general editing of my excusably ragged prose. Some proper names have been restored where their original disguise is no longer necessary.

If any passage still gives offence after all those years, I hope to be forgiven.

Deyá, Majorca, Spain, 1957   R.G.

Goodbye to All That

I

As a proof of my readiness to accept autobiographical convention, let me at once record my two earliest memories. The first is being loyally held up at a window to watch a procession of decorated carriages and waggons for Queen Victoria's Diamond Jubilee in 1897 (this was at Wimbledon, where I had been born on July 24th, 1895). The second is gazing upwards with a sort of despondent terror at a cupboard in the nursery, which stood accidentally open, filled to the ceiling with octavo volumes of Shakespeare. My father had organized a Shakespeare reading circle. I did not know until long afterwards that this was the Shakespeare cupboard but, apparently, I already had a strong instinct against drawing-room activities. And when distinguished visitors came to the house, such as Sir Sidney Lee with his Shakespearean scholarship, or Lord Ashbourne, not yet a peer, with his loud talk of 'Ireland for the Irish', and his saffron kilt, or Mr Eustace Miles the English real-tennis champion and vegetarian with his samples of exotic nuts, I knew all about them in my way.

Nor had I any illusions about Algernon Charles Swinburne, who often used to stop my perambulator when he met it on Nurses' Walk, at the edge of Wimbledon Common, and pat me on the head and kiss me: he was an inveterate pram-stopper and patter and kisser. Nurses' Walk lay between 'The Pines', Putney (where he lived with Watts-Dunton), and the Rose and Crown public house, where he went for his daily pint of beer; Watts-Dunton allowed him twopence for it and no more. I did not know that Swinburne was a poet, but I knew that he was a public menace. Swinburne, by the way, when a very young man, had gone to Walter Savage Landor, then a very old man, and been given the poet's blessing he asked for; and Landor when a child had been patted on the head by Dr Samuel Johnson;

and Johnson when a child had been taken to London to be touched by Queen Anne for scrofula, the King's evil; and Queen Anne when a child. . . .

But I mentioned the Shakespeare reading circle. It went on for years, and when I was sixteen, curiosity finally sent me to one of the meetings. I remember the vivacity with which my utterly unshrewish mother read the part of Katherine in *The Taming of the Shrew* to my amiable father's Petruchio. Mr and Mrs Maurice Hill were two of the most popular members of the circle. This meeting took place some years before they became Mr Justice Hill and Lady Hill, and some years, too, before I looked into *The Shrew*. I remember the lemonade glasses, the cucumber sandwiches, the *petits fours*, the drawing-room knick-knacks, the chrysanthemums in bowls, and the semicircle of easy chairs around the fire. The gentle voice of Maurice Hill as Hortensio admonished my father: 'Thou go thy ways, thou hast tamed a cursed shrew.' I myself as Lucio ended the performance with: ''Tis a wonder by your leave she will be tamed so.' I must go one day to hear him speak his lines as Judge of the Divorce Courts; his admonitions have become famous.

After 'earliest memories', I should perhaps give a passport description of myself and let the items enlarge themselves. Date of birth. . . . Place of birth. . . . I have already given those. Profession. . . . In my passport I am down as 'University Professor'. That was a convenience for 1926, when I first took out a passport. I thought of putting 'Writer', but passport officials often have complicated reactions to the word. 'University professor' wins a simple reaction: dull respect. No questions asked. So also with 'army captain (pensioned list)'.

My height is given as six feet two inches, my eyes as grey, and my hair as black. To 'black' should be added 'thick and curly'. I am untruthfully described as having no special peculiarity. For a start, there is my big, once aquiline nose, which I broke at Charterhouse while foolishly playing rugger with soccer players. (I broke another player's nose myself in the same game.) That unsteadied it, and boxing sent it askew. Finally, it was operated on by an unskilful army surgeon, and no longer serves as a vertical line of demarcation between the left and right sides of my face, which are naturally unassorted – my eyes, eyebrows, and ears being all set noticeably crooked, and my cheekbones, which are rather high, being on different levels. My mouth is what is known as 'full', and my smile is tight-lipped: when I was thirteen I broke two front teeth and became sensitive about showing them. My hands and feet are large. I weigh about twelve stone four. My best comic turn is a double-jointed pelvis; I can sit on a table and tap like the Fox sisters with it. One shoulder is distinctly lower than the other, because of a lung wound. I do not carry a watch because I always magnetize the main-spring; during the war when an order went out that officers should carry watches and synchronize them daily, I had to buy two new ones every month. Medically, I am a good life.

My passport gives my nationality as 'British subject'. Here I might parody Marcus Aurelius, who begins his *Golden Book* with the various ancestors and relatives to whom he owes the virtues of a worthy Roman Emperor: explaining why I am not a Roman Emperor or even, except on occasions, an English gentleman. My mother's father's family, the von Rankes, were Saxon country pastors, not anciently noble. Leopold von Ranke, the first modern historian, my great-uncle, introduced the 'von'. I owe something to him. He wrote, to the scandal of his contemporaries: 'I am a historian before I am a Christian; my object is simply to find out how the things actually occurred,' and when discussing Michelet the French historian: 'He wrote history in a style in which the truth could not be told.' That Thomas Carlyle decried him as 'Dry-as-Dust' is no discredit. To Heinrich von Ranke, my grandfather, I owe my clumsy largeness, my endurance, energy, seriousness, and my thick hair. He was rebellious and even atheistic in his youth. As a medical student at a Prussian university he took part in the political disturbances of 1848, when students demonstrated in favour of Karl Marx at the time of his trial for high treason. Like Marx, they had to leave the country. My grandfather came to London, and finished his medical course there. In 1854, he went to the Crimea with the British Army as a regimental surgeon. All I know about this is a chance remark that he made to me when I was a child: 'It is not always the big bodies which are the strongest. At Sevastopol in the trenches I saw the great British Guards crack up and die by the score, while the little sappers took no harm.' Still, his big body carried him very well.

He married, in London, my grandmother, a tiny, saintly, frightened Schleswig-Dane, daughter of Tiarks, the Greenwich astronomer. Before her father took to astronomy the Tiarks family had, it seems, followed the Danish country system – not at all a bad one – of alternate professions for father and son. The odd generations were tinsmiths, and the even generations were pastors. My gentler characteristics trace back to my grandmother. She had ten children; the eldest of these, my mother, was born in London. My grandfather's atheism and radicalism sobered down. He eventually returned to Germany, where he became a well-known children's doctor at Munich, and about the first in Europe to insist on clean milk for his child patients. Finding that he could not get clean milk to the hospitals by ordinary means, he started a model dairy-farm himself. His agnosticism grieved my devoutly Lutheran grandmother; she never ceased to pray for him, but concentrated more particularly on saving the souls of her children.

My grandfather did not die entirely unregenerate; his last words were: 'The God of my fathers, to Him at least I hold.' I do not know what he meant by that, but it was a statement consistent with his angry patriarchal moods, with his acceptance of a prominent place in Bavarian society as Herr Geheimrat Ritter von Ranke, and with his loyalty to the Kaiser, with whom once or twice he went deer-shooting. It meant, practically, that he considered himself a good Liberal in religion as in politics, and that my grandmother need not have worried. I admire my German relatives; they have high principles, are easy, generous, and serious. The men have fought duels not for cheap personal honour, but in the public interest – called out, for example, because they have protested against the scandalous behaviour of some superior officer or official. One of them lost seniority in the German consular service, because he refused to use the consulate in London as a clearing-house for secret service reports. They are not heavy drinkers either. My grandfather, as a student at the regular university 'drunks', had a habit of pouring superfluous beer into his eighteen-fortyish riding-boots, when nobody was watching. He brought up his children to speak English at home, and always looked to England as the centre of culture and progress. The women were noble and patient, and used to keep their eyes on the ground when out walking.

At the age of eighteen, my mother went to England as companion to Miss Britain, a lonely old woman who had befriended my grandmother as an orphan, and waited hand and foot on her for seventeen years. When she finally died, under the senile impression that my mother, her sole heiress, would benefit hardly at all from the will, it turned out that she had been worth £100,000. Characteristically, my mother divided the inheritance among her four younger sisters, keeping only a fifth share. She was determined to go to India, after a short training as a medical missionary. This ambition was presently baulked by her meeting my father, a widower with five children; it became plain to her that she could do as good work on the home-mission field.

The Graves family have a pedigree that goes back to a French knight who landed with Henry VII at Milford Haven in 1485. Colonel Graves the Roundhead is claimed as the founder of the Irish branch of the family. He was once wounded and left for dead in the market-place at Thame, afterwards had charge of King Charles I's person at Carisbrooke Castle, and later turned Royalist. Limerick was the centre of this branch. The occasional soldiers and doctors in it were mainly collaterals; the direct male line had a sequence of rectors, deans, and bishops, apart from my great-grandfather John Crosbie Graves, who was Chief Police Magistrate of Dublin. The Limerick Graves's have no 'hands' or mechanical sense; but a wide reputation as conversationalists. In those of my relatives who have the family characteristics most strongly marked, unnecessary talk is a nervous disorder. Not bad talk as talk goes: usually informative, often witty, but it goes on and on and on. The von Ranke's seem to have little mechanical aptitude either. I find it most inconvenient to be born into the age of the internal-combustion engine and the electric dynamo and to have no sympathy with them: a bicycle, a Primus stove, and an army rifle mark the bounds of my mechanical capacity.

My paternal grandfather, the Protestant Bishop of Limerick, had eight children. He was a remarkable mathematician – he first formulated some theory or other of spherical conics – and also the leading authority on the Irish Brehon Laws and Ogham script, but by reputation, far from generous. He and O'Connell, the Catholic Bishop, lived on the very best of terms. They cracked Latin jokes at each other, discussed fine points of scholarship, and were unclerical enough not to take their religious differences too seriously.

While in Limerick as a soldier of the garrison, some nineteen years after my grandfather's death, I heard stories about him from the townsfolk. Bishop O'Connell had once rallied him on the size of his family, and my grandfather had retorted warmly with the text about the blessedness of the man who has his quiver full of arrows; to which O'Connell answered briefly: 'The ancient Jewish quiver only held six.' My grandfather's wake, they said, was the longest ever seen in the town of Limerick: it stretched from the Cathedral right down O'Connell Street and over Sarfield Bridge, and I do not know how many miles Irish beyond. He had blessed me as a child, but I do not remember that.

Of my father's mother, a Cheyne from Aberdeen, I have been able to get no information at all beyond the fact that she was 'a very beautiful woman', and daughter of the Physician-general to the Forces of Ireland. I can only conclude that most of what she said or did passed unnoticed in the rivalry of family conversations. The Cheyne pedigree was flawless right back to Sir Reginald Cheyne, Lord Chamberlain of Scotland in 1267. In later times the Cheynes had been lawyers and physicians. But my father is at present engaged on his autobiography and, no doubt, will write at length about all this.

My father, then, met my mother some time in the early nineties. He had previously married one of the Irish Coopers, of Cooper's Hill, near Limerick. The Coopers were an even more Irish family than the Graves's. The story goes that when Cromwell came to Ireland and ravaged the country, Moira O'Brien, the last surviving member of the great clan O'Brien, who were the paramount chiefs of the country around Limerick, came to him one day with: 'General, you have killed my father and my uncles, my husband and my brothers. I am left as the sole heiress of these lands. Do you intend to confiscate them?' Cromwell is said to have been struck by her magnificent presence, and to have answered that this certainly had been his intention. But that she could keep her lands, or a part of them, on condition that she married one of his officers, Ensign Cooper. Jane Cooper, whom my father married, died of consumption.

The Graves family were thin-nosed and inclined to petulance, but never depraved, cruel, or hysterical. A persistent literary tradition: of Richard, a minor poet and a friend of Shenstone; and John Thomas, who was a mathematician and contributed to Sir William Rowan Hamilton's discovery of quaternions; and Richard, a divine and regius Professor of Greek; and James, an archaeologist; and Robert, who invented the disease called after him and was a friend of Turner's; and Robert, classicist, and theologian, and a friend of Wordsworth's; and Richard, another divine; and Robert, another divine; and various

Roberts, Jameses, Thomases, and Richards; and Clarissa, one of the toasts of Ireland, who married Leopold von Ranke (at Windermere church), and linked the Graves and von Ranke families a couple of generations before my father and mother married. (See the *British Museum Catalogue* for an eighteen- and nineteenth-century record of Graves' literary history.)

It was through this Clarissa-Leopold relationship that my father met my mother. My mother told him at once that she liked *Father O'Flynn*, the song for writing which my father will be chiefly remembered. He had put the words to a traditional jig tune *The Top of Cork Road*, which he remembered from his boyhood. Sir Charles Stanford supplied a few chords for the setting. My father sold the complete rights for one guinea. Boosey, the publisher, made thousands. Sir Charles Stanford, who drew a royalty as the composer, also collected a very large sum. Recently my father has been sent a few pounds from gramophone rights. He is not bitter about all this, but has more than once impressed upon me almost religiously never to sell for a sum down the complete rights of any work of mine whatsoever.

That my father is a poet has, at least, saved me from any false reverence for poets. I am even delighted when I meet people who know of him and not me. I sing some of his songs while washing up after meals, or shelling peas, or on similar occasions. He never once tried to teach me how to write, or showed any understanding of my serious poetry; being always more ready to ask advice about his own. Nor did he ever try to stop me writing. His light-hearted early work is the best. His *Invention of Wine*, for instance, which begins:

> *Ere Bacchus could talk*
> *Or dacently walk*
> *Down Olympus he jumped*
> *From the arms of his nurse,*
> *And though ten years in all*
> *Were consumed by the fall,*
> *He might have fallen farther*
> *And fared a dale worse . . .*

After marrying my mother and turning teetotaller, he is said to have lost something of his playfulness.

My father resisted the family temptation to take holy orders, never rising higher than lay-reader; and he broke the geographical connexion with Ireland, for which I cannot be too grateful to him. Though much harder on my relatives, and much more careful of associating with them than I am with strangers, I can admire my father and mother: my father for his simplicity and persistence, and my mother for her seriousness and strength. Both for their generosity. They never bullied me, and were grieved rather than angered by my default from formal religion. In physique and general characteristics my mother's side is, on the whole, stronger in me. But I have many habits of speech and movements peculiar to the Graves's, most of them eccentric. Such as finding it difficult to walk straight down a street; fidgeting with bits of bread at table; getting tired of sentences when half-way through and leaving them in the air; walking with the hands folded in a particular way behind the back; and being subject to sudden and most disconcerting spells of complete amnesia. These fits, so far as I can discover, serve no useful purpose, and tend to produce in the victim the same sort of dishonesty that afflicts deaf people who miss the thread of conversation – they hate to be left behind and rely on intuition and bluff to get them through. This disability is most marked in very cold weather. I do not now talk too much, except when I have been drinking, or when I meet someone who fought with me in France. The Graves's have good minds for such purposes as examinations, writing graceful Latin verse, filling in forms, and solving puzzles (when invited, as children, to parties where guessing games and brain-tests were played, we never failed to win). They have a good eye for ball games, and a graceful style. I inherited the eye, but not the style; my mother's family are entirely without style. I have an ugly but secure seat on a horse. There is a coldness in the Graves's which is anti-sentimental to the point of insolence, a necessary check to the goodness of heart from which my mother's family suffers. The Graves's, it is fair to generalize, though loyal to the British governing class to which they belong, and so to the Constitution, are individualists; the von Rankes regard their membership of the corresponding class in Germany as a sacred trust enabling them to do the more responsible work for the service of humanity. Recently, when a von Ranke entered a film studio, the family felt itself disgraced.

The most useful and, at the same time, most dangerous gift that I owe to my father's side of the family – probably more to the Cheynes than to the Graves's – is that I am always able, when dealing with officials, or getting privileges from public institutions which grudge them, to masquerade as a gentleman. Whatever I happen to be wearing; and because my clothes are not what gentlemen usually wear, and yet I do not seem to be an artist or effeminate, and my accent and gestures are irreproachable, I have been placed as the heir to a dukedom, whose perfect confidence in his rank would explain all such eccentricity. Thus I may seem, by a paradox, to be more of a gentleman even than one of my elder brothers, who spent a number of years as a consular official in the Near East. His wardrobe is almost too obviously a gentleman's, and he does not allow himself the pseudo-ducal privilege of having disreputable acquaintances, and saying on all occasions what he really means.

About this business of being a gentleman: I paid so heavily for the fourteen years of my gentleman's education that I feel entitled, now and then, to get some sort of return.

2

My mother married my father largely, it seems, to help him out with his five motherless children. Having any herself was a secondary consideration. Yet first she had a girl, then she had another girl, and it was very nice, of course, to have them, but slightly disappointing, because she belonged to the generation and tradition that made a son the really important event; then I came, a fine healthy child. She was forty at my birth; and my father forty-nine. Four years later she had another son, and four years later still another son. The desired preponderance of male over female had been established, and twice five made ten. I found the gap of two generations between my parents and me easier, in a way, to bridge than a single generation gap. Children seldom quarrel with their grand-parents, and I have been able to think of my mother and father as grand-parents. Also, a family of ten means a dilution of parental affection; the members tend to become indistinct. I have often been called: 'Philip, Richard, Charles, I mean Robert.'

My father being a very busy man, an inspector of schools for the Southwark district of London, we children saw practically nothing of him except during the holidays. Then he behaved very sweetly, and told us stories with the formal beginning, not 'once upon a time', but always: 'And so the old gardener blew his nose on a red pocket handkerchief. . . .' He occasionally played games with us, but for the most part, when not busy with educational work, was writing poems, or being president of literary or temperance societies. My mother, kept busy running the household and conscientiously carrying out her social obligations as my father's wife, did not see so much of us as she would have liked, except on Sundays or when we happened to be ill. We had a nurse, and one another, and found that companionship sufficient. My father's chief part in our education was to insist on our speaking grammatically, pronouncing words correctly, and using no slang. He left our religious instruction entirely to my mother, though he officiated at family prayers, which the servants were expected to attend, every morning before breakfast. Light punishments, such as being sent to bed early or being stood in a corner, were in the hands of my mother; the infliction of corporal punishment, never severe and given with a slipper, she reserved for my father. We learned to be strong moralists, and spent much of our time on self-examination and good resolutions. My sister Rosaleen put up a printed notice in her corner of the nursery – it might just as well have been put up by me: 'I must not say "bang bust" or "pig bucket", for it is rude.'

We were given very little pocket-money – a penny a week with a rise to twopence at the age of twelve or so – and encouraged to give part at least of any odd money that came to us from uncles or other visitors to Dr Barnardo's Homes, and to beggars. A blind beggar used to sit on the Wimbledon Hill pavement, reading the Bible aloud in Braille; he was not really blind, but could turn up his eyes and keep the pupils concealed for minutes at a time under drooping lids, which were artificially inflamed. We often gave to him. He died a rich man, and had been able to provide his son with a college education.

The first distinguished writer I remember meeting after Swinburne was P. G. Wodehouse, a friend of my brother Perceval. Wodehouse was then in his early twenties, on the staff of *The Globe*, and writing school-stories for *The Captain* magazine. He gave me a penny, advising me to get marshmallows with it. Though too shy to express my gratitude at the time, I have never since permitted myself to be critical about his work.

I had great religious fervour, which persisted until shortly after my confirmation at the age of sixteen, and remember the incredulity with which I first heard that there actually were people, people baptized like myself into the Church of England, who did not believe in Jesus's divinity. I had never met an unbeliever.

Though I have asked many of my acquaintances at what stage in their childhood or adolescence they became class-conscious none has ever given me a satisfactory answer. I remember how it happened to me. At the age of four and a half I caught scarlet fever; my younger brother had just been born, and I could not be nursed at home, so my parents sent me off to a public fever hospital. The ward contained twenty little proletarians, and only one bourgeois child besides myself. I did not notice particularly that the nurses and my fellow-patients had a different attitude towards me; I accepted the kindness and spoiling easily, being accustomed to it. But the respect and even reverence given to this other little boy, a clergyman's child, astonished me. 'Oh,' the nurses would cry after he had gone, 'oh, he did look a little gentleman in his pretty white pelisse when they took him away!' 'That young Matthew was a fair toff,' echoed the little proletarians. On my return from two months in hospital, my accent was deplored, and I learned that the boys in the ward had been very vulgar. I did not know what 'vulgar' meant; it had to be explained to me. About a year later I met Arthur, a boy of nine, who had been in the ward and taught me how to play cricket when we were convalescent together. He turned out to be a ragged errand-boy. In hospital, we had all worn the same institutional night-gowns, and I did not know that we came off such different shelves. But I suddenly realized with my first shudder of gentility that two sorts of Christians existed – ourselves, and the lower classes. The servants were trained to call us children, even when we were tiny, 'Master Robert', 'Miss Rosaleen', and 'Miss Clarissa', but I had not recognized these as titles of respect. I had thought of 'Master' and 'Miss' merely as vocative prefixes used for addressing other people's children; but now I found that the servants were the lower classes, and that we were 'ourselves'.

I accepted this class separation as naturally as I had accepted religious dogma, and did not finally discard it until nearly twenty years later. My parents were never of the aggressive, shoot-'em-down type, but Liberals or, more strictly, Liberal-Unionists. In religious theory, at least, they treated their employees as fellow-creatures; but social distinctions remained clearly defined. The hymn-book sanctioned these:

> He made them high or lowly,
> And ordered their estates . . .

I can well recall the tone of my mother's voice when she informed the maids that they could have what was left of the pudding, or scolded the cook for some carelessness. It had a forced hardness, made almost harsh by embarrassment. My mother, being *gemütlich* by nature, would, I believe, have loved to dispense with servants altogether. They seemed a foreign body in the house. I remember the servants' bedrooms. They were on the top landing, at the dullest side of the house, and by a convention of the times, the only rooms without carpets or linoleum. Those gaunt, unfriendly-looking beds and the hanging-cupboards with faded cotton curtains, instead of wardrobes with glass doors as in the other rooms. All this uncouthness made me think of the servants as somehow not quite human. Besides, the servants who came to us were distinctly below the average standard; only those with no particularly good references would apply for a situation in a family of ten. And because we had such a large house, and hardly a single person in the household kept his or her room tidy, they were constantly giving notice. Too much work, they said.

Our nurse made a bridge between the servants and ourselves. She gave us her own passport immediately on arrival: 'Emily Dykes is my name; England is my nation; Netheravon is my dwelling-place; and Christ is my salvation.' Though calling us Miss and Master, she used no menial tone. In a practical way Emily came to be more to us than our mother. I did not despise her until about the age of twelve – she was then nurse to my younger brothers – when I found that my education now exceeded hers, and that if I struggled with her I could trip her up and bruise her quite easily. Besides, she went to a Baptist chapel; I had learned by that time that the Baptists were, like the Wesleyans and Congregationalists, the social inferiors of the Church of England.

My mother taught me a horror of Roman Catholicism, which I retained for a very long time. In fact, I discarded Protestantism not because I had outgrown its ethics, but in horror of its Catholic element. My religious training developed in me a great capacity for fear – I was perpetually tortured by the fear of hell – a superstitious conscience, and a sexual embarrassment from which I have found it very difficult to free myself.

The last thing that Protestants lose when they cease to believe is a vision of Christ as the perfect man. That persisted with me, sentimentally, for years. At the age of eighteen I wrote a poem called 'In the Wilderness', about Christ greeting the scapegoat as it roamed the desert – which, of course, would have been impossible since the scapegoat always got pushed over a cliff by its Levite attendants. 'In the Wilderness' has since appeared in at least seventy anthologies. Strangers are always writing to me to say how much strength it has given them, and would I, etc.?

3

I WENT to several preparatory schools, beginning at the age of six. The very first was a dame's school at Wimbledon, but my father, as an educational expert, would not let me stay there long. He found me crying one day at the difficulty of the twenty-three-times table, and disapproved of a Question and Answer history book that we used, which began:

> Question: Why were the Britons so called?
> Answer: Because they painted themselves blue.

Also, they made me do mental arithmetic to a metronome; I once wetted myself with nervousness under this torture. So my father sent me to King's College School, Wimbledon. I was just seven years old, the youngest boy there, and they went up to nineteen. My father took me away after a couple of terms because he heard me using naughty words, and because I did not understand the lessons. I had started Latin, but nobody explained what 'Latin' meant; its declensions and conjugations were pure incantations to me. For that matter, so were the strings of naughty words. And I felt oppressed by the huge hall, the enormous boys, the frightening rowdiness of the corridors, and compulsory Rugby football of which nobody told me the rules. From there I went to Rokeby, a pre-paratory school of the ordinary type, also at Wimbledon, where I stayed for about three years. Here I began playing games seriously, grew quarrelsome, boastful, and domineering, won prizes, and collected things. The main difference between myself and the other boys was that I collected coins instead of stamps. The value of coins seemed less fictitious to me. The headmaster caned me only once: for forgetting to bring my gym-shoes to school, and then gave me no more than two strokes on the hand. Yet even now the memory makes me hot with resentment. My serious training as a gentleman began here.

I seem to have left out one school – Penrallt, right away in the hills behind Llanbedr. I had never been away from home before. I went there just for a term, for my health. Here I had my first beating. The headmaster, a parson, caned me on the bottom because I learned the wrong collect one Sunday by mistake. I had never before come upon forcible training in religion. At my dame's school we learned collects too, but were not punished for mistakes; we competed for prizes – ornamental texts to take home and hang over our beds. A boy at Penrallt called Ronny was the greatest hero I had ever met. He had a house at the top of a pine-tree which nobody else could climb, and a huge knife, made from the tip of a scythe which he had stolen; and he killed pigeons with a catapult, cooked them, and ate them in the tree-house. Ronny treated me very kindly; he went into the Navy afterwards, deserted on his first voyage, and, we were told, was never heard of again. He used to steal rides on cows and horses which he found in the fields. At Penrallt I found a book that had the ballads of 'Chevy Chase' and 'Sir Andrew Barton' in it; these were the first two real poems I remember reading. I saw how good they were. But, on the other hand, there was an open-air swimming bath where all the boys bathed naked, and I was overcome by horror at the sight. One boy of nineteen had red hair, real bad, Irish, red hair all over his body. I did not know that hair grew on bodies. Also, the headmaster had a little daughter with a little girl friend, and I sweated with terror whenever I met them; because, having no brothers, they once tried to find out about male anatomy from me by exploring down my shirt-neck when we were digging up pig-nuts in the garden.

Another frightening experience from this part of my life. I once had to wait in the school cloak-room for my sisters, who went to the Wimbledon High School. We were going on to be photographed together. I waited for perhaps a quarter of an hour in a corner of the cloak-room. I must have been ten years old, and hundreds and hundreds of girls went to and fro; they all looked at me and giggled, and whispered to one another. I knew they hated me because I was a boy sitting in the cloak-room of a girls' school; and my sisters, when they arrived, looked ashamed of me and seemed quite different from the sisters I knew at home. I had blundered into a secret world, and for months and even years afterwards my worst nightmares were of this girls' school, which was always filled with coloured toy balloons. 'Very Freudian', as one says now. My normal impulses were set back for years by these two experiences. In 1912, we spent our Christmas holidays in Brussels. An Irish girl staying at the same pension made love to me in a way that, I see now, was really very sweet. It frightened me so much, I could have killed her.

In English preparatory and public schools romance is necessarily homosexual. The opposite sex is despised and treated as something obscene. Many boys never recover from this perversion. For every one born homosexual, at least ten permanent pseudo-homosexuals are made by the public school system: nine of these ten as honourably chaste and sentimental as I was.

I left the day-school at Wimbledon because my father decided that the standard of work was not high enough to get me a scholarship at a public school. He sent me to another preparatory school at Rugby, where the headmaster's wife happened to be a sister of an old literary friend of his. I did not like the place. There was a secret about the headmaster which some of the elder boys shared – a somehow sinister secret. Nobody ever let me into it, but he came weeping into the class-room one day, beating his head with his fists, and groaning: 'Would to God I hadn't done it! Would to God I hadn't done it!' My father took me away suddenly, a week later. The headmaster, having been given twenty-four hours to leave the country, was succeeded by the second master – a good man, who had taught me how to write English by eliminating all phrases that could be done without, and using verbs and nouns instead of adjectives and adverbs wherever possible. And when to start new paragraphs, and the difference between 'O' and 'Oh'. Mr Lush was a very heavy man, who used to stand at his desk and lean on his thumbs until they bent at right angles. A fortnight after taking over the school, he fell out of a train on his head, and that was the end of him; but the school seems to be still in being. I am occasionally asked to subscribe to Old Boys' funds for memorial windows and miniature rifle ranges and so on.

I first learned rugger here. What surprised me most at this school was when a boy of about twelve, whose father and mother were in India, heard by cable that they had both suddenly died of cholera. We all watched him sympathetically for weeks after, expecting him to die of grief, or turn black in the face, or do something to match the occasion. Yet he seemed entirely unmoved, and because nobody dared discuss the tragedy with him he seemed oblivious of it – playing about and ragging just as he had done before. We found that rather monstrous. But he had not seen his parents for two years; and preparatory schoolboys live in a world completely dissociated from home life. They have a different vocabulary, a different moral system, even different voices. On their return to school from the holidays the change-over from home-self to school-self is almost instantaneous, whereas the reverse process takes a fortnight at least. A preparatory schoolboy, when caught off his guard, will call his mother 'Please, matron,' and always addresses any male relative or friend of the family as 'Sir', like a master. I used to do it. School life becomes the reality, and home life the illusion. In England, parents of the governing classes virtually lose all intimate touch with their children from about the age of eight, and any attempts on their parts to insinuate home feeling into school life are resented.

Next, I went to Copthorne, a typically good school in Sussex. The headmaster had been chary of admitting me at my age, particularly since I came from a school with such a bad recent history. However, family literary connexions did the trick, and the headmaster saw that I could win a scholarship if he took trouble over me. The depressed state I had been in ended the moment I arrived. My younger brother Charles followed me to this school, being taken away from the day-school at Wimbledon; and, later, my youngest brother John went there straight from home. How good and typical the school was can be seen in the case of John, a typical, good, normal person who, as I say, went straight there from home. He spent five or six years at Copthorne – played in the elevens – got the top scholarship at a public school, became head-boy with athletic distinctions, won a scholarship at Oxford and further athletic distinctions – and a good degree – and then, what did he do? Because he was such a typically good, normal person he naturally went back as a master to his old, typically good preparatory school, and now that he has been there some years and needs a change, he is applying for a mastership at his old public school. If he gets it, and becomes a housemaster after a few years, he will at last, I suppose,

24

become a headmaster and eventually take the next step as head of his old college at Oxford. That is the sort of typically good preparatory school it was.

There I learned to keep a straight bat at cricket, and to have a high moral sense; and mastered my fifth different pronunciation of Latin, and my fifth or sixth different way of doing simple arithmetic. They put me into the top class, and I got a scholarship – in fact, I got the first scholarship of the year. At Charterhouse. And why at Charterhouse? Because of ἵστημι and ἵημι. Charterhouse was the only public school whose scholarship examination did not contain a Greek grammar paper and, though smart enough at Greek Unseen and Greek composition, I could not conjugate ἵστημι and ἵημι conventionally. But for these two verbs, I should almost certainly have gone to the very different atmosphere of Winchester.

4

MY mother took us abroad to stay at my grandfather's house in Germany five times between my second and twelfth year. Then he died, and we never went again. He owned a big old manorhouse at Deisenhofen, ten miles from Munich; by name 'Laufzorn', which means 'Begone, anger!' Our summers there were easily the best things of my early childhood. Pine forests and hot sun, red deer, black and red squirrels, acres of blueberries and wild strawberries; nine or ten different kinds of edible mushrooms which we went into the forest to pick, and unfamiliar flowers in the fields – Munich lies high, and outcrops of Alpine flowers occur here and there; a farm with all the usual animals except sheep; drives through the countryside in a brake behind my grandfather's greys; and bathing in the Isar under a waterfall. The Isar was bright green, and said to be the fastest river of Europe. We used to visit the uncles who kept a peacock farm a few miles away; and a grand-uncle, Johannes von Ranke, the ethnologist, who lived on the lakeshore of Tegernsee, where everyone had buttercup-blonde hair; and occasionally my Aunt Agnes, Freifrau Baronin von Aufsess of Aufsess Castle, some hours away by train, high up in the Bavarian Alps.

Aufsess, built in the ninth century, stood so remote that it had never been sacked, but remained Aufsess property ever since. To the original building, a keep with only a ladder-entrance half-way up, a medieval castle had been added. Its treasures of plate and armour were amazing. My Uncle Siegfried showed us children the chapel: its walls hung with enamelled shields of each Aufsess baron, impaled with the arms of the noble family into which he had married. He pointed to a stone in the floor which pulled up by a ring, and said: 'That is the family vault where all Aufsesses go when they die. I'll be down there one day.' He scowled comically. (But he got killed in the war as an officer of the Imperial German Staff and, I believe, they never found his body.) Uncle Siegfried had a peculiar sense of humour. One day we children saw him on the garden path, eating pebbles. He told us to go away, but of course we stayed, sat down, and tried to eat pebbles too; only to be told very seriously that children should not eat pebbles: we would break our teeth. We agreed, after trying one or two; so he chose us each a pebble which looked just like all the rest, but which crushed easily and had a chocolate centre. This was on condition that we went away and left him to his picking and crunching. When we returned, later in the day, we searched and searched, but found only the ordinary hard pebbles. He never once let us down in a joke.

Among the castle treasures were a baby's lace cap that had taken two years to make; and a wine glass which my uncle's old father had noticed in the Franco-Prussian War standing upright in the middle of the square in an entirely ruined French village. For dinner, when we went there, we ate some enormous trout. My father, a practised fisherman, asked my uncle in astonishment where they came from. He explained that an underground river welled up close to the castle, and the fish which emerged with it were quite white from the darkness, of extraordinary size, and stone-blind.

They also gave us jam made of wild rose-berries, which they called 'Hetchi-Petch', and showed us an iron chest in a small, thick-walled, white-washed room at the top of the keep – a tremendous chest, twice the size of the door, and obviously made inside the room, which had no windows except arrow-slits. It had two keys, and must have been twelfth- or thirteenth-century work. Tradition ruled that it should never be opened, unless the castle stood in the most extreme danger. The baron held one key; his steward, the other. The chest could be opened only by using both keys, and nobody knew what lay inside; it was even considered unlucky to speculate. Of course, we speculated. It might be gold; more likely a store of corn in sealed jars; or even some sort of weapon – Greek fire, perhaps. From what I know of the Aufsesses and their stewards, it is inconceivable that the chest ever got the better of their curiosity. A ghost walked the castle, the ghost of a former baron known as the 'Red Knight'; his terrifying portrait hung half-way up the turret staircase which led to our bedrooms. We slept on feather beds for the first time in our lives.

Laufzorn, which my grandfather had bought and restored from a ruinous condition, could not compare in tradition with Aufsess, though it had for a time been a shooting lodge of the Bavarian kings. Still, two ghosts went with the place; the farm labourers used to see them frequently. One of them was a carriage which drove furiously along without horses and, before the days of motor cars, horrible enough. Not having visited the banqueting hall since childhood, I find it difficult to recall its true dimensions. It seemed as big as a cathedral, with stained-glass armorial windows, and bare floorboards furnished only at the four corners with small islands of tables and chairs; swallows had built rows of nests all along the sides of the ceiling. There were roundels of coloured light from the windows, the many-tined stags' heads (shot by my grandfather) mounted on the walls, swallow-droppings under the nests, and a little harmonium in one corner where we sang German songs. These concentrate my memories of Laufzorn. The bottom storey formed part of the farm. A carriage-drive ran right through it, with a wide, covered courtyard in the centre, where cattle were once driven to safety in times of baronial feud. On one side of the drive lay the estate steward's quarters, on the other the farm servants' inn and kitchen. In the middle storey lived my grandfather and his family. The top storey was a store for corn, apples, and other farm produce; and up here my cousin Wilhelm – later shot down in an air battle by a schoolfellow of mine – used to lie for hours picking off mice with an air-gun.

Bavarian food had a richness and spiciness that we always missed on our return to England. We liked the rye bread, the dark pine-honey, the huge ice-cream puddings made with fresh raspberry juice and the help of snow stored during the winter in an ice-house, my grandfather's venison, the honey cakes, the pastries, and particularly the sauces made with different kinds of mushrooms. Also the pretzels,

27

the carrots cooked in sugar, and summer pudding of cranberries and blueberries. In the orchard, close to the house, we could eat as many apples, pears, and greengages as we liked. There were also rows of blackcurrant and gooseberry bushes in the garden. The estate, despite the recency of my grandfather's tenure, his liberalism, and his experiments in modern agricultural methods, remained feudalistic. The poor, sweaty, savage-looking farm servants, who talked a dialect we could not understand, frightened us. They ranked lower even than the servants at home; and as for the colony of Italians, settled about half a mile from the house, whom my grandfather had imported as cheap labour for his brick factory – we associated them in our minds with 'the gipsies in the wood' of the song. My grandfather took us over the factory one day and made me taste a lump of Italian *polenta*. My mother told us afterwards – when milk pudding at Wimbledon came to table burned, and we complained – 'Those poor Italians in your grandfather's brick yard used to burn their *polenta* on purpose, sometimes, just for a change of flavour.'

Beyond the farm buildings at Laufzorn lay a large pond, fringed with irises and full of carp; my uncles netted it every three or four years. Once we watched the fun, and shouted when we saw the net pulled closer and closer to the shallow landing corner. It bulged with wriggling carp, and a big pike threshed about among them. I waded in to help, and came out with six leeches, like black rubber tubes, fastened to my legs; salt had to be put on their tails before they would leave go. The farm labourers grew wildly excited; one of them gutted a fish with his thumb, and ate it raw. I also remember the truck line between the railway station, two miles away, and the brick yard. Since the land had a fall of perhaps one in a hundred between the factory and the station, the Italians used to load their trucks with bricks; then a squad of them would give the trucks a hard shove and run along the line pushing for twenty or thirty yards; after which the trucks sailed off all by themselves towards the station.

We were allowed to climb up into the rafters of the big hay barn, and jump down into the springy hay; we gradually increased the height of the jumps. It was exciting to feel our insides left behind us in the air. Once we visited the Laufzorn cellar, not the ordinary beer cellar, but another into which one descended from the courtyard – quite dark except for a little slit window. A huge heap of potatoes lay on the floor; to get to the light, they had put out a twisted mass of long white feelers. In one corner was a dark hole closed by a gate: a secret passage from the house to a ruined monastery, a mile away – so we were told. My uncles had once been down some distance, but the air got bad and they came back; the gate had been put up to prevent anyone else trying it and never returning. Come to think of it, they were probably teasing us, and the hole led to the bottom of the *garde-robe* – which is a polite name for a medieval earth-closet.

When we drove out beside my grandfather, he was acclaimed with '*Grüss Gott, Herr Professor!*' by the principal personages of each village we went through. It always had a big inn with a rumbling skittle-alley, and a tall Maypole, banded like a barber's pole with blue and white, the Bavarian national colours. Apple and pear trees lined every road. The idea of these unguarded public fruit-trees astonished us. We could not understand why any fruit remained on them. On Wimbledon Common even the horse-chestnut trees were pelted with sticks and stones, long before the chestnuts ripened, and in defiance of an energetic common-keeper. What we least liked in Bavaria were the wayside crucifixes with their realistic blood and wounds, and the *ex-voto* pictures, like sign-boards, of naked souls in purgatory, grinning for anguish among high red and yellow flames. Though taught to believe in Hell, we did not like to be reminded of it.

Munich we found sinister – disgusting fumes of beer and cigar smoke, and intense sounds of eating in the restaurants; the hotly dressed, enormously stout population in trams and trains; the ferocious officials. Then the terrifying Morgue, which children were not allowed to visit. Any notable who died was taken to the Morgue, they told us, and put in a chair, to sit in state for a day or two. If a general, he had his uniform on; or if a burgomaster's wife, she had on her silks and jewels. Strings were tied to their fingers, and the slightest movement of a single string would ring a great bell, in case any life remained in the corpse after all. I have never verified the truth of this, but it was true enough to me. When my grandfather died, about a year after our last visit, I pictured him in the Morgue with his bushy white hair, his morning coat, his striped trousers, his decorations, and his stethoscope. And perhaps, I thought, a silk hat, gloves, and cane on a table beside him. Trying, in a nightmare, to be alive; but knowing himself dead.

The headmaster of Rokeby school who caned me for forgetting

my gymnastic shoes loved German culture, and impressed this feeling on the school, so that it stood to my credit that I could speak German and had visited Germany. At my other preparatory schools this German connexion seemed something at least excusable, and perhaps even interesting. Only at Charterhouse did it rank as a social offence. My history from the age of fourteen, when I went to Charterhouse, until just before the end of the war, when I began to think for myself, is a forced rejection of the German in me. I used to insist indignantly on being Irish, and took my self-protective stand on the technical point that solely the father's nationality counted. Of course, I also accepted the whole patriarchal system of things, convinced of the natural supremacy of male over female. My mother took the 'love, honour, and obey' contract literally; my sisters were brought up to wish themselves boys, to be shocked at the idea of woman's suffrage, and not to expect so expensive an education as their brothers. The final decision in any domestic matter always rested with my father. My mother would say: 'If two ride together, one must ride behind.'

We children did not talk German well; our genders and minor parts of speech were shaky, and we never learned to read Gothic characters or script. Yet we had the sense of German so strongly that I feel I know German far better than French, though able to read French almost as fast as I can read English, and German only very painfully and slowly, with the help of a dictionary. I use different parts of my mind for the two languages. French is a surface acquirement which I could forget quite easily if I had no reason to speak it every now and then.

5

I SPENT a good part of my early life at Wimbledon. We did not get rid of the house, a big one near the common, until soon after the end of the war; yet I can recall little or nothing of significance that happened there. But after the age of eleven or twelve I was always at some boarding school, and in the spring and summer holidays we went to the country, so that I saw Wimbledon only at

Christmas and for a day or two at the beginning and end of the other holidays. London lay half an hour away, yet I seldom went there. We were never taken to the theatre, even to pantomimes, and by the middle of the war I had been to the theatre exactly twice in my life, and then merely to children's plays, by courtesy of an aunt. My mother brought us up to be serious and to benefit humanity in some practical way, but allowed us no hint of its dirtiness, intrigue, and lustfulness, believing that innocence would be the surest protection against them. She carefully censored our reading. I was destined to be 'if not a great man, at least a good man'. Our treats were educational or aesthetic: to Kew Gardens, Hampton Court, the Zoo, the British Museum, or the National History Museum. I remember my mother, in the treasure room of the British Museum, telling us with bright eyes that all these wonderful things were ours. We looked at her astonished. She said: 'Yes, they belong to us as members of the public. We can look at them, admire them, and study them for as long as we like. If we had them back at home, we couldn't do better. Besides, they might get stolen.'

We read more books than most children do. There must have been four or five thousand books in the house altogether. They consisted of an old-fashioned scholar's library bequeathed to my father by my namesake, whom I have mentioned as a friend of Wordsworth, but who had a tenderer friendship with Felicia Hemans; to this were added my father's own collection of books, mostly poetry, with a particular cupboard for Anglo-Irish literature; devotional works contributed by my mother; educational books sent to my father by publishers in the hope that he would recommend them for use in Government schools; and novels and adventure books brought into the house by my elder brothers and sisters.

My mother used to tell us stories about inventors and doctors who gave their lives for the suffering, and poor boys who struggled to the top of the tree, and saintly men who made examples of themselves. Also the parable of the king who had a very beautiful garden which he threw open to the public. Two students entered; and one, of whom my mother spoke with a slight sneer in her voice, noticed occasional weeds even in the tulip-beds; but the other (and here she brightened up) found beautiful flowers even on rubbish heaps. She kept off the subject of war as much as possible, always finding it difficult to explain how it was that God permitted wars. The Boer War clouded my early childhood: Philip, my eldest brother (who

31

called himself a Fenian), also called himself a pro-Boer, and I remember great tension at the breakfast-table between him and my father, whose political views were never extreme.

The eventual sale of the Wimbledon house solved a good many problems. My mother hated throwing away anything that could possibly, in the most remote contingency, be of any service to anyone and, after twenty-five years, lumber had piled high. The medicine-cupboard was perhaps the most tell-tale corner of the house. Nobody could call it untidy; all the bottles had stoppers, but stood so crowded together that nobody except my mother, who had a long memory, could recognize the ones at the back. Every few years, no doubt, she went through them. Any doubtful bottle she would tentatively re-label: 'This must be Alfred's old bunion salve,' or 'Strychnine - query?' Even special medicines prescribed for scarlet fever or whooping cough were kept, in case of re-infection. An energetic labeller, she wrote in one of my school prizes: 'Robert Ranke Graves won this book as a prize for being first in his class in the term's work and second in examinations. He also won a special prize for divinity, though the youngest boy in the class. Written by his affectionate mother, Amy Graves. Summer, 1908.' Home-made jam used always to arrive at table well documented. One small pot read: 'Gooseberry, lemon, and rhubarb - a little shop-gooseberry added - Nelly re-boiled.'

Three sayings and a favourite story of my mother's:

'Children, I command you, as your mother, never to swing objects around in your hands. The King of Hanover put out his eye by swinging a bead purse.'

'Children, I command you, as your mother, to be careful when you carry your candles upstairs. The candle is a little cup of grease.'

'There was a man once, a Frenchman, who died of grief because he could never become a mother.'

She used to tell the story by candle-light:

There was once a peasant family living in Schleswig-Holstein, where they all have crooked mouths. One night they wished to blow out the candle. The father's mouth was twisted to the left, so! and he tried to blow out the candle, so! but he was too proud to stand anywhere but directly before the candle, so he puffed and he puffed but could not blow the candle out. And then the mother tried, but her mouth was twisted to the right, so! and she tried to blow, so! and she was too proud to stand anywhere but directly before the candle, and she puffed and puffed, but could not blow the candle out. Then there was the brother with mouth twisted upward, so! and the sister with the mouth twisted downward, so! and they tried each in turn, so! and so! and the idiot baby with his mouth twisted in an eternal grin, so! At last the maid, a beautiful girl from Copenhagen with a perfectly formed mouth, put it out with her shoe. So! Flap!

These quotations make it clear how much I owe, as a writer, to my mother. She also taught me to 'speak the truth and shame the devil!' Her favourite Biblical exhortation went: 'My son, whatever thy hand findeth to do, do it with all thy might.'

I always considered Wimbledon a wrong place: neither town nor country. The house was at its worst on Wednesday, my mother's 'At Home' day. We went down in our Sunday clothes to eat cakes in the drawing-room, be kissed, and behave politely. My sisters had to recite. Around Christmas, celebrated in the German style, came a dozen or so children's parties; we would make ourselves sick with excitement. I don't like thinking of Wimbledon.

Every spring and summer, unless we happened to visit Germany, or France as we did once, we went to Harlech in North Wales. My mother had built a house there. Before motor traffic reached the North Welsh coast, Harlech was a very quiet place and little known, even as a golf centre. It consisted of three parts. First, the village itself, five hundred feet up on a steep range of hills: granite houses with slate roofs and ugly windows and gables, chapels of seven or eight different denominations, enough shops to make it the marketing centre of the smaller villages around, and the castle, a favourite playground of ours. Second, the Morfa, a flat sandy plain from which the sea had receded; part of this formed the golf links, but to the north lay a stretch of wild country which we used to search in the spring for plovers' eggs. The seaside stretched beyond the links – good, hard sand for miles, safe bathing, sandhills for hide-and-seek.

The third part of Harlech was never visited by golfers or the few other summer visitors, and seldom by the village people themselves: the desolate, rocky hill-country at the back of the village. As we grew older, we spent more and more of our time up here, and less and less on the beach and the links. There were occasional farms and crofts in these hills, but one could easily walk fifteen or twenty miles without crossing a road, or passing close to a farm. Originally we went up with some practical excuse. For the blueberries on the hills near Maes-y-garnedd; or the cranberries at Gwlawllyn; or bits of Roman hypocaust tiling (with the potter's thumb-marks still on them) in the ruined Roman villas by Castell Tomen-y-mur; or globe flowers on the banks of the upper Artro; or a sight of the wild goats which lived behind Rhinog Fawr, the biggest of the hills in the next range; or raspberries from the thickets near Cwmbychan Lake; or white heather from a nameless hill, away to the north of the Roman Steps. But after a time we visited those hills simply because they were good to walk about on. Their penny-plain quality pleased us even more than the twopence-coloured quality of the Bavarian Alps. My best friend at the time, my sister Rosaleen, was one year older than myself.

This country (and I know no country like it) seemed to be independent of formal nature. One hardly noticed the passage of the seasons there; the wind always blew across the stunted grass, the black streams always ran cold and clear, over black stones. The mountain sheep were wild and free, capable of scrambling over a six-foot stone wall (unlike the slow, heavy, smutty-fleeced South-down flocks that fattened in the fields beyond Wimbledon) and, when in repose, easily mistaken for the lichen-covered granite boulders strewn everywhere. Few trees grew except hazels, rowans, stunted oaks, and thorn bushes in the valleys. Winters were always mild, so that last year's bracken and last year's heather survived in a faded way through to the next spring. We saw hardly any birds, bar an occasional buzzard, and curlews wheeling in the distance; and wherever we went the rocky skeleton of the hill seemed only an inch or two beneath the turf.

Having no Welsh blood in us, we felt little temptation to learn Welsh, still less to pretend ourselves Welsh, but knew that country as a quite ungeographical region. Any stray sheep-farmers whom we met seemed intruders on our privacy. Clarissa, Rosaleen, and I were once out on the remotest hills and had not seen a soul all day. At last we came to a waterfall and found two trout lying on the bank beside it; ten yards away stood the fisherman, disentangling his line from a thorn-bush. He had not seen us, so I crept up quietly to the fish and put a sprig of white bell-heather (which we had picked that afternoon) in the mouth of each. We hurried back to cover, and I asked: 'Shall we watch?' But Clarissa said: 'No, don't spoil

it.' We came home and never spoke of it again, even to each other:
and never knew the sequel. . . .

Had this been Ireland, we should have self-consciously learned
Irish and local legends; but we did not go to Ireland, except once
when I was an infant in arms. Instead we came to know Wales more
purely, as a place with a history too old for local legends; while
walking there we made up our own. We decided who lay buried
under the Standing Stone, and who had lived in the ruined round-hut
encampment, and in the caves of the valley where the big rowans
grew. On our visits to Germany I had felt a sense of home in a natural
human way, but above Harlech I found a personal peace independent
of history or geography. The first poem I wrote as myself concerned
those hills. (The first poem I wrote as a Graves was a neat translation
of one of Catullus's satires.)

Our busy and absent-minded father would never worry about us
children; our mother did worry. Yet she allowed us to go off into the
hills immediately after breakfast, and did not complain much when
we came back long after supper-time. Though she had a bad head for
heights, she never restrained us from climbing in dangerous places;
and we never got hurt. Having a bad head for heights myself, I trained
myself deliberately and painfully to overcome it. We used to go
climbing in the turrets and towers of Harlech Castle. I have worked
hard on myself in defining and dispersing my terrors. The simple fear
of heights was the first to be overcome.

A quarry-face in the garden of our Harlech house provided one or
two easy climbs, but gradually I invented more and more difficult
ones. With each new success behind me I would lie down, twitching
with nervousness, in the safe meadow grass at the top. Once I lost my
foothold on a ledge and should have been killed; but it seemed as
though I improvised a foothold in the air and kicked myself up to
safety from it. When I examined the place afterwards, I recalled the
Devil's Temptation to Jesus: the freedom to cast oneself from the
rock and be restored to safety by the angels. Yet such events are not
uncommon in mountain climbing. My friend George Mallory, for
instance, who later disappeared close to the summit of Mount Everest,
once did an inexplicable climb on Snowdon. He had left his pipe on a
ledge, half-way down one of the Lliwedd precipices, and scrambled
back by a short cut to retrieve it, then up again by the same route. No
one saw what route he took, but when they came to examine it the
next day for official record, they found an overhang nearly all the

35

way. By a rule of the Climbers' Club climbs are never named in honour of their inventors, but only describe natural features. An exception was made here. The climb was recorded as follows: '*Mallory's Pipe*, a variation on Route 2; see adjoining map. This climb is totally impossible. It has been perfomed once, in failing light, by Mr G. H. L. Mallory.'

6

LET me begin my account of Charterhouse School by recalling the day that I left, a week before the outbreak of war. I discussed my feelings with Nevill Barbour, then Head of the School. First, we agreed that there were perhaps even more typical public schools than Charterhouse in existence, but that we preferred not to believe it. Next, that no possible remedy could be found, because tradition was so strong that to break it one would have to dismiss the whole school and staff, and start all over again. However, even this would not be enough, the school buildings being so impregnated with what passed as the public school spirit, but what we felt as fundamental evil, that they would have to be demolished and the school rebuilt elsewhere under a different name. Finally, that our only regret at leaving the place was that for the last year we had been in a position, as members of the Sixth Form, to do more or less what we pleased. Now we were both going on to St John's College, Oxford, which promised to be merely a more boisterous repetition of Charterhouse. We should be freshmen there, but would naturally refuse to be hearty and public schoolish, and therefore be faced with the stupidity of having our rooms raided, and being forced to lose our temper and hurt somebody and get hurt ourselves. There would be no peace probably until we reached our third year, when we should be back again in the same sort of position as now, and in the same sort of position as in our last year at our preparatory school. 'In 1917,' said Nevill, 'the official seal will be put on all this dreariness. We'll get our degrees, and then have to start as new boys again in some dreadful profession.'

'Correct,' I told him.

'My God,' he said, turning to me suddenly, 'I can't stand the prospect. Something has to be put in between me and Oxford; I must at least go abroad for the whole vacation.'

Three months were not long enough, to my mind. I had a vague thought of running away to sea.

'Do you realize,' Nevill asked me, 'that we have spent fourteen years of our lives principally at Latin and Greek, not even competently taught, and that we're now going to start another three years of the same thing?'

Yet when we had said our very worst of Charterhouse, I reminded him, or he me, I forget which: 'Of course, the trouble is that at any given time one always finds at least two really decent masters in the school, among the forty or fifty, and ten really decent fellows among the five or six hundred. We shall always remember them, and have Lot's feeling about not damning Sodom for the sake of ten persons. And in another twenty years' time we'll forget this conversation and think that we were mistaken, and that perhaps everybody, with a few criminal exceptions, was fairly average decent, and say: "I was a young fool then, insisting on impossible perfection," and we'll send our sons to Charterhouse for sentiment's sake, and they'll go through all we did.'

This must not be construed as an attack on my old school; it is merely a record of my mood at the time. No doubt, I was unappreciative of the hard knocks and character-training that public schools are advertised as providing; and a typical Old Carthusian remarked to me recently: 'The moral tone of the school has improved out of all recognition since those days.' But so it always will have.

As a matter of fact I did not go up to Oxford until five years later, in 1919, when my brother Charles, four years younger than myself, was already in residence; and did not take my degree until 1926, by which time my brother John had caught up with me, though eight years younger than myself.

From my first moment at Charterhouse I suffered an oppression of spirit that I hesitate to recall in its full intensity. Something like being in that chilly cellar at Laufzorn among the potatoes, but a potato out of a different sack from the rest. The school consisted of about six hundred boys, whose chief interests were games and romantic friendships. Everyone despised school-work; the scholars were not concentrated in a single dormitory house as at Winchester or Eton, but divided among ten, and known as 'pro's'. Unless good at games, and able to pretend that they hated work even more than the non-scholars, and ready whenever called on to help these with their work, they always had a bad time. I happened to be a scholar who really liked work, and the apathy of the class-rooms surprised and disappointed me. My first term, I was left alone more or less, it being a rule that new boys should be neither encouraged nor baited. The other boys seldom addressed me except to send me on errands, or coldly point out breaches of school convention.

In the second term the trouble began. A number of things naturally made for my unpopularity. Besides being a scholar and not outstandingly good at games, I was always short of pocket-money. Since I could not conform to the social custom of treating my contemporaries to tuck at the school shop, I could not accept their treating. My clothes, though conforming outwardly to the school pattern, were ready-made and not of the best-quality cloth that all the other boys wore. Even so, I had not been taught how to make the best of them. Neither my mother nor my father had any regard for the niceties of dress, and my elder brothers were abroad by this time. Nearly all the other boys in my house, except for five scholars, were the sons of businessmen: a class of whose interests and prejudices I knew nothing, having hitherto met only boys of the professional class. Also, I talked too much for their liking. A further disability was that I remained as prudishly innocent as my mother had planned I should. I knew nothing about simple sex, let alone the many refinements of sex constantly referred to in school conversation, to which I reacted with horror. I wanted to run away.

The most unfortunate disability of all was that my name appeared on the school list as 'R. von R. Graves'. I had hitherto believed my second name to be 'Ranke'; the 'von', encountered on my birth certificate, disconcerted me. Carthusians behaved secretively about their second names, and usually managed to conceal fancy ones. I could no doubt have passed off 'Ranke', without the 'von', as monosyllabic and English, but 'von Ranke' was glaring. Businessmen's sons, at this time, used to discuss hotly the threat, and even the necessity, of a trade war with the Reich. 'German' meant 'dirty German'. It meant: 'cheap, shoddy goods competing with our sterling industries.' It also meant military menace, Prussianism, useless philosophy, tedious scholarship, loving music and sabre-rattling. Another boy in my house with a German name, though English by birth and upbringing, got much the same treatment as I did. On the other hand, a French boy in the house became very popular, though poor at games; King Edward VII had done his *entente cordiale* work thoroughly. Considerable anti-Jewish feeling worsened the situation: someone started the rumour that I was not only a German, but a German Jew.

Of course, I always claimed to be Irish, but an Irish boy who had been in the house about a year and a half longer than myself resented this claim. He went out of his way to hurt me, not only by physical acts of spite like throwing ink over my school-books, hiding my games-clothes, attacking me suddenly from behind corners, pouring water over my bed at night, but by continually forcing his bawdy humour on my prudishness, and inviting everybody to laugh at my disgust. He also built up a humorous legend of my hypocrisy and concealed depravity. I came near a nervous breakdown. School ethics prevented me from informing the housemaster of my troubles. The house-monitors, though supposed to keep order and preserve the moral tone of the house, never interfered in any case of bullying among the juniors. I tried violent resistance, but as the odds were always heavily against me this merely encouraged the ragging. Complete passive resistance would probably have been wiser. I got accustomed to bawdy-talk only during my last two years at the school, and had been a soldier for some little time before I got hardened and could reply in kind to insults.

G. H. Rendall, the then Headmaster at Charterhouse, is reported to have innocently said at a Headmasters' Conference: 'My boys are amorous, but seldom erotic.' Few cases of eroticism, indeed, came to his notice; I remember no more than five or six big rows during my time at Charterhouse, and expulsions were rare. The housemasters knew little about what went on in their houses, their living quarters being removed from the boys'. Yet I agree with Rendall's distinction between 'amorousness' (by which he meant a sentimental falling in love with younger boys) and eroticism, or adolescent lust. The intimacy that frequently took place was very seldom between an elder boy and the object of his affection – that would have spoiled the romantic illusion – but almost always between boys of the same age who were not in love, and used each other as convenient sex-instruments. So the atmosphere was always heavy with romance of a conventional early-Victorian type, complicated by cynicism and foulness.

7

HALF-WAY through my second year I wrote to tell my parents that they must take me away, because I could not stand life at Charterhouse any longer: the House had made it plain that I did not belong, and was not wanted. I gave them details, in confidence, to make them take my demand seriously; but they failed to respect this confidence, believing that their religious duty would be to inform the housemaster of all I had written them. Nor did they even warn me what they were doing; but contented themselves with visiting me and preaching the power of prayer and faith. I must endure all, they said, for the sake of . . . I have forgotten what exactly – perhaps my career. Fortunately I had withheld any account of sex-irregularities in the house, so all that the housemaster did was to make a speech that night, after prayers, deterrent of bullying in general. He told us that he had just received a complaint from a boy's parents; making it plain at the same time how much he disliked informers and outside interference in affairs of the house. My name did not come up, but the visit of my parents on a non-holiday had excited comment. I was obliged to stay on, and be treated as an informer. Being now in the upper school, I had a study of my own. But studies could not be locked, and mine was always being wrecked. I could no longer even use the ordinary house changing-room, so removed my games-clothes to a disused shower-bath. Then my heart went wrong, and the school doctor decided that I must play no more football. My last resource, to sham insanity, succeeded unexpectedly well. Soon nobody troubled except to avoid any contact with me. I got the idea from *The Book of Kings*, where David had 'scrabbled on the prison wall'.

This is not to charge my parents with treachery. Their honour is beyond reproach. Next term, I went to Charterhouse by the special train, but arrived at Waterloo too late to take a ticket; I just managed to get into a compartment before the train started. The railway company not having provided enough coaches, I had to stand all the way. At Godalming station, the crowd of boys rushing out into the station yard to secure taxis swept me past the ticket collectors, so I got a very uncomfortable ride free. I mentioned this in my next letter home, just for something to say, and my father wrote to reproach me. He said that he had himself made a special visit to Waterloo station, bought a ticket to Godalming, and torn it up. . . . My mother could be even more scrupulous. A young couple on their honeymoon once stopped the night with us at Wimbledon, and left behind a packet of sandwiches, two already half-eaten. My mother sent them on.

Thrown entirely on myself, I began to write poems; which the house considered stronger proof of insanity than the formal straws I wore in my hair. On the strength of a poem I had sent to the school magazine, *The Carthusian*, I was invited to join the school Poetry Society – a most anomalous organization for Charterhouse. It consisted of seven members. The meetings, for the reading and discussion of poetry, were held once a month at the house of Guy Kendall, then a form-master at the school, now headmaster of University College School at Hampstead. The members were four sixth-form boys, and two boys a year and a half older than me. None was in the same house as myself. At Charterhouse, no friendship might exist between boys of different houses or ages (though related, or next-door neighbours at home), beyond a formal acquaintance at work or organized games like cricket and football. Even if they played a friendly game of tennis or squash-rackets together, they would never hear the last of it.

So the friendship that began between me and Raymond Roda-kowski, one of the two younger members, was highly unconventional. Coming home one evening from a meeting of the society, I told Raymond about life in the house. A week or two before my study had been raided, and one of my more personal poems seized and pinned up on the public notice board in 'Writing School' – the living-room for members of the lower school. As a member of the fifth form, I was excluded from Writing School, and therefore could not rescue the poem. Raymond, the first Carthusian to whom I had·been able to talk humanly, grew indignant, and took my arm in his. 'They are bloody barbarians!' He told me that I must pull myself together and do something positive, because I was a good poet, and a good person. I loved Raymond for that. He said: 'You're not allowed to play football; why don't you box? It's supposed to improve the heart.' I laughed and promised that I would. Then Raymond asked: 'I expect they rag you about your initials?' 'Yes, they call me a dirty German.' 'I had trouble, too,' he told me, 'before I took up boxing.' Raymond's mother was Scottish; his father an Austrian Pole, a founder of the Brooklands Racing Track.

Very few boys boxed, and the boxing-room, over the school

tuck-shop, made a convenient place to meet Raymond whom, otherwise, I would not have seen, except at Poetry Society meetings. I began boxing seriously and savagely. Raymond said: 'These cricketers and footballers are all afraid of boxers, almost superstitious. They won't box themselves for fear of losing their good looks – the annual interhouse competitions are such bloody affairs. But do you remember the Mansfield, Waller, and Taylor show? That's a useful tradition to keep up.'

Of course, I remembered. Two terms previously, there had been a famous meeting of the school Debating Society, the committee of which consisted of sixth-form boys. Though the debates were pretty dull, what passed for intellectual life at Charterhouse was represented by the Debating Society, and *The Carthusian*, always edited by two members of this committee – both institutions being free from the control of masters. One Saturday debate-night the usual decorous conventions were broken by a riotous entry of 'bloods' – members of the cricket and football elevens. The bloods were the ruling caste at Charterhouse; the eleventh man in the football eleven, though he might be a member of the under-fourth form, enjoyed far more prestige that the most brilliant scholar in the sixth. Even 'Head of the School' was an empty title. But the sixth-form intellectuals and the bloods never fought. The bloods had nothing to gain by a clash; the intellectuals were happy to be left alone. So this invasion of the bloods, just returned from winning an 'away' match against the *Casuals*, and full of beer, caused the Debating Society a good deal of embarrassment. The bloods disturbed the meeting by cheers and cat-calls, and slammed the library magazine-folders on the table. Mansfield, as president of the society, called them to order, and when they continued the disturbance, closed the debate.

The bloods thought the incident finished, but they thought wrong. A letter appeared in *The Carthusian* a few days later, protesting against the bad behaviour in the Debating Society of 'certain First Eleven babies'. The three sets of initials signed were those of Mansfield, Waller, and Taylor. The school, astonished by this suicidally daring act, waited for Korah, Dathan, and Abiram to be swallowed up. The Captain of Football swore that he'd chuck the three signatories into the fountain in Founder's Court. But somehow he did not. The fact was that this happened early in the autumn term, and only two other First Eleven colours had been left over from the preceding year; new colours were given gradually as the football season advanced. The other rowdies had been merely embryo bloods. So the matter had to be settled between these three sixth-form intellectuals and the three colours of the First Eleven. But the First Eleven were uncomfortably aware that Mansfield was the heavy-weight boxing champion of the school, Waller the runner-up for the middle-weights, and that Taylor was also a tough fellow to be reckoned with. While they were wondering what on earth to do, Mansfield decided to take the war into his enemies' country.

The social code of Charterhouse rested on a strict caste system; the caste marks, or *post-te*'s, being slight distinctions in dress. A new boy had no privileges at all; a boy in his second term might wear a knitted tie instead of a plain one; a boy in his second year might wear coloured socks; the third year gave most of the main privileges – turned down collars, coloured handkerchiefs, a coat with a long roll, and so on; fourth year, a few more, such as the right to get up raffles; but peculiar distinctions were reserved for the bloods. These included light-grey flannel trousers, butterfly collars, jackets slit up the back, and the right of walking arm-in-arm.

So the next Sunday Mansfield, Waller, and Taylor did the bravest deed ever done at Charterhouse. Chapel began at eleven in the morning, but the school had to be in its seats by five minutes to eleven and sit waiting there. At two minutes to eleven the bloods used to stalk up; at one and a half minute to, came the masters; at one minute to, came the choir in their surplices; then the headmaster arrived, and the service began. If any boy, accidentally late, sneaked in between five minutes to, and two minutes to, the hour, six hundred pairs of eyes followed him; he heard whispering and giggling at his apparent foolhardiness in pretending to be a blood. On this Sunday, then, when the bloods had entered with their usual swaggering assurance, an extraordinary thing happened.

The three sixth-formers slowly walked up the aisle, magnificent in light-grey flannel trousers, slit jackets, butterfly collars, and each wore a pink carnation in his lapel. Astonished and horrified by this spectacle, everyone turned to gaze at the Captain of the First Eleven; he had gone quite white. But by this time the masters had entered, followed by the choir, and the opening hymn, though raggedly sung, ended the tension. When chapel emptied, it always emptied according to 'school order', that is, according to position in work: the sixth form therefore went out first. The bloods not being at all high in school order, Mansfield, Waller, and Taylor had the start of them. After chapel on Sunday, the custom in the autumn term was for boys to meet and gossip in the library; so to the library Mansfield, Waller, and Taylor went. On the way, they buttonholed a talkative master, drew him in with them and kept him talking until dinner-time. If the bloods had dared to do anything violent they would have had to do it at once, but to make a scene in the presence of a master was impossible. Mansfield, Waller, and Taylor went down to their houses for dinner, still talking to the master. After that, they always went about together in public, and the school, particularly the lower school, which had long chafed under the dress regulations, made heroes of them and began scoffing at the bloods as weak-kneed.

Finally, the captain of the eleven complained to Rendall about this breach of school conventions, asking for permission to enforce the bloods' rights by disciplinary measures. Rendall, who was a scholar and disliked the games tradition, refused his request, insisting that the sixth form deserved as distinctive privileges as the First Eleven, and were, in his opinion, entitled to hold what they had assumed. The prestige of the bloods declined greatly.

On Raymond's encouragement, I pulled myself together and when the next school year started found things very much easier. My chief persecutor, the Irishman, had gone away with a nervous breakdown. He wrote me a hysterical demand for forgiveness – saying at the same time that, if I refused it, he still had a friend in the house to give me a bad time. I did not answer the letter.

8

I STILL had no friends except among the junior members of the house, from whom I did not conceal my dislike of the seniors; I found the juniors on the whole a decent lot. Towards the end of this year, in the annual boxing and gymnastic display, I fought three rounds with Raymond. There is a lot of love in boxing – the dual play, the reciprocity, the pain not felt as pain. We were out neither to hurt nor win, though we hit each other hard.

This public appearance improved my position in the house. Then the doctor allowed me to play football again, and I played it fairly well; but things went wrong in a different way. It began with confirmation, for which I was prepared by a zealous evangelical master. For a whole term I concentrated all my thoughts on religion, looking forward to the ceremony as a spiritual climax. When it came, and the Holy Ghost failed to descend in the form of a dove, and I did not find myself gifted with tongues, and nothing spectacular happened (except that the boy whom the Bishop of Zululand was blessing at the same time as myself slipped off the narrow foot-stool on which we were both kneeling), I was bound to feel a reaction. Raymond had not been confirmed, and astonished me by admitting, and even boasting, that he was an atheist. I argued with him about the existence of God, and the divinity of Christ, and the necessity of the Trinity. He said, of the Trinity, that anybody who could agree with the Athanasian Creed that 'whoever will be saved must confess that there are not Three Incomprehensible but One Incomprehensible' was asserting that a man must go to Hell if he does not believe something that is, by definition, impossible to understand. His own respect for himself as a reasonable being forbade him to believe such things. He also asked me: 'What's the good of having a soul if you have a mind? What's the function of the soul? It seems a mere pawn in the game.'

Because I loved and respected Raymond, I felt bound to find an answer to this shocking question. But the more I considered it, the less certain I became of my ground. So in order not to prejudice religion (and I set religion and my chances of salvation before human love) I at first broke my friendship with Raymond entirely. Later I weakened, but as a complete and ruthless atheist he would not even meet me, when I approached him, with any broad-Church compromise. For the rest of our time at Charterhouse I kept my distance. Yet in 1917, when he was serving with the Irish Guards, I rode over to his billets one afternoon, having by then become a complete agnostic, and felt as close to him as ever. He got killed at Cambrai soon after.

My relations with Raymond were comradely, not amorous; but in my fourth year I fell in love with a boy three years younger than myself, who was exceptionally intelligent and fine-spirited. Call him Dick. Dick was not in my house, but I had recently joined the school choir and so had he, which gave me opportunities for speaking to him occasionally after choir practice. I was unconscious of any sexual desire for him, and our conversations were always impersonal. This illicit acquaintance did not escape comment, and one of the masters, who sang in the choir, warned me to end it. I replied that I would not have my friendships in any way limited, pointing out that Dick was interested in the same things as myself, particularly in books; that, though the disparity in our ages might seem unfortunate, a lack of intelligence among the boys of my own age obliged me to find friends where I could. Finally the headmaster took me to task for it. I lectured him loftily on the advantage of friendship between elder and younger boys, citing Plato, the Greek poets, Shakespeare, Michelangelo, and others, who had felt as I did. He let me go without taking any action.

In my fifth year I reached the sixth form, and became a house-monitor. There were six of us. One of them, Jack Young, the house games-captain, a friendly, easy-going fellow, said one day: 'Look here, Graves, I have to send in a list of competitors for the inter-house boxing competitions; shall I put your name down?' Since my coolness with Raymond, boxing had lost its interest; I had been busy with football, and played for the house-team now. 'I'm not boxing these days,' I told Young. 'Well,' he said, 'young Alan is entering for the welter-weights. He's got a fair chance. Why don't you enter for the welter-weights too? You might be able to damage one or two of the stronger men, and make things easier for him.' I did not altogether like the idea of making things easier for Alan, but obviously I had to enter the competition. Realizing that my wind, though all right for football, would not be equal to boxing round after round, I decided that my fights must be short. The house-butler smuggled a bottle of cherry-whisky in for me – I would shorten the fights on that.

I had never drunk anything alcoholic before in my life. At seven years old my mother persuaded me to sign a pledge card, which bound me to abstain by the grace of God from all spirituous liquors so long as I retained it. But my mother took the card away and put it safely in the box-room, with the Queen Anne silver inherited from my Cheyne grandmother, Bishop Graves's diamond ring which Queen Victoria gave him when he preached before her at Dublin, our christening mugs, and the heavy early-Victorian jewellery bequeathed by Miss Britain. And since box-room treasures never left the box-room, I regarded myself as permanently parted from my pledge. This cherry-whisky delighted me.

The competitions began at about one o'clock on a Saturday afternoon, and went on until seven. I was drawn for the very first fight and my opponent, by ill luck, was Alan. Alan wanted me to scratch. I told him it would look bad to do so. We consulted Jack Young,

46

who said: 'No, the most sporting thing will be to box it out, and let the decision be given on points; but don't either of you hurt each other!' so we boxed. Alan started showing off to his friends, who were sitting in the front row. I muttered: 'Stop that, we're boxing, not fighting!' but a few seconds later he hit me again, unnecessarily hard. I got angry and knocked him out with a right swing on the side of his neck. This was the first time I had ever knocked anyone out, and the feeling combined well with my cherry-whisky exaltation. I muzzily realized that the swing did not form part of the ordinary school-boxing curriculum. Straight lefts; lefts to body, rights to head; left and right hooks; all these were known, but the swing had somehow been neglected, probably because it was not so 'pretty'.

I went to the changing-room for my coat, and stout Sergeant Harris, the boxing instructor, said: 'Look here, Mr Graves, why don't you put down your name for the middle-weight competition too?' I cheerfully agreed. Then I went back to the house, where I took a cold bath and more cherry-whisky. My next fight, for the first round of the middle-weights, would take place half an hour later. This time my opponent, who was a stone heavier than myself but had little science, bustled me about for the first round, and I could see that he would tire me out unless I did something pretty soon. In the second round I knocked him down with my right swing, but he got up. Feeling a bit winded, I hastened to knock him down again. I must have knocked him down four or five times that round, but he refused to take the count. I discovered afterwards that he, like myself, was conscious of Dick watching the fight. Finally I thought, as he lurched towards me once more: 'If you don't go down, and stay down, this time, I won't be able to hit you again at all.' I just pushed at his jaw as it offered itself to me, but that was enough. He went down, and he stayed down. This second knock-out made quite a stir. Knock-outs were rare in these boxing competitions. As I returned to the house for another cold bath and some more cherry-whisky, I noticed the fellows looking at me curiously, almost with admiration.

The later stages of the competition are vague in my memory. I now had to worry only about Raymond – nearly a stone heavier than my-self, and expected to win the middle-weights; but he had also gone in for two weights, the middle and the heavy, and just been through a tough fight with the eventual winner of the heavy-weights, that left him in no proper state to continue. So he scratched his fight with me. I believe that Raymond would have fought all the same, had it been against anyone else; but he wanted me to win, and knew that his scratching would give me a rest between bouts. Then a semi-finalist scratched against me in the welter-weights, so only three more fights remained, and I let none of them go beyond the first round. The swing won me both weights, for which I received two silver cups. But I had also dislocated both my thumbs by not getting my elbow high enough over. When I tried to sell the cups some years later, to keep food in my mouth, they turned out to be only silver-plated.

The most important thing that happened in my last two years, apart from my attachment to Dick, was that I got to know George Mallory: a twenty-six or twenty-seven-year-old master, not long up from Cambridge and so youthful-looking as to be often mistaken for a member of the school. From the first, he treated me as an equal, and I used to spend my spare time reading in his room, or going for walks with him in the country. He told me of the existence of modern authors. My father being two generations older than myself and my only link with books, I had never heard of people like Shaw, Samuel Butler, Rupert Brooke, Wells, Flecker, or Masefield, and the dis-covery excited me. It was in George Mallory's rooms that I first met Edward Marsh (then secretary to the Prime Minister, Mr Asquith), who has always been a good friend to me, and with whom, though we seldom see each other now, I have never quarrelled: in this he is almost unique among my pre-war friends. Marsh liked my poems, which Mallory had showed him, but pointed out that they were written in the poetic diction of fifty years ago and that, though the quality of the poem was not necessarily impaired by this, many readers would be prejudiced against work written in 1913 in the fashions of 1863.

George Mallory, Cyril Hartmann, Raymond, and I published a magazine in the summer of 1913, called *Green Chartreuse*. It was intended to have only one number; new magazines at a public school always sell out the first number, and lose heavily on the second. From *Green Chartreuse* I shall quote one of my own contributions, of autobiographical interest, written in the school dialect:

MY NEW-BUG'S EXAM

When lights went out at half past nine in the evening of the second Friday in the Quarter, and the faint footfalls of the departing House-master were heard no more, the fun began.

The Head of Under Cubicles constituted himself examiner and executioner, and was ably assisted by a time keeper, a question-recorder, and a staff of disreputable friends. I was a timorous 'new-bug' then, and my pyjamas were damp with the perspiration of fear. Three of my fellows had been examined and sentenced before the inquisition was directed against me.

'It's Jones's turn now,' said a voice. 'He's the little hash-pro who hacked me in run-about today. We must set him some tight questions!'

'I say, Jones, what's the colour of the House-master – I mean what's the name of the House-master of the House whose colours are black and white? One, two, three . . .'

'Mr Girdlestone,' my voice quivered in the darkness.

'He evidently knows the simpler colours. We'll muddle him. What are the colours of the Club to which Block Houses belong? One, two, three, four . . .'

I had been slaving at getting up these questions for days, and just managed to blurt out the answer before being counted out.

'Two questions. No misses. We must buck up,' said someone.

'I say, Jones, how do you get to Farncombe from Weekites? One, two, three . . .'

I had issued directions only as far as Bridge before being counted out.

'Three questions. One miss. You're allowed three misses out of ten.'

'Where is Charterhouse Magazine? One, two, three, four . . .'

'Do you mean *The Carthusian* office?' I asked.

Everyone laughed.

'Four questions. Two misses. I say, Robinson, he's answered far too many. We'll set him a couple of stingers.'

Much whispering.

'What is the age of the horse that rolls Under Green? One, two, three . . .'

'Six!' I said, at a venture.

'Wrong; thirty-eight. Six questions. Three misses! Think yourself lucky you weren't asked its pedigree.'

'What are canoeing colours? One, two, thr . . .'

'There aren't any!'

'You'll get cocked-up for festivity; but you can count it. Seven questions. Three misses. Jones?'

'Yes!'

'What was the name of the girl to whom rumour stated that last year's football secretary was violently attached? One, two, three, four . . .'

'Daisy!' (It sounded a likely name.)

'Oh, really! Well, I happen to know last year's football secretary; and he'll simply kill you for spreading scandal. You're wrong anyhow.

Eight questions. Four misses! You'll come to my "cube" at seven to-morrow morning. See? Good night!'

Here he waved his hair-brush over the candle, and a colossal shadow appeared on the ceiling.

The Poetry Society died about this time – and this is how it died. Two of its sixth-form members came to a meeting, and each read a rather dull and formal poem about love and nature; none of us paid much attention to them. But the following week they came out in *The Carthusian*, and soon everyone began pointing and giggling; because both poems, signed with pseudonyms, were acrostics, the initial letters spelling out a 'case'. 'Case' meant 'romance', a formal coupling of two boys' names, with the name of the elder boy first. In both poems the first names mentioned were those of bloods. It was a foolish act of aggression in the feud between sixth form and the bloods. But nothing much would have come of it, had not another of the sixth-form members of the Poetry Society been idealistically in love with one of the smaller boys whose name appeared in the acrostics. In rage and jealousy he went to the headmaster (Frank Fletcher, who had superseded G. H. Rendall), and called his attention to the acrostic – which otherwise none of the masters would have noticed. He pretended not to know the authors; but though he had missed the particular Poetry Meeting at which the verses were read, he could easily have guessed them from the style. Meanwhile, I had incautiously told someone the authors' names; so I got dragged into the row as a witness against them.

The headmaster took a very serious view of the matter. The two poets lost their monitorial privileges; the editor of *The Carthusian* who, though aware of the acrostics, had accepted the poems, lost his editorship and his position as Head of School. The informer, who happened to be next in school order, succeeded him in both capacities; he had not expected this development, which made him most un-popular. His consolation was a real one: that he had done it all for love, to avenge the public insult done his young friend. The Poetry Society was ignominiously dissolved by the headmaster's orders. It was an 'I told you so' for the other masters, who did not believe either in poetry, or in school uplift societies. But I owed a great debt of gratitude to Kendall (one of the few masters who insisted on treating the boys better than they deserved); the meetings of the Poetry Society had been all that I could look forward to when things were at their worst for me.

My last year at Charterhouse I did everything possible to show how little respect I had for school tradition. In the winter of 1913 I won a classical exhibition at St John's College, Oxford, which allowed me to go slow on school work. Nevill Barbour and I were editing *The Carthusian*, and a good deal of my time went on that. Nevill, who as a scholar had met the same sort of difficulties as myself, shared my dislike of most Charterhouse traditions, and decided that compulsory games were among the worst. Of these, we considered cricket the most objectionable, because it wasted most time in the best part of the year. Nevill suggested a campaign in favour of lawn-tennis. We were not seriously devoted to tennis, but found it our handiest weapon against cricket – the game, we wrote, in which the selfishness of the few did not excuse the boredom of the many. Tennis was quick and busy. We asked Old Carthusian tennis internationals to contribute letters proposing tennis as the manlier and more vigorous game. We even persuaded Anthony Wilding, the world champion, to write. The games-masters, who called tennis 'pat-ball', a game for girls, were scandalized at this assault on cricket, and even more so by an ironical letter in its support, which I had signed 'Judas Iscariot'. One of them came to Nevill and asked would he please be less controversial. 'This is not a deputation,' he explained. 'No?' said Nevill. 'I thought it was. You were the only member of the Staff considered tactful enough to approach the Governing Body for a rise of salary last year.'

The result of our campaign surprised us. When we revealed the scandal that subscriptions to the two derelict school tennis-courts had been, for several years, appropriated by the cricket committee, not only did we double our sales, but a fund was started for providing several more tennis-courts, and making Charterhouse the cradle of public-school tennis. Though delayed by the war, these courts did, in fact, appear one day. I noticed them recently as I drove past in a car; there seemed to be plenty of them. I wonder, are there tennis bloods at Charterhouse now?

Poetry and Dick were still almost all that really mattered. Life with my fellow house-monitors was one of perpetual discord. I had grudges against every one of them, except Jack Young and the head-monitor. Young, the only blood in the house, spent most of his time with fellow-bloods in other houses. The head-monitor was a scholar who, though well-principled, had been embittered by his first three years in the house, and now stood too much on his dignity. He did more or less what the other monitors wanted him to do, and I hated having to lump him in with the rest. My love for Dick provoked a constant facetiousness, but they never dared go too far. I once caught one of them in the bathroom, scratching up a pair of hearts conjoined, with Dick's initials and mine above them. I pushed him into the bath and turned the taps on. The next day, he got hold of a manuscript note-book of mine which I had left, with some other books, in the moni-tors' room. He and all the others, except Jack Young, annotated it critically in blue chalk, and signed their initials. Jack would have nothing to do with this ungentlemanly behaviour. When I discovered what had been done, I demanded a signed apology, threatening that if it did not arrive within five minutes, I would choose one of them as being solely responsible and punish him. I was now off to take a cold bath, and the first monitor whom I met afterwards would get knocked down.

Whether by accident, or whether he thought that his position protected him, the first I met in the corridor was the head-monitor. I knocked him down. It was the time of evening preparation, from which we were excused. But a fag happened to pass on an errand, and saw the spurt of blood; so the incident could not be hushed up. Presently the housemaster sent for me. He was an excitable, elderly man, with some difficulty in controlling his spittle when angry; a trait that had earned him the name of 'Gosh' Parry. I went to his study, where he made me sit down in a chair, then stood over me, clenching his fists and crying in falsetto: 'Do you realize that you have com-mitted a very brutal act?' His mouth bubbled with spittle. I jumped up and clenched my fists too, saying that I would do the same thing again to anyone else who, after scribbling impertinent remarks on my private papers, refused to apologize. 'Private papers? Filthy poems!' said Gosh Parry.

I had another difficulty with the headmaster as a result. But, this being my last term, he allowed me to finish my five years without ignominy. I puzzled him by the frankness with which I confessed my love for Dick, when he re-opened the question. I refused to be ashamed, and heard afterwards that he had described this as one of the rare friendships between boys of unequal ages which, he felt, was essentially moral. A week or two later I went through one of the worst quarters of an hour of my life on Dick's account. When the master who sang in the choir warned me about exchanging glances with Dick in chapel I had been infuriated. But when one of the choir-boys told me that he had seen the master surreptitiously kissing Dick once, on a choir-treat, I went quite mad without asking for any details or confirmation. I went to the master and told him that unless he resigned, I would report the matter to the headmaster – he already had a reputation in the school for this sort of thing and kissing boys was a criminal offence. No doubt my sense of moral outrage concealed a murderous jealousy. When he vigorously denied the charge, I could not guess what would happen next. But I said: 'Well, come to the headmaster and deny it in his presence.' He asked: 'Did the boy tell you this himself?' 'No.' 'Well, then I'll send for him, and he'll tell us the truth.'

Dick was sent for, and arrived looking very scared. The master said menacingly: 'Graves tells me that I once kissed you. Is that true?' Dick answered: 'Yes, it is!' So Dick was dismissed, the master collapsed, and I felt thoroughly miserable. He undertook to resign at the end of the term, which was quite close, on grounds of ill-health. He even thanked me for speaking directly to him and not going to the headmaster. This was the summer of 1914; he went into the army and was killed the following year. Dick told me later that he had not been kissed at all, but he saw I was in a jam – it must have been some other member of the choir!

One of my last recollections at Charterhouse is a school debate on the motion 'that this House is in favour of compulsory military service'. The Empire Service League, with Earl Roberts of Kandahar, V.C., as its President, sent down a propagandist in support. Only six votes out of one hundred and nineteen were noes. I was the principal opposition speaker, having recently resigned from the Officers' Training Corps in revolt against the theory of implicit obedience to orders. And during a fortnight spent the previous summer at the O.T.C. camp near Tidworth on Salisbury Plain, I had been frightened by a special display of the latest military fortifications: barbed-wire entanglements, machine-guns, and field artillery in action. General, now Field-Marshal Sir William Robertson, who had a son at the school, visited the camp and impressed upon us that war with Germany must inevitably break out within two or three years, and that we must be prepared to take our part in it as leaders of the new forces which would assuredly be called into being. Of the six noes, Nevill Barbour and I are, I believe, the only ones who survived the war.

My last memory is the headmaster's parting shot: 'Well, goodbye, Graves, and remember that your best friend is the waste-paper basket.' This has proved good advice, though not perhaps in the sense he intended: few writers seem to send their work through as many drafts as I do.

I used to speculate on which of my contemporaries would distinguish themselves after they left school. The war upset these calculations. Many dull boys had brief brilliant military careers, particularly as air-fighters, becoming squadron and flight commanders. 'Fuzzy' McNair, the Head of the school, won the V.C. as a Rifleman. Young Sturgess, who had been my study fag, distinguished himself more unfortunately by flying the first heavy bombing machine of a new pattern across the Channel on his first trip to France: he made a perfect landing (having mistaken his course) at an aerodrome behind the German lines. A boy whom I had admired during my first year at Charterhouse was the Honourable Desmond O'Brien: the only Carthusian of that time who cheerfully disregarded all school rules. Having cut skeleton-keys for the library, chapel, and science laboratories, he used to break out of his house at night and carefully disarrange things there. O'Brien had the key to the headmaster's study too and, entering one night with an electric torch, carried off a memorandum which he showed me: 'Must expel O'Brien.' He had a wireless receiving-station in one of the out-of-bounds copses on the school grounds; and discovered a ventilator shaft down which he could hoot like an owl into the library without detection. Once we were threatened with the loss of a half-holiday because some member of the school had catapulted a cow, which died of shock, and nobody would own up. O'Brien was away at the time, on special leave for a sister's wedding. A friend wrote to tell him about the half-holiday. He sent Rendall a telegram: 'Killed cow sorry coming O'Brien.' At last Rendall did expel him for having absented himself from every lesson and chapel for three whole days. O'Brien was killed, early in the war, while bombing Bruges.

At least one in three of my generation at school died; because they all took commissions as soon as they could, most of them in the infantry and Royal Flying Corps. The average life expectancy of an infantry subaltern on the Western Front was, at some stages of the war, only about three months; by which time he had been either wounded or killed. The proportions worked out at about four wounded to every one killed. Of these four, one got wounded seriously, and the remaining three more or less lightly. The three lightly wounded returned to the front after a few weeks or months of absence, and again faced the same odds. Flying casualties were even higher. Since the war lasted for four and a half years, it is easy to see why most of the survivors, if not permanently disabled, got wounded several times.

Two well-known sportsmen were contemporaries of mine: A. G. Bower, late captain of England at soccer, but only an average player at Charterhouse; and Woolf Barnato, the Surrey cricketer (and millionaire racing motorist), also only an average player. Though Barnato was in the same house as myself, we had not a word to exchange for the four years we were together. Five scholars have so far made names for themselves: Richard Hughes as a playwright; Richard Goolden as an actor of old-man parts; Vincent Seligman as author of a propagandist life of Venizelos; Cyril Hartmann as an authority on historical French scandals; and my brother Charles as society columnist on the middle page of the *Daily Mail*. Occasionally I see another name or two in the papers. The other day, M— was in the news for escaping from a private lunatic asylum; he had once offered a boy ten shillings to hold his hand in a thunderstorm, and frequently threatened to run away from Charterhouse.

9

GEORGE MALLORY did something better than lend me books: he took me climbing on Snowdon in the school vacations. I knew Snowdon very well from my bedroom window at Harlech. In the spring, its distant white cap lent a sentimental glory to the landscape. The first time I went with George to Snowdon we stayed at the Snowdon Ranger Hotel, near Quellyn Lake. It was January, and we found the mountain covered in snow. We did little rock-climbing, but went up some good snow slopes with rope and ice-axe. I remember one climb to the summit. Finding the hotel there with its roof blown off in the previous night's blizzard, we sat by the cairn and ate Carlsbad plums and liver-sausage sandwiches. Geoffrey Keynes, the editor of the *Nonesuch Blake*, was in the team. He and George, who used to go drunk with excitement at the end of his climbs, picked stones off the cairn and shied them at the hotel chimney-stack until it joined the ruins of the roof.

George is still rated as one of the three or four best climbers in climbing history. Nobody had expected him to survive his first spectacular season in the Alps. He never afterwards lost his almost foolhardy daring, yet knew all there could be known about mountaineering technique. I always felt absolutely safe with him on the rope. George went through the war as a gunner lieutenant, but kept his nerve – by rock-climbing while on leave.

When the war ended, George loved mountains more than ever. His death on Mount Everest came five years later. No one knows whether he and Irvine actually made the last five hundred yards of the ascent, or whether they turned back, or what happened; but anyone who has climbed with George is convinced that he got to the summit and rejoiced in his accustomed way without leaving himself sufficient reserve of strength for the descent. I did not see it mentioned in the newspaper account of his death that he originally took to climbing while a scholar at Winchester, as a corrective to his weak heart. He told me that life at Winchester had made him so miserable that he once ran away: taking nothing with him but his beloved mathematics books. George's other claim to fame is that he wrote the first modern biography of James Boswell.

He was wasted at Charterhouse where, in my time at least, the boys generally despised him as neither a disciplinarian nor interested in cricket or football. He tried to treat his class in a friendly way, which puzzled and offended them, because of the school tradition of concealed warfare between boys and masters. We considered it no shame to cheat, lie, or deceive where a master was concerned, though the same treatment of a school-fellow would have been immoral. George also antagonized the housemasters by refusing to accept this state of war and fraternizing with the boys whenever possible. When two housemasters, who had been unfriendly to him, happened to die within a short time of each other, he joked to me: 'See, Robert, how mine enemies flee before my face!' I always called him by his Christian name, and so did three or four more of his friends in the school. This lack of dignity put him beyond the pale with most boys, and all masters. Eventually the falseness of his position told on his temper; yet he always managed to find four or five boys who were, like him, out of their element, befriending and making life tolerable for them. Before the final Everest expedition, he had decided to resign and take a job at Cambridge with the

Workers' Educational Association; tired of trying to teach gentlemen to be gentlemen.

I spent a season with George and a large number of climbers at the Pen-y-Pass Hotel on Snowdon in the spring of 1914. This time we did real precipice climbing, and I had the luck to climb with George, H. E. L. Porter (a renowned technician), Kitty O'Brien, and Conor O'Brien, her brother, who afterwards made a famous voyage round the world in a ridiculously small boat. Conor climbed, he told us, principally as a corrective to bad nerves. He would get very excited when any slight hitch occurred; his voice usually rose to a scream. Kitty used to chide him: 'Ach, Conor, dear, have a bit of wit!' and Conor would apologize. Being a sailor, he used to climb in bare feet. Often in climbing one has to support the entire weight of one's body on a couple of toes – but toes in stiff boots. Conor claimed that he could force his naked toes farther into crevices than a boot would go.

The most honoured man there was Geoffrey Young, an Eton master, and the President of the Climbers' Club. His four closest friends had all been killed climbing; a comment on the extraordinary care which he always took himself. It appeared not merely in his preparations for an ascent – the careful examination strand by strand of the Alpine rope, the attention to his boot-nails, and the balanced loading of his rucksack – but also in his caution on the rock-face. Before making any move he thought it out foot by foot, as though it were a chess problem. If the next hand-hold happened to be just a little out of his reach, or the next foot-hold seemed at all precarious, he would stop to think of a safe way round the difficulty. George used sometimes to grow impatient, but Geoffrey refused to be hurried. His shortness put him at a disadvantage in the matter of reach. Though not as double-jointed and prehensile as Porter, or as magnificent as George, he was the perfect climber; and still remains so. This, in spite of having lost a leg with a Red Cross unit on the Italian front. He climbs with an artificial leg, and has recently published the only reliable textbook on rock-climbing. I felt very proud to be on the same rope as Geoffrey Young, and when he told me one day: 'Robert, you have the finest natural balance that I have ever seen in a climber,' this compliment pleased me far more than if the Poet Laureate had told me that I had the finest sense of rhythm that he had ever met in a young poet.

I certainly must have a good balance. Once, in Switzerland, it saved me from a broken leg or legs. My mother took us there in the Christmas holidays of 1913–14, ostensibly for winter sports, but really because she thought that my sisters should be given a chance to meet nice young men of means. About my third day on skis I went up from Champéry, where we were staying and the snow was too soft, to Morgins, a thousand feet higher, where it closely resembled castor sugar. Here I found an ice-run for skeleton-toboggans. Without pausing to consider that skis have no purchase on ice at all, I launched myself down it. After a few yards, my speed increased alarmingly and I realized with a shock what I was in for. There were several sharp turns in the run, protected by high banks, and I had to trust entirely to body-balance in swerving round them. On reaching the terminus still upright, I had my eyes damned by a frightened sports-club official for having endangered my life on his territory.

In an essay on climbing written at the time, I said that the sport made all others seem trivial. 'New climbs, or new variations of old climbs, are not made in a competitive spirit, but only because it is good to stand somewhere on the earth's surface where nobody else has stood before. It is good, too, to be alone with a specially chosen band of people – people in whom one can trust completely. Rock-climbing, one of the most dangerous sports possible, unless one keeps to the rules, becomes reasonably safe if one does keep to them. With physical fitness in every member of the team, a careful watch on the weather, proper overhauling of climbing apparatus, and no hurry, anxiety, or stunts, mountaineering can be much safer than fox-hunting. Hunting implies uncontrollable factors, such as hidden wire, holes in which a horse may stumble, caprice or vice in the horse. Climbers trust entirely to their own feet, legs, hands, shoulders, sense of balance, judgement of distance.'

My first precipice was Crib-y-ddysgel: a test climb for beginners. About fifty feet above the scree – a height that is more frightening than five hundred, because death seems almost as certain and far more immediate – a long, sloping shelf of rock, about the length of an ordinary room, had to be crossed from right to left. This offered no hand-holds or foot-holds worth mentioning, and was too steep to stand or kneel on without slipping. It shelved at an angle of, I suppose, forty-five or fifty degrees. One rolled across upright, and trusted in friction as a maintaining force. Once across the shelf without disaster, I felt that the rest of the climb would be easy.

They called this climb 'The Gambit'. Robert Trevelyan, the poet, had been given the test in the previous season, but been unlucky enough to fall off. He was pulled up short, after a few feet, by the leader's well-belayed rope; but the experience disgusted him with climbing and he spent the rest of his time at Pen-y-Pass just walking about.

Belaying means making fast, on a projection of rock, a loop of the rope which is wound round one's waist, and so disposing the weight of the body that, if the climber above or below happens to fall, the belay will keep the whole party from going down together. Alpine rope has a breaking-point of a third of its own length. Only one member of the climbing team moves at any given time, the others wait, belayed. Sometimes the leader has to move up fifty or sixty feet until he finds a secure belay from which to start the next upward movement, so that if he slips, and cannot put on any sort of brake, he must fall more than twice that length before being pulled up.

That same day I was taken on a spectacular, though not particularly difficult climb on Crib Goch. At one point we traversed around a knife-edge buttress. From this knife-edge a pillar-like rock, technically known as a monolith, had split away. We scrambled up the monolith, which overhung the valley with a clear five hundred feet drop, and each in turn stood on the top balanced. Next, he had to make a long, careful stride from the top of the monolith to the rock-face; here there was a ledge just wide enough to admit the toe of a boot, and a hand-hold at convenient height to give an easy pull-up to the next ledge. I remember George shouting down from above: 'Be careful of that foot-hold, Robert! Don't chip the edge off, or the climb will be impossible for anyone who wants to do it again. It's got to last another five hundred years at least.'

I was in danger only once. Porter took me climbing on an out-of-the-way part of the mountain. The climb, known as the Ribbon Track and Girdle Traverse, had not been attempted for ten years. About half-way up we reached a chimney. A 'chimney' is a vertical fissure in the rock wide enough to admit the body; whereas a 'crack' is only wide enough to admit the boot. One works up a chimney sideways, with back and knees; but up a crack with one's face to the rock. Porter, fifty feet above me in the chimney, made a spring to a hand-hold slightly out of reach. In doing so, he dislodged a pile of stones which had been wedged in the chimney. They rattled down, and one, rather bigger than a cricket ball, struck me unconscious. Fortunately I was well belayed, and Porter had made his objective. The rope held me up; I recovered my senses a few seconds later and managed to continue.

At Pen-y-Pass we used to take a leisurely breakfast and lie in the sun with a tankard of beer before starting for the precipice foot in the late morning. Snowdon is a perfect mountain for climbers, its rock being sound and not slippery. And once they reach the top of any of the precipices, some of which are a thousand feet high, but all just climbable, one way or another, there is always an easy track to jog home down. In the evening, when we got back to the hotel, we lay and stewed in hot baths. I remember wondering at my body – the worn fingernails, the bruised knees, and the lump of climbing muscle which had begun to bunch above my instep, seeing it as beautiful in relation to this new purpose. My worst climb was on Lliwedd, the most formidable of the precipices when, at a point that needed most concentration, a raven circled round the party in great sweep. I found this curiously unsettling, because one climbs only up and down, or sideways, and the raven seemed to be suggesting diverse other possible dimensions of movement – tempting us to let go our hold and join him.

IO

I HAD just finished with Charterhouse and gone up to Harlech, when England declared war on Germany. A day or two later I decided to enlist. In the first place, though the papers predicted only a very short war – over by Christmas at the outside – I hoped that it might last long enough to delay my going to Oxford in October, which I dreaded. Nor did I work out the possibilities of getting actively engaged in the fighting, expecting garrison service at home, while the regular forces were away. In the second place, I was outraged to read of the Germans' cynical violation of Belgian neutrality. Though I discounted perhaps twenty per cent of the atrocity details as wartime exaggeration, that was not, of course, sufficient. Recently

I saw the following contemporary newspaper cuttings put in chrono-
logical sequence:

When the fall of Antwerp became known, the church bells were
rung [i.e. at Cologne and elsewhere in Germany]. – *Kölnische Zeitung*.

According to the *Kölnische Zeitung*, the clergy of Antwerp were
compelled to ring the church bells when the fortress was taken. – *Le
Matin*.

According to what *The Times* has heard from Cologne, via Paris,
the unfortunate Belgian priests who refused to ring the church bells
when Antwerp was taken, have been sentenced to hard labour. –
Corriere della Sera.

According to information which has reached the *Corriere della Sera*
from Cologne, via London, it is confirmed that the barbaric conquerors
of Antwerp punished the unfortunate Belgian priests for their heroic
refusal to ring the church bells by hanging them as living clappers to the
bells with their heads down. – *Le Matin*.

In the trenches, a few months later, I happened to belong to a
company mess in which four of us young officers out of five had,
by a coincidence, either German mothers or naturalized German
fathers. One of them said: 'I'm glad I joined when I did. If I'd put
it off for a month or two, they'd have accused me of being a German
spy. As it is, I have an uncle interned in Alexandra Palace, and my
father's only been allowed to retain the membership of his golf club
because he has two sons in the trenches.' I told him: 'Well, I have
three or four uncles sitting somewhere opposite, and a number of
cousins, too. One of those uncles is a general. But that's all right.
I don't brag about them. I only advertise my uncle Dick Poore,
the British admiral commanding at the Nore.'

Among these enemy relatives was my cousin Conrad, only son
of the German Consul at Zürich. In January 1914, I had gone ski-
ing with him between the trees in the woods above the city. And
once we tobogganed together down the Dolderstrasse in Zürich itself, where the lamp-posts were sandbagged and family toboggans,
skidding broadside on at the turns, were often crashed into by single-
seater skeletons; arms and legs got broken by the score, and the
crowds thought it a great joke. Conrad served with a crack Bavarian
regiment throughout the war, and won the 'Pour le Mérite', an
order even more rarely awarded than the British Victoria Cross.
Soon after the war ended, a party of Bolsheviks killed him in a

Baltic village, where he had been sent to make requisitions. Conrad was a gentle, proud creature, chiefly interested in natural history, who used to spend hours in the woods studying the habits of wild animals; he had strong feelings against shooting them.

Perhaps my family's most outstanding military feat was a German uncle's; he had been dug out at the age of forty-five as a lieutenant in the Bavarian artillery. My brother John met him a year or two ago, and happened to mention a coming visit to Rheims. My uncle nudged him: 'Have a look at the cathedral. One day, during the war, my divisional general called for me. "Gunner-lieutenant von Ranke, I understand that you are a Lutheran, not a Roman Catholic?" I admitted this was so. Then he said: "I have a very disagreeable service for you to perform, Lieutenant. Those misbegotten French are using the cathedral for an observation post. They think they can get away with it because it's Rheims Cathedral, but they have our trenches taped from there. I call upon you to dislodge them." I fired only two rounds, and down came the pinnacle and the Frenchmen with it. A very neat bit of shooting. I felt proud to have limited the damage like that. Really, you must take a look at it.'

The Harlech golf club secretary suggested my taking a commission instead of enlisting. He rang up the nearest regimental depôt – the Royal Welch Fusiliers at Wrexham – and told the adjutant that I had served in the Officers Training Corps at Charterhouse. The adjutant said: 'Send him right along.' On August 11th I began my training, and immediately became a hero. My mother announced: 'Our race has gone mad!' and regarded my going as a religious act; my father felt proud that I had 'done the right thing'. I even recovered, for a time, the respect of C. L. Graves, of the *Spectator* and *Punch*, the uncle with whom I had recently had a tiff. When he tipped me a sovereign, two terms previously, I had written to thank him, saying that I was at last able to buy Samuel Butler's *Note Books*, *The Way of All Flesh*, and the two *Erewhons*. This had infuriated him, as a good Victorian.

Most of the other applicants for commissions at Wrexham were boys who had recently failed to pass into the Royal Military College at Sandhurst, and were now trying to get into the regular army at the old militia back-door – re-named the Special Reserve. Only one or two fellows had come, like myself, for the sake of the war, and not for the sake of a career. There were about a dozen of us recruit officers on the Square, learning to drill and be drilled. My

O.T.C. experience helped me here, but I knew nothing of Army tradition and made all the worst mistakes – saluting the bandmaster, failing to recognize the colonel when in mufti, walking in the street without a belt, talking shop in the mess. Though I soon learned to conform, my greatest difficulty was talking to the men of my platoon with the proper air of authority. Many of them were re-enlisted old soldiers, and I disliked bluffing that I knew more than they did. We had two or three very old soldiers employed on the depôt staff, wearing ribbons of Burma, 1885, and even earlier campaigns, and usually also the ribbon of the 'Rooti', or good service, medal awarded for 'eighteen years of undetected crime'. Of one old fellow, called Jackie Barrett, a Kipling character, I heard it said: 'There goes Jackie Barrett. He and his mucking-in chum deserted the regiment at Quetta, and crossed the North-West Frontier on foot. Three months later, Jackie gave himself up as a deserter to the British Consul in Jerusalem. He buried his chum by the way.'

After only three weeks on the Square, I went off on detachment duty, to a newly-formed internment camp for enemy aliens at Lancaster. The camp was a disused waggon-works near the river, a dirty, draughty place, littered with old scrap metal and guarded by high barbed-wire fences. About three thousand prisoners had already arrived there, and more and more crowded in every day: seamen arrested on German vessels in Liverpool harbour, waiters from large hotels in the North, an odd German band or two, harmless German commercial travellers and shopkeepers. The prisoners resented being interned, particularly family men who had lived at peace in England for many years. The one comfort that we could offer them was: 'You are safer inside than out.' For anti-German feeling had begun to run high; shops with German names were continually raided; and even German women made to feel that they were personally responsible for the alleged Belgian atrocities. Besides, we pointed out, in Germany they would be forced to join the army. At this time, we could make a boast of our voluntary system, and never foresaw the time when these internees would be bitterly envied by forcibly-enlisted Englishmen for being kept safe until the war ended.

In the summer of 1915, *The Times* reprinted a German newspaper account by Herr Wolff, an exchanged prisoner, of his experiences at Lancaster in 1914. *The Times* amused itself with Wolff's allegations that he and forty other waiters from the Midland Hotel, Manchester, had been arrested and taken, handcuffed and fettered, in special railway carriages to Lancaster, escorted by fifty Manchester policemen armed with carbines. But it was true, because I myself took over from the Chief Inspector, a fine figure in a frogged tunic, who gave me a splendid salute. He had done his job well and seemed proud of it, the only mishap being the accidental breaking of two carriage windows by the slung carbines. Wolff reported that even children were interned in the camp; and this also was true. A dozen or so little boys from the German bands had been interned because it seemed more humane to keep them with their friends than to send them to a workhouse. But their moral safety in the camp caused the commandant great concern.

I commanded a detachment of fifty Special Reservists, most of them with only six weeks' service: a rough lot of Welshmen from the border counties. They had joined the army just before war started, as a cheap way of getting a training camp holiday; being forced to continue beyond the usual fortnight exasperated them. They were constantly deserting and having to be fetched back by the police, and seemed more scared of the prisoners than the prisoners were of them. I hated doing my round of sentries on a dark night at 2 or 3 a.m. Very often the lantern used to blow out and, fumbling to light it again in the dark, I would hear the frightened voice of a sentry roar: 'Halt! Who goes there?' I knew that he would be standing with his rifle aimed and five live rounds in his magazine; but always gave him the pass-word just in time. Sentries often fired at shadows. The prisoners, particularly the sailors, fought a good deal among themselves. I saw a prisoner spit out teeth and blood one morning, and asked him what was wrong. 'Oh, sir, one no-good friend give me one clap on the chops.' Frequent deputations came to complain of the dullness of the food – the same ration food served to the troops. But after a while the prisoners settled down to sullen docility, starting hobbies, glee parties, games, and plans for escape. I had far more trouble with my Welshmen, who were always escaping from their quarters, though I guarded all possible exits. Finally I discovered that they had been crawling out through a sewer. They boasted of their successes with the women. Private Kirby said to me: 'Do you know, sir? On the Sunday after we arrived, all the preachers in Lancashire took as their text: "Mothers, take care of your daughters; the Royal Welch have come to town."'

An inconvenient accident happened to me at Lancaster. The telephone was installed at an office where I slept on a sloping desk. One night, Pack Saddle (the code name for the Chief Supply Officer, Western Command) rang up from Chester after midnight, with orders for the commandant. They concerned the rationing of another batch of four hundred prisoners, who were being sent to him from Chester and North Wales. In the middle of a conversation made difficult by a thunderstorm, my sleepiness, and Pack Saddle's irritability, the line got struck by lightning somewhere. An electric shock spun me round, and I could not use a telephone again without sweating and stammering until some twelve years later.

Guarding prisoners seemed an unheroic part to be playing in the war which, by October, had reached a critical stage; I wanted to be abroad fighting. My training had been interrupted, and I knew that even when recalled from detachment duty, I should have to wait a month or two at least before getting sent out. When I returned to the depôt, 'Tibs' Crawshay, the adjutant, a keen regular soldier, found two things wrong with me. First of all – I had not only gone to an inefficient tailor, but also had a soldier-servant who neglected to polish my buttons and shine my belt and boots as he should have done. Never having owned a valet before, I did not know what to expect of him. Crawshay finally summoned me to the Orderly Room. He would not send me to France, he said, until I had entirely overhauled my wardrobe and looked more like a soldier – my company commander's report on me was 'unsoldierlike and a nuisance'. But my pay only just covered the mess bills, and I could hardly ask my parents to buy me another outfit so soon after assuring them that I had everything necessary. Crawshay next decided that I must be a poor sportsman – probably because on the day of the Grand National, in which a horse of his was running, all the young officers applied for leave to see the race, except myself. I volunteered to take the job of Orderly Officer for the Day for someone who wanted to go.

One by one my contemporaries were sent out to France to take the place of casualties in the First and Second Battalions, while I remained despondently at the depôt. But again boxing helped me. Johnny Basham, a sergeant in the regiment, was training at the time for his fight – which he won – with Boswell for the Lonsdale Belt, welter-weight. I visited the training camp one evening, where Basham was offering to fight three rounds with any member of the regiment – the more the merrier. A young officer pulled on the gloves, and

Basham got roars of laughter from the crowd as soon as he had taken his opponent's measure, by dodging around and playing the fool with him. I asked Basham's manager if I could have a go. He lent me some shorts, and I stepped into the ring. Pretending to know nothing of boxing, I led off with my right and moved clumsily. Basham saw a chance of getting another laugh; he dropped his guard and danced about with a you-can't-hit-me challenge. I caught him off his balance, and knocked him across the ring. He recovered and went for me, but I managed to keep on my feet. When I laughed at him, he laughed too. We had three very brisk rounds, and he very decently made me seem a much better boxer than I was, by accommodating his pace to mine. As soon as Crawshay heard the story, he rang me up at my billet and told me that he had learned with pleasure of my performance; that for an officer to box like that was a great encouragement for the men; that he was mistaken about my sportsmanship; and that, to show his appreciation, he would put me down for a draft to France in a week's time.

Of the officers sent out before me, several had already been killed or wounded. The killed included a Liberal M.P., Second-Lieutenant W. G. Gladstone, whom we called 'Glad Eyes'. He was in his early thirties, a grandson of old Gladstone, whom he resembled in feature, and Lord-Lieutenant of his county. While war hung in the balance he had declared himself against it, whereupon his Hawarden tenantry, much ashamed, threatened to duck him in the pond. Realizing that, once war was declared, further protest would be useless, he joined the regiment as a second-lieutenant. His political convictions remained unaltered but, being a man of great integrity, he refused to take the non-combative employment as a staff-colonel offered him in the War Office. Soon after joining the First Battalion in France he was killed by a sniper while unnecessarily exposing himself. General French sent his body home for a military funeral at Hawarden; I attended it.

One or two random memories remain of this training period at Wrexham. The landlord of my billet, a Welsh solicitor, greatly overcharged us though pretending amicability. He wore a wig – or, to be more exact, three wigs, with hair of progressive lengths. After wearing the medium-sized hair for a few days, he would put on the long-haired wig, and say that, dear him! he really ought to get a hair-cut. Then he would leave the house and, in a public lavatory perhaps, or a wayside copse, change into the short-haired wig, which he wore until he thought it time to change to the medium once more. The deception came to light when one of the officers billeted with me got drunk and raided his bedroom. This officer, a Williams, was an extreme example of the sly Border Welshman. The drunker he became, the more shocking his confessions. He told me once about a Dublin girl whom he had promised to marry, and even slept with on the strength of a diamond engagement ring. 'Only paste, really,' he boasted. The day before the wedding she lost a foot – cut off by a Dalkey tram, and he hurriedly left Dublin. 'But, Graves, she was a lovely, lovely girl until that happened!' Williams had been a medical student at Trinity College, Dublin. Whenever he visited Chester, the nearest town, to pick up a prostitute, he would not only appeal to her patriotism to charge him nothing, but always gave my name. I knew of this because these women wrote me reproachful letters. At last I told him in the mess: 'In future you are going to be distinguished from all the other Williamses in the regiment by being called "Dirty Williams".' The name stuck. By one shift or another he escaped all trench-service, except for a short spell in a quiet sector, and lasted the war out safely.

Private Probert came from Anglesey, and had joined the Special Reserve in peacetime for his health. In September, the entire battalion volunteered for service overseas, except Probert. He refused to go, and could be neither coaxed nor bullied. Finally he came before the colonel, whom he genuinely puzzled by his obstinacy. Probert explained: 'I'm not afraid, colonel, sir. But I don't want to be shot at. I have a wife and pigs at home.' The battalion was now rigged out in a temporary navy-blue uniform until khaki might be available – all but Probert. The colonel decided to shame him, and he continued, by order, to wear the peacetime scarlet tunic and blue trousers with a red stripe: a very dirty scarlet tunic, too, because he had been put on the kitchen staff. His mates called him 'Cock Robin', and sang a popular chorus in his honour:

> And I never get a knock
> When the boys call Cock
> Cockity ock, ock,
> Cock Robin!
> In my old red vest I mean to cut a shine,
> Walking down the street they call me 'Danger on
>   the line' . . .

But Probert did not care:

> *For the more they call me Robin Redbreast*
> *I'll wear it longer still.*
> *I will wear a red waistcoat, I will,*
> *I will, I will, I will, I will, I will!*

So, in October, he got discharged as medically unfit: 'Of under-developed intelligence, unlikely to be of service in His Majesty's Forces', and went happily home to his wife and pigs. Of the singers, few who survived Festubert in the following May, survived Loos in the following September.

Recruit officers spent a good deal of their time at Company and Battalion Orderly Room, learning how to deal with crime. 'Crime' meant any breach of King's Regulations; and there was plenty of it. Battalion Orderly Room would last four or five hours every day, at the rate of one crime dealt with every three or four minutes – this being apart from the scores of less serious offences tried by company commanders. The usual Battalion Orderly Room crimes were deser-tion, refusing to obey an order, using obscene language to a non-commissioned officer, drunk and disorderly, robbing a comrade, and so forth. On pay-nights, hardly a man stayed sober; but no attention was paid if silence reigned as soon as the company officer came on his rounds at Lights Out. Two years later, serious crime had dimin-ished to a twentieth of that amount, though the battalion was treble its original strength, and though many of the cases that the company officer had dealt with summarily now came before the colonel; and drunkenness practically vanished.

Taylor, a young soldier in my company, had been with me at Lancaster, where I bought him a piccolo to play when the detach-ment went on route marches; he would give us one tune after an-other for mile after mile. The other fellows carried his pack and rifle. At Wrexham, on pay-nights, he used to sit on an upturned bucket in the company billet – a drill-hall near the railway station – and play jigs for the drunks to dance to. He never drank himself. The music began slow, but gradually quickened, until he had worked them into a frenzy, delaying this climax for my arrival with the company orderly-sergeant. As the sergeant flung open the door and bellowed: '"F" Company, Attention!' Taylor would break off, thrust the piccolo under his blankets, and jump to his feet. The drunks were left frozen in the middle of their capers, blinking stupidly.

At the first Battalion Orderly Room that I attended, a case went like this:

SERGEANT-MAJOR (*off-stage*): Now, then, you 99 Davies, F-Company, cap off, as you were, cap off, as you were, cap off! That's better. Escort and prisoner, right *turn*! Quick *march*! Right wheel! (*On stage*) Left wheel! Mark time! Escort and prisoner, *halt*! Left *turn*!

COLONEL: Read the charge, sergeant-major.

SERGEANT-MAJOR: No. 99 Pte W. Davies, F-Company, at Wrexham on 20th August: improper conduct. Committing a nuisance on the barrack square. Witnesses: Sergeant Timmins, Corporal Jones.

COLONEL: Sergeant Timmins, your evidence.

SERGEANT TIMMINS: Sir, on the said date about two p.m., I was hacting horderly sar'nt. Corporal Jones reported the nuisance to me. I hinspected it. It was the prisoner's, sir.

COLONEL: Corporal Jones! Your evidence.

CORPORAL JONES: Sir, on the said date I was crossing the barrack square, when I saw prisoner in a sitting posture. He was committing excreta, sir. I took his name and reported to the orderly sergeant, sir.

COLONEL: Well, Private Davies, what have you to say for yourself?

99 DAVIES (*in a nervous sing-song*): Sir, I came over queer all of a sudden, sir. I haad the diarrhoeas terrible baad. I haad to do it, sir.

COLONEL: But my good man, the latrine was only a few yards away.

99 DAVIES: Colonel, sir, you caan't stop nature!

SERGEANT-MAJOR: Don't answer an officer like that!

(*Pause.*)

SERGEANT TIMMINS (*coughs*): Sir?

COLONEL: Yes, Sergeant Timmins?

SERGEANT TIMMINS: Sir, I had occasion to hexamine the nuisance, sir, *and it was done with a heffort, sir*!

COLONEL: Do you take my punishment, Private Davies?

99 DAVIES: Yes, colonel, sir.

COLONEL: You have done a very dirty act, and disgraced the regiment and your comrades. I shall make an example of you. Ten days' detention.

SERGEANT-MAJOR: Escort and prisoner, left *turn*! Quick *march*! Left wheel!

(*Off-stage*): Escort and prisoner, *halt*! Cap on! March him off to the guard-room. Get ready the next case!

Orderly Room always embarrassed and dispirited me. I never got used to it, even after sentencing thousands of men myself. The sole change brought by the introduction of the civilian element into the army was that, about half-way through the war, an Army Council

Instruction laid down that henceforth the word of command must be: 'Accused and escort, right turn, quick march ...' instead of 'Prisoner and escort, right turn, quick march ...' Few interesting cases ever came up. Even the obscene language, always quoted verbatim, continued drearily the same; the only variation I remember from the four stock words was provided by the man, charged with using threatening and obscene language to an N.C.O., who had told a lance-corporal: 'Corporal Smith, two men shall meet before two mountains.' When the colonel asked what this meant, the lance-corporal explained that though two mountains could never meet, two men might, and these two might be himself and the prisoner; and the meeting might be in peacetime, and the prisoner might then be tempted to strike him. Despite the remoteness of this contingency, the prisoner got seven days' detention – in the Camp Prison. Humour was mainly supplied by the very Welsh Welshmen from the hills, who had an imperfect command of English. One of them, charged with being absent off ceremonial parade and using obscene language to the sergeant, became very indignant in Orderly Room and cried out to the colonel: 'Colonel, sir, sergeant tole me wass I for guard; I axed him no, and now the bloody bastard says wass I.'

The greatest number of simultaneous charges that I ever heard brought against a soldier occurred in the case of Boy Jones, at Liverpool in 1917. They accused him, first, of using obscene language to the bandmaster. (The bandmaster, who was squeamish, reported it as: 'Sir, he called me a double effing c—.') Next, breaking out of the detention awarded for this crime. Then, 'absenting himself from the regiment until apprehended in the Hindenburg Line, France.' Fourth resisting an escort. Fifth, being found in possession of regimental property belonging to the Cheshire Regiment. Boy Jones, who was only fourteen, and looked thirteen, had wriggled through the bars of his detention-cell and, after getting a few things together in his hut, gone to Liverpool Exchange Station to wait for a victim – who proved to be a private in a Cheshire Bantam Battalion, just returning to France from leave. Bantam Battalions consisted of volunteers hitherto too short to qualify for the army. Boy Jones treated the bantam to a lot of drink and robbed him of his rifle, equipment, badges, and papers. He then went off in his place. Arrived in France, he proceeded to the Bantam Battalion; but this did not suit him. He wanted to be with his own regiment; so he deserted the Bantams,

70

who were billeted somewhere north of Arras, and walked south along the trenches looking for his regiment, having now resumed his proper badges. A couple of days' walk brought him to the Second Battalion Headquarters where he reported, but was immediately sent home, after a tough struggle with his escort at the railhead. The punishment awarded for all these heinous offences – 'ten days confined to camp', and a spanking by the bandmaster – seemed to us very nicely calculated.

A most unusual charge, against the regimental goat-major (a corporal), was first framed as lese majesty, but later reduced to 'disrespect to an officer: in that he, at Wrexham – on such and such a date – did prostitute the Royal Goat, being the gift of His Majesty, the Colonel-in-Chief, from His Royal Herd at Windsor, by offering its stud-services for a fee to —, Esq., farmer and goat breeder, of Wrexham.' Though the goat-major pleaded that he had done this out of consideration for the goat, to which he was much attached, the Colonel reduced him to the ranks and took away his job.

In peacetime, the regular battalions of the regiment, though officered mainly by Anglo-Welshmen of county families, did not contain more than about one Welsh-speaking Welshman in fifty. Most recruits came from Birmingham. The only Harlech man besides myself, who joined the regiment at the start was a golf caddie. He had got into trouble a short time before for stealing clubs. The chapels held soldiering to be sinful, and in Merioneth the chapels had the last word. Prayers were offered for me by the chapels, not because of the physical dangers I would run in France, but because of the moral dangers threatening me at home. However, when Lloyd George became Minister of Munitions in 1915, and persuaded the chapels that war was a Crusade, we had a sudden tremendous influx of Welshmen from North Wales. They were difficult soldiers, who particularly resented having to stand still while N.C.O.s swore at them.

At Wrexham, we second-lieutenants learned regimental history, drill, musketry, Boer War field-tactics, military law and organization, how to recognize bugle calls, how to work a machine-gun, and how to conduct ourselves on formal occasions. We dug no trenches, handled no bombs, thought of the company, not of the platoon, still less of the section, as the smallest independent tactical unit. Only two wounded officers were back from the front at the time; both had left the Second Battalion on the retreat from Mons. Neither would talk much of his experiences. One of them, 'Emu' Jones, would tell us no more than this: 'The first queer sight I saw in France was three naked women hanging by their feet in a butcher's shop.' The other used to say: 'The German shells knock hell out of a man, especially the big black ones. Just hell. And that fellow Emu – he wasn't any good. We marched and marched, and with his weak heart he used to faint daily and expect his poor bloody platoon to carry him as well as the rest of their load. Everyone swore he was skrimshanking. Don't believe what old Emu tells you of the Retreat.'

II

I USED to congratulate myself on having quite blindly chosen the Royal Welch Fusiliers, of all regiments in the army. 'Good God!' I used to think. 'Suppose that when the war broke out I had been living in Cheshire, and had applied for a commission in the Cheshire Regiment.' How ashamed I should have been to find in the history of that regiment – the old Twenty-second Foot, just senior in the line to the Royal Welch, the Twenty-third – that it had been deprived of its old title 'The Royal Cheshires' as a punishment for losing a battle. (This was a quite unhistorical libel, but we all believed it.) Or how lucky not to have joined the Bedfords, who were making a name for themselves in this war, but were still called 'The Peacemakers'; for they had only four battle-honours on their colours, none more recent than the year 1711, and we misquoted their regimental motto as: 'Thou shalt not kill!' Even the Black Watch had a stain on its record; and everyone knew about it. If a Tommy of another regiment went into a public bar where men of the Black Watch were drinking, and felt brave enough to start a fight, he would ask the barmaid not for 'pig's ear', which is rhyming-slang for beer, but for a pint of 'broken square'. Then belts would be unbuckled.

The Royal Welch had twenty-nine battle-honours, a number equalled only by a couple of other two-battalion regiments. And here, too, the Royal Welch had the advantage, since these were not single regiments, but 1888 combinations of two each with its separate history. The First Battalion of the Royal Welch Fusiliers could boast twenty-six battle-honours of its own, the remaining three having fallen to the Second Battalion in its short and interrupted existence. They were all good bloody battle-honours, none of them like that battle into which, it was said, the Argyll and Sutherland Highlanders had gone with nine hundred men and from which they emerged with nine hundred and one – no casualties, and a band-boy come of age and promoted a private. For many hard fights, such as The Boyne and Aughrim and the capture of Lille, the Royal Welch had never been honoured. The regiment shared in each of the four hardest fought victories of the British Army, as listed by Sir John Fortescue. My regimental history is rusty now, but I believe that they were Malplaquet, Albuhera, Waterloo, and Inkerman. The Royal Welch was also one of the six Minden regiments, who performed the unprecedented feat of charging a body of cavalry many times their own strength and driving it off the field. Even the surrender at York Town in the American War of Independence, the regiment's single disaster, could not be accounted a disgrace. The Navy had let the Army down; and the Royal Welch were accorded the full honours of war, won by their conduct in the hard fighting at Lexington and Guildford Court House, and their suicidal advance up Bunker Hill. The original 'Thomas Atkins' was a Royal Welch Fusilier in that war.

I caught the sense of regimental tradition a day or two after my arrival at the depôt. In a cupboard at the mess, I came across a big leather-bound ledger and pulled it out to read. It proved to be the Daily Order Book of the First Battalion in the trenches before Sevastopol, and I opened it at the page giving orders for an attack on the Redan Redoubt. Such and such a company was desired to supply volunteers for the storming party under Lieutenant So-and-so. Next followed details of their arms and equipment, the number of ladders they must carry, and the support to be afforded by other companies. Then details of rations and supply of ammunition, with an earnest 'Godspeed!' from the commanding officer. (A sketch of the commanding officer hung on the wall above my head, lying sick in his tent at Scutari, wearing a 'Balaclava helmet', or cap-comforter, against the intense cold.) The attack failed, and among subsequent entries were orders for the burial of the dead, appreciation from headquarters of the gallantry vainly displayed, and a notice that the effects of Lieutenant So-and-so, who had led the storming party, would be sold at public auction in the trenches next day. Another

Daily Order contained the citation of a certain Sergeant Luke O'Connor's gallantry, for which he received one of the first Victoria Crosses when the award was instituted in 1856. He still lived – Lieutenant-General Sir Luke O'Connor, now colonel of the regiment.

The most immediate piece of regimental history that I met as a recruit-officer was the flash: a fan-like bunch of five black ribbons, each two inches wide, seven and a half inches long, and ending in a dove-tail. The angle at which the fan must be spread has been exactly regulated by regimental convention. The flash is stitched to the back of the tunic collar, and only the Royal Welch are privileged to wear it. The story goes that the Royal Welch were abroad on foreign service for several years in the 1830s, and by some mischance never received the army order abolishing the queue. When the regiment returned and paraded at Plymouth, the inspecting general reprimanded the commanding officer because his men were still wearing their hair in the old fashion. The commanding officer, angered by the slight, immediately rode up to London and won from King William IV, through the intercession of some Court official, a regimental privilege of continuing to wear the bunch of ribbons with which the end of the queue was tied – the flash. The King made it a distinctive badge to be worn by all ranks in recognition of exemplary service during the Napoleonic Wars.

The Army Council, which is usually composed of cavalry, engineer, artillery, and Guards generals, with the Line hardly represented, had never encouraged regimental peculiarities, and could not easily forget the irregularity of our direct appeal to the Sovereign. The Army Council did not, at any rate, sanction the flash on the new khaki service-dress. Yet our officers and warrant-officers continued to wear it. In a pre-war correspondence between the regiment and the Army Council, Sir Luke O'Connor maintained that the flash, being a distinctive mark honourably won, should be worn with service-dress, and not merely with peacetime scarlet. The Army Council objected that it would be a distinctive mark for enemy snipers, and particularly dangerous when worn by officers. Sir Luke retorted by inquiring on what occasion, since the retreat from Corunna, when the regiment was the last to leave Spain, with the key of the town postern in the pocket of one of its officers, had any of His Majesty's enemies seen the back of a Royal Welch Fusilier officer? The Army Council stood firm; and the matter remained in abeyance throughout the war. Once, in 1917, when an officer of my company went to be

74

decorated with the Military Cross at Buckingham Palace, King George, as Colonel-in-chief of the regiment, showed a personal interest in the flash. He asked: 'You are serving in one of the line battalions?' 'The Second Battalion, sir.' So the King gave him the order 'About turn!' for a look at the flash, and then 'About turn!' again. 'Good,' he said, 'you're still wearing it, I see,' and then, in a stage whisper: 'Don't ever let anyone take it from you!'

After the war, when scarlet was abandoned on the grounds of expense, the Army Council saw that it could now reasonably sanction the flash on service-dress for all ranks. As an additional favour it consented to recognize another defiant regimental peculiarity: the spelling of the word 'Welch' with a *c*. This permission was published in a special Army Council Instruction of 1919. The ignorant *Daily Herald* commented ''Strewth!' as though it were unimportant, but the spelling with a *c* was as important to us as the miniature cap-badge worn at the back of the cap was to the Gloucesters (a commemoration of the time when they fought back to back in Egypt). I have seen a young officer sent off Battalion Parade because his buttons read 'Welsh' instead of 'Welch'. 'Welch' referred us somehow to the archaic North Wales of Henry Tudor and Owen Glendower and Lord Herbert of Cherbury, the founder of the regiment; it dissociated us from the modern North Wales of chapels, Liberalism, the dairy and drapery business, slate mines, and the tourist trade.

The regiment insisted strictly on the standard measurements of the flash. When New Army battalions were formed, and rumours came to Wrexham that in the Eighteenth Battalion officers were wearing flashes nearly down to their waists, great consternation ensued. Our adjutant sent off the youngest subaltern on a special mission to the Eighteenth Battalion, the colonel of which had been borrowed from some Yorkshire regiment. The subaltern had orders to present himself at the Orderly Room with a large pair of shears.

The New Army battalions were, however, as anxious to be regimental as the line battalions. Once in France a regular major of the Royal Fusiliers entered the mess of the Nineteenth (Bantam) Battalion of the Royal Welch Fusiliers. He greeted the mess with 'Good afternoon, gentlemen,' and called for a drink from the mess-sergeant. After he had chatted for a while, he asked the senior officer present: 'Do you know why I ordered that drink from the mess-sergeant?' 'Of course, you wanted to see whether we remembered the Peninsular War.' The Royal Fusilier nodded: 'Our mess is just along behind that wood there. We haven't forgotten either.' After Albuhera, the few survivors of the Royal Welch Fusiliers and the Royal Fusiliers had messed together on the captured hill; deciding that henceforth and for ever, the officers of each regiment would be honorary members of the other's mess, and the N.C.O.s the same.

I must tell of St David's Night: the raw leeks eaten to the roll of the drum, with one foot on a chair and one on the mess table enriched by spoils of the Summer Palace at Peking – 1900, when we struck up another solemn friendship with the U.S. Marine Corps. (Leeks are not at all bad to eat, despite Shakespeare.) And the Royal Goat with gilded horns, that once leaped over the mess table bearing a drummer-boy on its back. And the toast to Major Toby Purcell's golden spurs, worn at The Boyne and lost in a shipwreck off New-foundland about 1840. And the toast to Shenkin Ap Morgan, the First Gentleman of Wales. And *The British Grenadiers*, the regimental march-past: for the British Grenadiers does not mean, as most people think, merely the Grenadier Guards. The term includes all regiments, the Royal Welch among them, that wear a bursting grenade as a collar- and cap-badge, to recall their early employment as storm troops armed with bombs.

During the war, the Royal Welch Fusiliers swelled to a size that imperilled regimental *esprit de corps*. Before the war we had two line battalions and the depôt. The affiliated and flash-less territorials – four battalions recruited for home service – could be disregarded, despite their regular adjutants. The Special Reserve Battalion, which trained at the depôt, was a poor relation. Now more and more New Army battalions were added: even a Twenty-fifth Battalion went to Pales-tine in 1917, and proved as good as the Eighth. So the regiment (that is, consensus of opinion in the two line battalions) tentatively accepted the New Army battalions one by one as they proved them-selves worthy by service in the field. It never accepted the territorials, disowning them contemptuously as 'dog-shooters'. The fact was that three of the four territorial battalions failed signally in the Suvla Bay landing at Gallipoli. One battalion, it became known, had offered violence to its officers; the commanding officer, a regular, had not cared to survive a disgrace which even the good work that these battalions did later at Gaza could not cancel. The remaining territorial battalion joined the First Division in France early in 1915, and quite unnecessarily lost its machine-guns at Givenchy. Regimental machine-guns, in 1915, were regarded almost as sacred. To lose them before the wiping-out of the entire battalion was considered as shameful as losing the regimental colours would have been in any eighteenth- or nineteenth-century battle. The territorial machine-gun officer who abandoned his guns had congratulated himself on removing the bolts; this would make them useless to the enemy. But he had forgotten the boxes of spare-parts. The Second Battalion made a raid in the same sector, a year and a half later, and recaptured one of the guns, which had been busy against our trenches ever since.

On arrival at the depôt, we Special Reserve officers were reminded of our great good fortune: if the war lasted, we should have the privilege of serving with one or the other of the line battalions. In peacetime, a candidate for a commission had not only to distinguish himself in the passing-out examination at the Royal Military College, Sandhurst, and be strongly recommended by two officers of the regiment, but to possess a guaranteed independent income that would enable him to play polo and hunt and keep up the social reputation of the regiment. These requirements were waived in our case; but we were to understand that we did not belong to the 'regiment' in the special sense. Permission to serve with it in time of war should satisfy our highest military aspirations. We were not temporary officers, like those of the New Army, but held permanent commissions in the Special Reserve Battalion. The Royal Welch, we were reminded, considered themselves second to none, even to the Guards. Representations had been made to them, after the South African War, inquiring whether they would like to become the Welsh Guards, and the offer had been indignantly declined; such a change would have made the regiment junior, in the brigade, even to the recently formed Irish Guards.

We were warned that while serving with a line battalion, none of us must expect to be recommended for orders or decorations. An ordinary campaigning medal, inscribed with a record of battalion service, should suffice as reward. Decorations were not considered by the Royal Welch as personal awards, but as representative awards for the whole regiment. They would therefore be kept for the professional soldiers, who would find them useful as aids to extra-regimental promotion. This was what, in fact, happened. There must have been something like two or three hundred Special Reserve officers serving overseas with the regiment before the war ended. But except for three or four, who were not directly recommended by the battalion commander, but distinguished themselves while attached to brigade or divisional staffs, or who got sent to New Army battalions or other regiments, we continued undecorated. I can recall only three exceptions. The normal proportion of awards, considering the casualties we suffered, which was about sixty or seventy killed, should have been at least ten times that amount. Let me hasten to say that I myself never performed any feat for which I might conceivably have been decorated throughout my service in France.

The regimental spirit persistently survived all catastrophes. Our First Battalion, for instance, was practically annihilated within two months of joining the British Expeditionary Force. Young Orme, who joined straight from Sandhurst, at the crisis of the first battle of Ypres, found himself commanding a battalion reduced to only about forty rifles. With these, and another small force, the remnants of the Second Battalion of the Queen's Regiment, reduced to thirty men and two officers, he helped to recapture three lines of lost trenches and was himself killed. The reconstituted battalion saw heavy fighting at Bois Grenier in December, but got smashed up at the Aubers Ridge and Festubert in the following May; and again at Loos in September, when only one combatant officer survived the attack – a machine-gun officer on loan from the South Staffordshire Regiment. The same sort of thing happened time after time in fighting at Fricourt, the Quadrangle, High Wood, Delville Wood, and Ginchy on the Somme in 1916; and again at Puisieux and Bullecourt in the spring fighting of 1917; and again, and again, until the Armistice. In the course of the war, at least fifteen or twenty thousand men must have passed through each of the two line battalions, whose fighting strength never stood at more than eight hundred. After each catastrophe the ranks were filled up with new drafts from home, with the lightly wounded from the disaster of three or four months before, and with the more seriously wounded of earlier ones.

In the First and Second Battalions, throughout the war, not merely the officers and N.C.O.s knew their regimental history. The men had learned far more about Minden, Albuhera, and Waterloo, and the Battle of the Pyramids, than they had about the fighting on the other fronts, or the official causes of the war.

12

In 1916, when on leave in England after being wounded, I began an account of my first few months in France. Having stupidly written it as a novel, I have now to re-translate it into history. Here is one reconstituted chapter:

On arrival in France, we six Royal Welch Fusilier officers went to the Harfleur base camp near Le Havre. Later it became an educational centre for trench routine, use of bombs, trench-mortars, rifle-grenades, gas-helmets, and similar technicalities. But now we did a route-march or two through the French countryside and that was all, apart from fatigues at the Le Havre docks, helping the Army Service Corps unload stores from ships. The town was gay. As soon as we arrived, numerous little boys accosted us, pimping for their alleged sisters. 'I take you to my sister. She very nice. Very good jig-a-jig. Not much money. Very cheap. Very good. I take you now. Plenty champagne for me?' I was glad when we got orders to go 'up the line', though disgusted to find ourselves posted not to the Royal Welch Fusiliers, but to the Welsh Regiment.

I had heard little about the Welsh Regiment, except that it was tough and rough, and that the Second Battalion, to which we were going, had a peculiar regimental history as the old Sixty-ninth Foot. It had originally been formed as an emergency force from pensioners and boy-recruits, and sent overseas to do the work of a regular battalion – I forget in which eighteenth-century campaign. At one time, the Sixty-ninth had served as marines. They were nicknamed the 'Ups and Downs', partly because '69' makes the same sense whichever way up it is written. The 69 was certainly upside-down when we joined. All the company officers, with the exception of two boys recently posted from Sandhurst, and one Special Reserve captain, came from other regiments. There were six Royal Welch Fusiliers, two South Wales Borderers, two East Surreys, two Wiltshires, one from the Border Regiment, one from the King's Own Yorkshire Light Infantry. Even the quartermaster was an alien from the Connaught Rangers. There were still perhaps four time-serving N.C.O.s left in the battalion. Of the men, perhaps fifty or so had got more than a couple of months' training before being sent out; some had only three weeks' training; a great many had never fired a musketry course. All this, because the First Division had been in constant hard fighting since the previous August; in eight months the battalion had lost its full fighting strength five times over. The last occasion was at Richebourg, on May 9th, one of the worst disasters hitherto. The Division's epitaph in the official communiqué read: 'Meeting with considerable opposition in the direction of the Rue du Bois, our attacks were not pressed.'

The battalion's ranks were made up first with reservists of the later categories, then with re-enlisted men, then with Special Reservists of pre-war enlistment, then with 1914 recruits of three or four months' training; but each class in turn had been expended. Now, nothing remained to send, except recruits of the spring 1915 class, with various sweepings and scourings. The First Battalion had, meanwhile, suffered the same heavy losses. In Cardiff the Welsh Regiment advertised: 'Enlist at the depôt and get to France quick.' The recruits were mostly men either over-age or under-age – a repetition of regimental history – or with some slight physical disability which prevented them from enlisting in regiments more particular than the Welsh.

I still have the roll of my first platoon of forty men. The figures given for their ages are misleading. On enlistment, all over-age men had put themselves in the late thirties, and all under-age men had called themselves eighteen. But once in France, the over-age men did not mind adding on a few genuine years. No less than fourteen in the roll give their age as forty or over, and these were not all. Fred Prosser, a painter in civil life, who admitted to forty-eight, was really fifty-six. David Davies, collier, who admitted to forty-two, and Thomas Clark, another collier who admitted to forty-five, were only one or two years junior to Prosser. James Burford, collier and fitter, was the oldest soldier of all. When I first spoke to him in the trenches, he said: 'Excuse me, sir, will you explain what this here arrangement is on the side of my rifle?' 'That's the safety-catch. Didn't you do a musketry-course at the depôt?' 'No, sir, I was a re-enlisted man, and I spent only a fortnight there. The old Lee-Metford didn't have no safety-catch.' I asked him when he had last fired a rifle. 'In Egypt in 1882,' he said. 'Weren't you in the South African War?' 'I tried to re-enlist, but they told me I was too old, sir. I had been an old soldier in Egypt. My real age is sixty-three.' He spent all his summers as a tramp, and in the bad months of the year worked as a collier, choosing a new pit every season. I heard him and David Davies one night discussing the different seams of coal in Wales, and tracing them from county to county and pit to pit with technical comments.

The other half of the platoon contained the under-age section. I had five of these boys; William Bumford, collier, for instance, who gave his age as eighteen, was really only fifteen. He used to get into trouble for falling asleep on sentry duty, an offence punishable with death, but could not help it. I had seen him suddenly go to sleep, on his feet, while holding a sandbag open for another fellow to fill. So we got him a job as orderly to a chaplain for a while, and a few months later all men over fifty and all boys under eighteen got combed out. Bumford and Burford were both sent to the base; but neither escaped the war. Bumford grew old enough by 1917 to be sent back to the battalion, and was killed that summer; Burford died in a bombing accident at the base-camp. Or so I was told – the fate of hundreds of my comrades in France came to me merely as hearsay.

The troop-train consisted of forty-seven coaches, and took twenty-four hours to arrive at Béthune, the railhead, via Saint Omer. We detrained at about 9 p.m., hungry, cold, and dirty. Expecting a short journey, we had allowed our baggage to be locked in a van; and then played nap throughout the journey to keep our minds off the discomfort. I lost sixty francs, which was over two pounds at the existing rate of exchange. On the platform at Béthune, a little man in filthy khaki, wearing the Welsh cap-badge, came up with a friendly touch of the cap most unlike a salute. He had orders to guide us to the battalion, at present in the Cambrin trenches, about ten kilometres away. Collecting the draft of forty men we had with us, we followed him through the unlit suburbs of the town – all intensely excited by the noise and flashes of the guns in the distance. None of the draft had been out before, except the sergeant in charge. They began singing. Instead of the usual music-hall songs they sang Welsh hymns, each man taking a part. The Welsh always sang when pretending not to be scared; it kept them steady. And they never sang out of tune.

We marched towards the flashes, and could soon see the flare-lights curving across the distant trenches. The noise of the guns grew louder and louder. Presently we were among the batteries. From about two hundred yards behind us, on the left of the road, a salvo of four shells whizzed suddenly over our heads. This broke up *Aberystwyth* in the middle of a verse, and sent us off our balance for a few seconds; the column of fours tangled up. The shells went hissing away eastward; we saw the red flash and heard the hollow bang where they landed in

German territory. The men picked up their step again and began chaffing. A lance-corporal dictated a letter home: 'Dear auntie, this leaves me in the pink. We are at present wading in blood up to our necks. Send me fags and a life-belt. This war is a booger. Love and kisses.'

The roadside cottages were now showing more and more signs of. dilapidation. A German shell came over and then whoo – oo – ooo-oooOOO – bump – CRASH! landed twenty yards short of us. We threw ourselves flat on our faces. Presently we heard a curious singing noise in the air, and then flop! flop! little pieces of shell-casing came buzzing down all around. 'They calls them the musical instruments,' said the sergeant. 'Damn them,' said my friend Frank Jones-Bateman, cut across the hand by a jagged little piece, 'the devils have started on me early.' 'Aye, they'll have a lot of fun with you before they're done, sir,' grinned the sergeant. Another shell came over. Everyone threw himself down again, but it burst two hundred yards behind us. Only Sergeant Jones had remained on his feet. 'You're wasting your strength, lads,' he said to the draft. 'Listen by the noise they make where they're going to burst.'

At Cambrin village, about a mile from the front trenches, we were taken into a ruined chemist's shop with its coloured glass jars still in the window: the billet of the four Welsh company-quartermaster-sergeants. Here they gave us respirators and field-dressings. This, the first respirator issued in France, was a gauze-pad filled with chemically treated cotton waste, for tying across the mouth and nose. Reputedly it could not keep out the German gas, which had been used at Ypres against the Canadian Division; but we never put it to the test. A week or two later came the 'smoke-helmet', a greasy grey-felt bag with a talc window to look through, and no mouthpiece, certainly ineffective against gas. The talc was always cracking, and visible leaks showed at the stitches joining it to the helmet.

Those were early days of trench warfare, the days of the jam-tin bomb and the gas-pipe trench-mortar: still innocent of Lewis or Stokes guns, steel helmets, telescopic rifle-sights, gas-shells, pill-boxes, tanks, well-organized trench-raids, or any of the later refinements of trench warfare.

After a meal of bread, bacon, rum, and bitter stewed tea sickly with sugar, we went through the broken trees to the east of the village and up a long trench to battalion headquarters. The wet and slippery trench ran through dull red clay. I had a torch with me, and saw that hundreds of field mice and frogs had fallen into the trench but found no way out. The light dazzled them, and because I could not help treading on them, I put the torch back in my pocket. We had no mental picture of what the trenches would be like, and were almost as ignorant as a young soldier who joined us a week or two later. He called out excitely to old Burford, who was cooking up a bit of stew in a dixie, apart from the others: 'Hi, mate, where's the battle? I want to do my bit.'

The guide gave us hoarse directions all the time. 'Hole right.' 'Wire high.' 'Wire low.' 'Deep place here, sir.' 'Wire low.' The field-telephone wires had been fastened by staples to the side of the trench, and when it rained the staples were constantly falling out and the wire falling down and tripping people up. If it sagged too much, one stretched it across the trench to the other side to correct the sag, but then it would catch one's head. The holes were sump-pits used for draining the trenches.

We now came under rifle-fire, which I found more trying than shell-fire. The gunner, I knew, fired not at people but at map-references – crossroads, likely artillery positions, houses that suggested billets for troops, and so on. Even when an observation officer in an aeroplane or captive balloon, or on a church spire directed the guns, it seemed random, somehow. But a rifle-bullet, even when fired blindly, always seemed purposely aimed. And whereas we could usually hear a shell approaching, and take some sort of cover, the rifle-bullet gave no warning. So, though we learned not to duck a rifle-bullet because, once heard, it must have missed, it gave us a worse feeling of danger. Rifle-bullets in the open went hissing into the grass without much noise, but when we were in a trench, the bullets made a tremendous crack as they went over the hollow. Bullets often struck the barbed wire in front of the trenches, which sent them spinning with a head-over-heels motion – ping! rockety-ockety-ockety-ockety into the woods behind.

At battalion headquarters, a dug-out in the reserve line, about a quarter of a mile behind the front companies, the colonel, a twice-wounded regular, shook hands with us and offered us the whisky bottle. He hoped that we would soon grow to like the regiment as much as our own. This sector had not long before been taken over from a French territorial division of men in the forties, who had a local armistice with the Germans opposite – no firing, and apparently even civilian traffic allowed through the lines. So this dug-out happened to be unusually comfortable, with an ornamental lamp, a clean cloth, and polished silver on the table. The colonel, adjutant, doctor, second-in-command, and signalling officer had just finished dinner: it was civilized cooking – fresh meat and vegetables. Pictures pasted on the papered walls; spring-mattressed beds, a gramophone, easy chairs: we found it hard to reconcile these with the accounts we had read of troops standing waist-deep in mud, and gnawing a biscuit while shells burst all around. The adjutant posted us to our companies. 'Captain Dunn of "C" is your company commander,' he told me. 'The soundest officer in the battalion. By the way, remind him that I want him to send in that list of D.C.M. recommendations for the last show at once; but not more than two names, or else they won't give us any. Four is about the ration for any battalion in a dud show.'

Our guide took us up to the front line. We passed a group of men huddled over a brazier – small men, daubed with mud, talking quietly together in Welsh. They were wearing waterproof capes, for it had now started to rain, and cap-comforters, because the weather was cold for May. Although they could see we were officers, they did not jump to their feet and salute. I thought that this must be a convention of the trenches; and indeed it is laid down somewhere in the military text-books that the courtesy of the salute must be dispensed with in battle. But, no, it was just slackness. We overtook a fatigue-party struggling up the trench loaded with timber lengths and bundles of sandbags, cursing plaintively as they slipped into sump-holes or entangled their burdens in the telephone wire. Fatigue-parties were always encumbered by their rifles and equipment, which it was a crime ever to have out of reach. After squeezing past this party, we had to stand aside to let a stretcher-case pass. 'Who's the poor bastard, Dai?' the guide asked the leading stretcher-bearer. 'Sergeant Gallagher,' Dai answered. 'He thought he saw a Fritz in No Man's Land near our wire, so the silly booger takes one of them new issue percussion bombs and shots it at 'im. Silly booger aims too low, it hits the top of the parapet and bursts back. Deoul! man, it breaks his silly f—ing jaw and blows a great lump from his silly f—ing face, whatever. Poor silly booger! Not worth sweating to get him back! He's put paid to, whatever.' The wounded man had a sandbag over his face. He died before they got him to the dressing-station.

I felt tired out by the time I reached company headquarters, sweating under a pack-valise like the men, and with all the usual furnishings hung at my belt – revolver, field-glasses, compass, whisky-flask, wire-cutters, periscope, and a lot more. A 'Christmas-tree' that was called. Those were the days in which officers had their swords sharpened by the armourer before sailing to France. I had been advised to leave mine back in the quartermaster-sergeants' billet, and never saw it again, or bothered about it. My hands were sticky with the clay from the side of the trench, and my legs soaked up to the calves. At 'C' Company headquarters, a two-roomed timber-built shelter in the side of a trench connecting the front and support lines, I found table-cloth and lamp again, whisky bottle and glasses, shelves with books and magazines, and bunks in the next room. I reported to the company commander.

I had expected a grizzled veteran with a breastful of medals; but Dunn was actually two months younger than myself – one of the fellowship of 'only survivors'. Captain Miller of the Black Watch in the same division was another. Miller had escaped from the Rue du Bois massacre by swimming down a flooded trench. Only survivors had great reputations. Miller used to be pointed at in the streets when the battalion was back in reserve billets. 'See that fellow? That's Jock Miller. Out from the start and hasn't got it yet.' Dunn did not let the war affect his morale at all. He greeted me very easily with: 'Well, what's the news from England? Oh, sorry, first I must introduce you. This is Walker – clever chap from Cambridge, fancies himself as an athlete. This is Jenkins, one of those elder patriots who chucked up their jobs to come here. This is Price – joined us yesterday, but we liked him at once: he brought some damn good whisky with him. Well, how long is the war going to last, and who's winning? We don't know a thing out here. And what's all this talk about war-babies? Price pretends ignorance on the subject.' I told them about the war, and asked them about the trenches.

'About trenches,' said Dunn. 'Well, we don't know as much about trenches as the French do, and not near as much as Fritz does. We can't expect Fritz to help, but the French might do something. They are too greedy to let us have the benefit of their inventions. What wouldn't we give for their parachute-lights and aerial torpedoes! But there's never any connexion between the two armies, unless a battle is on, and then we generally let each other down.

'When I came out here first, all we did in trenches was to paddle about like ducks and use our rifles. We didn't think of them as places to live in, they were just temporary inconveniences. Now we work here all the time, not only for safety but for health. Night and day.

85

First, at fire-steps, then at building traverses, improving the communication trenches, and so on; last comes our personal comfort – shelters and dug-outs. The territorial battalion that used to relieve us were hopeless. They used to sit down in the trench and say: "Oh, my God, this is the limit." Then they'd pull out pencil and paper and write home about it. Did no work on the traverses or on fire positions. Consequence – they lost half their men from frost-bite and rheumatism, and one day the Germans broke in and scuppered a lot more of them. They'd allowed the work we'd done in the trench to go to ruin, and left the whole place like a sewage farm for us to take over again. We got sick as muck, and reported them several times to brigade headquarters; but they never improved. Slack officers, of course. Well, they got smashed, as I say, and were sent away to be lines-of-communication troops. Now we work with the First South Wales Borderers. They're all right. Awful swine, those territorials. Usen't to trouble about latrines at all; left food about to encourage rats; never filled a sandbag. I only once saw a job of work that they did: a steel loop-hole for sniping. But they put it facing square to the front, and quite unmasked, so two men got killed at it – absolute death-trap. Our chaps are all right, but not as right as they ought to be. The survivors of the show ten days ago are feeling pretty low, and the big new draft doesn't know a thing yet.'

'Listen,' said Walker, 'there's too much firing going on. The men have got the wind up over something. If Fritz thinks we're jumpy, he'll give us an extra bad time. I'll go up and stop them.'

Dunn went on: 'These Welshmen are peculiar. They won't stand being shouted at. They'll do anything if you explain the reason for it – do and die, but they have to know their reason why. The best way to make them behave is not to give them too much time to think. Work them off their feet. They are good workmen, too. But officers must work with them, not only direct the work. Our time-table is: breakfast at eight o'clock in the morning, clean trenches and inspect rifles, work all morning; lunch at twelve, work again from one till about six, when the men feed again. "Stand-to" at dusk for about an hour, work all night, "stand-to" for an hour before dawn. That's the general programme. Then there's sentry-duty. The men do two-hour sentry spells, then work two hours, then sleep two hours. At night, sentries are doubled, so working parties are smaller. We officers are on duty all day, and divide up the night into three-hourly watches.' He looked at his wristwatch. 'By the way,' he said, 'that carrying-party must have brought up the R.E. stuff by now. Time we all got to work. Look here, Graves, you lie down and have a doss on that bunk. I want you to take the watch before "stand-to". I'll wake you up and show you around. Where the hell's my revolver? I don't like to go out without it. Hello, Walker, what was wrong?'

Walker laughed. 'A chap from the new draft. He had never fired his musketry course at Cardiff, and tonight he fired ball for the first time. It went to his head. He'd had a brother killed up at Ypres, and sworn to avenge him. So he blazed off all his own ammunition at nothing, and two bandoliers out of the ammunition-box besides. They call him the "Human Maxim" now. His foresight's misty with heat. Corporal Parry should have stopped him; but he just leant up against the traverse and shrieked with laughter. I gave them both a good cursing. Some other new chaps started blazing away too. Fritz retaliated with machine-guns and whizz-bangs. No casualties. I don't know why. It's all quiet now. Everybody ready?'

When they went off, I rolled up in my blanket and fell asleep. Dunn woke me at about one o'clock. 'Your watch,' he said. I jumped out of the bunk with a rustle of straw; my feet were sore and clammy in my boots. I was cold, too. 'Here's the rocket-pistol and a few flares. Not a bad night. It's stopped raining. Put your equipment on over your raincoat, or you won't be able to get at your revolver. Got a torch? Good. About this flare business. Don't use the pistol too much. We haven't many flares, and if there's an attack we'll need as many as we can get. But use it if you think something's doing. Fritz is always sending up flare-lights; he's got as many as he wants.'

Dunn showed me around the line. The battalion frontage was about eight hundred yards. Each company held some two hundred of these, with two platoons in the front line, and two in the support line about a hundred yards back. He introduced me to the platoon sergeants, more particularly to Sergeant Eastmond and told him to give me any information I wanted; then went back to sleep, asking to be woken at once if anything went wrong. I found myself in charge of the line. Sergeant Eastmond being busy with a working-party, I went round by myself. The men of the working-party, whose job was to replace the traverses, or safety-buttresses, of the trench, looked curiously at me. They were filling sandbags with earth, piling them up bricklayer fashion, the headers and stretchers alternating, then patting them flat with spades. The sentries stood on the fire-step at the corners of the traverses, stamping their feet and blowing on their fingers. Every now and then they peered over the top for a few seconds. Two parties, each of an N.C.O. and two men, were out in the company listening-posts, connected with the front trench by a sap about fifty yards long. The German front line stretched some three hundred yards beyond. From berths hollowed in the sides of the trench and curtained with sandbags came the grunt of sleeping men.

I jumped up on the fire-step beside the sentry and cautiously raised my head, staring over the parapet. I could see nothing except the wooden pickets supporting our protecting barbed-wire entanglements, and a dark patch or two of bushes beyond. The darkness seemed to move and shake about as I looked at it; the bushes started travelling, singly at first, then both together. The pickets did the same. I was glad of the sentry beside me; he gave his name as Beaumont. 'They're quiet tonight, sir,' he said. 'A relief going on; I think so, surely.'

I said: 'It's funny how those bushes seem to move.'

'Aye, they do play queer tricks. Is this your first spell in trenches, sir?'

A German flare shot up, broke into bright flame, dropped slowly and went hissing into the grass just behind our trench, showing up the bushes and pickets. Instinctively I moved.

'It's bad to do that, sir,' he said, as a rifle-bullet cracked and seemed to pass right between us. 'Keep still, sir, and they can't spot you. Not but what a flare is a bad thing to fall on you. I've seen them burn a hole in a man.'

I spent the rest of my watch in acquainting myself with the geography of the trench-section, finding how easy it was to get lost among culs-de-sac and disused alleys. Twice I overshot the company frontage and wandered among the Munster Fusiliers on the left. Once I tripped and fell with a splash into deep mud. My watch ended when the first signs of dawn showed. I passed the word along the line for the company to stand-to-arms. The N.C.O.s whispered hoarsely into the dug-outs: 'Stand-to, stand-to,' and out the men tumbled with their rifles in their hands. Going towards company headquarters to wake the officers I saw a man lying on his face in a machine-gun shelter. I stopped and said: 'Stand-to, there!' I flashed my torch on him and saw that one of his feet was bare.

The machine-gunner beside him said: 'No good talking to him, sir.'

I asked: 'What's wrong? Why has he taken his boot and sock off?'

'Look for yourself, sir!'

I shook the sleeper by the arm and noticed suddenly the hole in the back of his head. He had taken off the boot and sock to pull the trigger of his rifle with one toe; the muzzle was in his mouth.

'Why did he do it?' I asked.

'He went through the last push, sir, and that sent him a bit queer; on top of that he got bad news from Limerick about his girl and another chap.'

He belonged to the Munsters – their machine-guns overlapped the left of our company – and his suicide had already been reported. Two Irish officers came up. 'We've had several of these lately,' one of them told me. Then he said to the other: 'While I remember, Callaghan, don't forget to write to his next-of-kin. Usual sort of letter; tell them he died a soldier's death, anything you like. I'm not going to report it as suicide.'

At stand-to, rum and tea were served out. I looked at the German trenches through a periscope – a distant streak of sandbags. Some of these were made of coloured cloth, whether for camouflage or from a shortage of plain sacking, I do not know. The enemy gave no sign, except for a wisp or two of wood-smoke where they, too, were boiling up a hot drink. Between us and them lay a flat meadow with cornflowers, marguerites, and poppies growing in the long grass, a few shell holes, the bushes I had seen the night before, the wreck of an aeroplane, our barbed wire and theirs. Three-quarters of a mile away stood a big ruined house; a quarter of a mile behind that, a red-brick village – Auchy – poplars and haystacks, a tall chimney, and another village – Haisnes. Half-right, pit-head and smaller slag-heaps. La Bassée lay half-left; the sun caught the weather-vane of the church and made it twinkle.

In the interval between stand-to and breakfast, the men who were not getting in a bit of extra sleep sat about talking and smoking, writing letters home, cleaning their rifles, running their thumb-nails up the seams of their shirts to kill lice, gambling. Lice were a standing joke. Young Bumford handed me one: 'We was just having an argument as to whether it's best to kill the old ones or the young ones, sir. Morgan here says that if you kill the old ones, the young ones die of grief; but Parry here, sir, he says that the young ones are easier to kill and you can catch the old ones when they go to the funeral.' He appealed to me as an arbiter: 'You've been to college, sir, haven't you?'

I said: 'Yes, I have, but so had Crawshay Bailey's brother Norwich.' The platoon treasured this as a wonderfully witty answer. *Crawshay Bailey* is one of the idiotic songs of Wales. Crawshay Bailey himself 'had an engine and he couldn't make it go', and all his relatives in the song had similar shortcomings. Crawshay Bailey's brother Norwich, for instance, was fond of oatmeal porridge, but was sent to Cardiff College, for to get a bit of knowledge. After that, I had no trouble with the platoon.

Breakfast at company headquarters consisted of bacon, eggs, coffee, toast, and marmalade. There were three chairs and two ammunition-boxes to sit on. Accustomed to company commanders who never took junior officers into their confidence, I liked the way that questions of the moment were settled at meal-times by a sort of board-meeting with Dunn as chairman. On this first morning we had a long debate on how to keep sentries awake. Dunn finally issued a company order forbidding them to lean against traverses; it made them sleepy. Besides, when they fired, the flash would come always from the same place. The Germans might fix a rifle on the spot after a time. I told Dunn of the bullet that passed between Beaumont and myself.

'Sounds like a fixed rifle,' he said, 'because not one aimed shot in a hundred comes as close as that at night. And we had a chap killed in that very traverse the night we came in.' The Bavarian Guards Reserve, who were opposite us at the time, seemed to have complete control of the sniping situation.

Dunn gave me the characters of the N.C.O.s in my platoon: which were trustworthy and which had to be watched. He had begun telling me just how much I could expect from the men at my platoon inspection of rifles and equipment, when a soldier came rushing in, his eyes blank with horror and excitement. 'Gas, sir, gas! They're using gas!'

'My God!' exclaimed Price. We all looked at Dunn, whose soldier-servant the man was.

Dunn said imperturbably: 'Very well, Kingdom, bring me my respirator from the other room, and another pot of marmalade.'

The alarm had originated with smoke blowing across from the German trenches, where breakfast must also have been in progress; we knew the German meal-times by a slackening down of rifle-fire. Gas had become a nightmare. Nobody believed in the efficacy of our respirators, though advertised as proof against any gas the enemy could send over. Pink army forms marked 'Urgent' constantly arrived from headquarters to explain how to use these accessories: all contradictory. First, the respirators were to be kept soaking wet, then they were to be kept dry, then they were to be worn in a satchel, then, again, the satchel was not to be used.

Frank Jones-Bateman, a quiet boy of nineteen, came to visit me from the company on our right. He mentioned with a false ease that he had shot a German just before breakfast: 'Sights at four hundred,' he said. He had just left Rugby with a scholarship waiting for him at Clare, Cambridge. His nickname was 'Silent Night'.

13

HERE are extracts from letters that I wrote at this time. I have restored the names of places, which we were forbidden to mention:

May 21st, 1915. Back in billets again at a coal-mining village called La Bourse. It is not more than three miles and a half from the front line, but the miners are still working. As we came out of the trenches the Germans were shelling the wood by Cambrin village, searching for one of our batteries. I don't think they got it, but it was fun to see the poplar-trees being lopped down like tulips when the whizz-bangs hit them square. As we marched down the *pavé* road from Cambrin, the men straggled along out of step and out of fours. Their feet were sore from having had their boots on for a week – they only have one spare pair of socks issued to them. I enclose a list of their minimum load, which weighs about sixty pounds. A lot of extras get put on top of this – rations, pick or shovel, periscope, and their own souvenirs to take home on leave:

Greatcoat	1	Towel	1
Tin, mess	1	Housewife	1
,, ,, cover . . .	1	Holdall	1
Shirt	1	Razor	1
Socks, pair	1	,, case	1
Soap	1	**Lather brush**	1

91

Comb	1	Field-service dressing . . .	1
Fork	1	Respirator	1
Knife	1	Spine protector	1
Spoon	1	Set of equipment. . . .	1
Toothbrush	1	Laces, pair	1
Cardigan	1	Rounds ammunition . .	150
Cap, fatigue comforter . .	1	Rifle and bayonet	
Pay-book	1	Rifle cover	1
Disc, identity	1	Oil-bottle and pull-through	1
Sheet, waterproof	1	Entrenching tool	1
Grease, tin of	1		

Well, anyhow, marching on cobbled roads is difficult, so when a staff-officer came by in a Rolls-Royce and cursed us for bad march-discipline, I felt like throwing something at him. Trench soldiers hate the staff and the staff know it. The principal disagreement seems to be about the extent to which trench conditions should modify discipline.

The La Bourse miners are old men and boys dressed in sloppy blue clothes with bulging pockets. Shell craters ring the pit-head. I am billeted with a fatherly old man called Monsieur Hojdés, who has three marriageable daughters; one of them, uninvited, lifted up her skirt to show me a shell-wound on the thigh that laid her up last winter.

May 22nd. A colossal bombardment by the French at Souchez, a few miles away – continuous roar of artillery, coloured flares, shells bursting all along the ridge by Notre Dame de Lorette. I couldn't sleep. The noise went on all night. Instead of dying away it grew and grew, till the whole air rocked and shook; the sky was lit up with huge flashes. I lay in my feather-bed and sweated. This morning they tell me there was a big thunderstorm in the middle of the bombardment. But, as Walker says: 'Where the gunder ended and the thunder began was hard to say.' The men took hot baths at the mines and cleaned up generally. Their rifles are all in an advanced state of disrepair, and many of their clothes are in rags, but neither can be replaced, we are told, until they get much worse. The platoon is billeted in a barn full of straw. Old Burford, who is so old that he refuses to sleep with the other men of the platoon, has found a private doss in an out-building among some farm tools. In trenches he will sleep on the fire-step even in the rain, rather than in a warm dug-out with the other men. He says that he remembers the C.O. as a baby in long skirts. Young Bumford is the only man he'll talk to. The platoon is always ragging Bumford for his childish simplicity. Bumford plays up to it, and begs them not to be too hard on 'a lad from the hills'.

May 23rd. We did company drill in the morning. Afterwards, Jones-Bateman and I lay on the warm grass and watched aeroplanes flying above the trenches pursued by a trail of white shrapnel puffs. In the evening I took a working-party over to Vermelles les Noyelles, to work on a second line of defence – trench digging and putting up barbed-wire under an R.E. officer. But the ground was hard, and the men were tired out when they got back at two o'clock in the morning, after singing songs all the way home. They have one about Company Quartermaster-Sergeant Finnigan, which goes to the Salvation Army tune of 'Whiter Than the Snow':

> *Coolness under fire,*
> *Coolness under fire,*
> *Mentioned in dispatches*
> *For pinching the Company rations,*
> *Coolness under fire.*

> *Now he's on the peg,*
> *Now he's on the peg,*
> *Mentioned in dispatches*
> *For drinking the Company rum,*
> *Now he's on the peg.*

The chorus is:

> *Whiter than the milky cokernuts,*
> *Whiter than the milky cokernuts,*
> *Wash me in the water*
> *That you washed your dirty daughter in*
> *And I shall be whiter than the*
> *Milky cokernuts,*
> > *Nuts,*
> > *Nuts,*
> *Oooooh nuts.*

Finnigan doesn't mind the libel at all.

Two young miners, in another company, disliked their sergeant,

93

who had a down on them and gave them all the most dirty and dangerous jobs. When they were in billets he crimed them for things they hadn't done; so they decided to kill him. Later, they reported at Battalion Orderly Room and asked to see the adjutant. This was irregular, because a private is forbidden to address an officer without an N.C.O. of his own company acting as go-between. The adjutant happened to see them and asked: 'Well, what is it you want?'

Smartly slapping the small-of-the-butt of their sloped rifles, they said: 'We've come to report, sir, that we're very sorry, but we've shot our company sergeant-major.'

The adjutant said: 'Good heavens, how did that happen?'

'It was an accident, sir.'

'What do you mean, you damn fools? Did you mistake him for a spy?'

'No, sir, we mistook him for our platoon sergeant.'

So they were both court-martialled and shot by a firing-squad of their own company against the wall of a convent at Béthune. Their last words were the battalion rallying-cry: 'Stick it, the Welch!' (They say that a certain Captain Haggard first used it in the battle of Ypres when he was mortally wounded.) The French military governor was present at the execution, and made a little speech saying how gloriously British soldiers can die.

You'd be surprised at the amount of waste that goes on in the trenches. Ration biscuits are in general use as fuel for boiling up dixies, because kindling is scarce. Our machine-gun crew boil their hot water by firing off belt after belt of ammunition at no particular target, just generally spraying the German line. After several pounds' worth of ammunition has been used, the water in the guns – which are water-cooled – begins to boil. They say they make German ration and carrying parties behind the line pay for their early-morning cup of tea. But the real charge will be on income-tax after the war.

May 24th. Tomorrow we return to the trenches. The men are pessimistic but cheerful. They all talk about getting a 'cushy' one to send them back to 'Blity'. *Blitey* is, it seems, Hindustani for 'home'. My servant, Fry, who works in a paper-bag factory at Cardiff in civil life, has been telling me stories about cushy ones. Here are two of them.

'A bloke in the Munsters once wanted a cushy, so he waves his hand above the parapet to catch Fritz's attention. Nothing doing. He waves his arms about for a couple of minutes. Nothing doing, not a shot. He puts his elbows on the fire-step, hoists his body upside-down and waves his legs about till he gets blood to the head. Not a shot did old Fritz fire. "Oh," says the Munster man, "I don't believe there's a damned square-head there. Where's the German army to?" He has a peek over the top – crack! he gets it in the head. Finee.'

Another story: 'Bloke in the Camerons wanted a cushy, bad. Fed up and far from home, he was. He puts his hand over the top and gets his trigger finger taken off, and two more beside. That done the trick. He comes laughing through our lines by the old boutillery. "See, lads," he says, "I'm off to bonny Scotland. Is it na a beauty?" But on the way down the trench to the dressing-station, he forgets to stoop low where the old sniper's working. *He* gets it through the head, too. Finee. We laugh, fit to die!'

To get a cushy one is all that the old hands think of. Only twelve men have been with the battalion from the beginning, and all are transport men except one, Beaumont, a man in my platoon. The few old hands who went through the last show infect the new men with pessimism; they don't believe in the war, they don't believe in the staff. But at least they would follow their officers anywhere, because the officers happen to be a decent lot. They look forward to a battle because that gives them more chances of a cushy one in the legs or arms than trench warfare. In trench warfare the proportion of head wounds is much greater. Haking commands this division. He's the author of our standard text-book, *Company Training*. The last shows have not been suitable ones for company commanders to profit by his directions. He came round this morning to an informal inspection of the battalion, and shook hands with the survivors, There were tears in his eyes. Sergeant Smith swore, half-aloud: 'Bloody lot of use that is: busts up his bloody division, and then weeps over what's bloody left.' Well, it had nothing to do with me; I didn't allow myself to feel either for the general or for the sergeant. It's said here that Haking told General French that the division's *morale* has gone completely. So far as I can see that is inaccurate; the division will fight all right, but with little enthusiasm. It's said, too, that when the New Army comes out, we are to be withdrawn and used on lines of communication for some months at least. I don't believe it. No one will mind smashing up over and over again the divisions that have got used to being smashed up. The general impression here is that the New Army divisions can't be of much military use.

May 28th. In trenches among the Cuinchy brick-stacks. Not my idea of trenches. There has been a lot of fighting hereabouts. The trenches have made themselves rather than been made, and run inconsequently in and out of the big thirty-foot high stacks of bricks; it is most confusing. The parapet of a trench which we don't occupy is built up with ammunition boxes and corpses. Everything here is wet and smelly. The Germans are very close: they have half the brick-stacks, we have the other half. Each side snipes down from the top of its brick-stacks into the other's trenches. This is also a great place for German rifle-grenades and trench-mortars. We can't reply properly; we have only a meagre supply of rifle-grenades and nothing to equal the German sausage mortar-bomb. This morning about breakfast time, just as I came out of my dug-out, a rifle-grenade landed within six feet of me. For some reason, instead of falling on its head and exploding, it landed with its stick in the wet clay and stood there looking at me. They are difficult to see coming; they are shot from a rifle, with its butt on the ground, tilted, and go up a long way before turning over and coming down head first. I can't understand why this particular rifle-grenade fell as it did; the chances were impossibly against it.

'Sausages' are easy to see and dodge, but they make a terrible noise when they drop. We have had about ten casualties in our company today from them. I find that my reactions to danger are extraordinarily quick; but everyone gets like that. We can sort out all the different explosions and disregard whichever don't concern us – such as the artillery duel, machine-gun fire at the next company to us, desultory rifle-fire. But we pick out at once the faint plop! of the mortar that sends off a sausage, or the muffled rifle noise when a grenade is fired. The men are much afraid, yet always joking. The company sergeant-major stands behind Number Eleven brick-stack and shoots at sausages with a rifle as they come over; trying to explode them in the air. He says that it's better than pigeon-shooting. He hasn't hit one yet.

Last night a lot of German stuff was flying about, including shrapnel. I heard one shell whish-whishing towards me and dropped flat. It burst just over the trench where 'Petticoat Lane' runs into 'Lowndes Square'. My ears sang as though there were gnats in them, and a bright scarlet light shone over everything. My shoulder got twisted in falling and I thought I had been hit, but I hadn't been. The vibration made my chest sing, too, in a curious way, and I lost my sense of equilibrium. I was ashamed when the sergeant-major came along the trench and found me on all fours, still unable to stand up straight

A corpse is lying on the fire-step waiting to be taken down to the grave-yard tonight: a sanitary-man, killed last night in the open while burying lavatory stuff between our front and support lines. His arm was stretched out stiff when they carried him in and laid him on the fire-step; it stretched right across the trench. His comrades joke as they push it out of the way to get by. 'Out of the light, you old bastard! Do you own this bloody trench?' Or else they shake hands with him familiarly. 'Put it there, Billy Boy.' Of course, they're miners, and accustomed to death. They have a very limited morality, but they keep to it. It's moral, for instance, to rob anyone of anything, except a man in their own platoon. They treat every stranger as an enemy until he proves himself their friend, and then there's nothing they won't do for him. They are lecherous, the young ones at least, but without the false shame of the English lecher. I had a letter to censor the other day, written by a lance-corporal to his wife. He said that the French girls were nice to sleep with, so she mustn't worry on his account, but that he far preferred sleeping with her and missed her a great deal.

June 6th. We have been billeted in Béthune, a fair-sized town about seven miles behind the front line. It has everything one wants: a swimming bath, all sorts of shops, especially a cake-shop, the best I've ever met, a hotel where you can get a really good dinner, and a theatre where we have brigade 'gaffs'. I saw a notice this morning on a building by the Béthune-La Bassée canal – 'Troops are forbidden to bomb fish. By order of the Town Major.' Béthune is very little knocked about, except the part called Faubourg d'Arras, near the station. I am billeted with a family called Averlant Paul, in the Avenue de Bruay, people of the official class: refugees from Poimbert. There are two little boys and an elder sister, who goes to what corresponds with the under-fifth of the local high-school. She was worrying last night over her lessons and asked me to help her write out the theory of decimal division. She showed me her notes; they were full of abbreviations. I asked why she'd used abbreviations. She said: 'The lady professor talked very fast because we were much hurried.' 'Why were you hurried?' 'Oh, because part of the school is used as a billet for your troops, and the Germans were shelling it, and we were always having to take shelter in the cellar, and when we came back each time there was less and less time left.'

June 9th. I am beginning to realize how lucky I was in my gentle introduction to the Cambrin trenches. We are now in a nasty salient, a little to the south of the brick-stacks, where casualties are always heavy. The company had seventeen casualties yesterday from bombs and grenades. The front trench averages thirty yards from the Germans. Today, at one part, which is only twenty yards away from an occupied German sap, I went along whistling 'The Farmer's Boy', to keep up my spirits, when suddenly I saw a group bending over a man lying at the bottom of the trench. He was making a snoring noise mixed with animal groans. At my feet lay the cap he had worn, splashed with his brains. I had never seen human brains before; I somehow regarded them as a poetical figment. One can joke with a badly-wounded man and congratulate him on being out of it. One can disregard a dead man. But even a miner can't make a joke that sounds like a joke over a man who takes three hours to die, after the top part of his head has been taken off by a bullet fired at twenty yards' range.

Beaumont, of whom I told you in my last letter, also got killed – the last unwounded survivor of the original battalion, except for the transport men. He had his legs blown against his back. Everyone was swearing angrily, but an R.E. officer came up and told me that he had a tunnel driven under the German front line, and that if my chaps wanted to do a bit of bombing, now was the time. So he sent the mine up – it was not a big one, he said, but it made a tremendous noise and covered us with dirt – and we waited for a few seconds for the other Germans to rush up to help the wounded away, and then chucked all the bombs we had.

Beaumont had been telling how he had won about five pounds' worth of francs in the sweepstake after the Rue du Bois show: a sweepstake of the sort that leaves no bitterness behind it. Before a show, the platoon pools all its available cash and the survivors divide it up afterwards. Those who are killed can't complain, the wounded would have given far more than that to escape as they have, and the unwounded regard the money as a consolation prize for still being here.

June 24th. We are billeted in the cellars of Vermelles, which was taken and re-taken eight times last October. Not a single house has remained undamaged in the town, which once must have had two or three thousand inhabitants. It is beautiful now in a fantastic way. We came up two nights ago; there was a moon shining behind the houses and the shells had broken up all the hard lines of roofs and quaintly perforated the grim walls of a brewery. Next morning we found the deserted gardens of the town very pleasant to walk about in; they are quite overgrown and flowers have seeded themselves about wildly. Red cabbages and rose and madonna lilies are the chief ornaments. One garden has currant bushes in it. I and the company sergeant-major started eating along the line from opposite ends without noticing each other. When we did, we both remembered our dignity, he as a company sergeant-major, and I as an officer. He saluted, I acknowledged the salute, we both walked away. A minute or two later, we both came back hoping that the coast was clear and again, after an exchange of salutes, had to leave the currants and pretend that we were merely admiring the flowers. I don't quite know why I behaved like that. The C.M.S. is a regular, and therefore obliged to stop eating in the presence of an officer. So, I suppose, courtesy to his scruples made me stop too. Anyhow, along came a couple of privates and stripped the bushes clean.

This afternoon we had a cricket match, officers *versus* sergeants, in an enclosure between some house out of observation from the enemy. Our front line is perhaps three-quarters of a mile away. I made top score, twenty-four; the bat was a bit of a rafter; the ball, a piece of rag tied round with string; and the wicket, a parrot cage with the clean, dry corpse of a parrot inside. It had evidently died of starvation when the French evacuated the town. I recalled a verse of Skelton's:

> Parrot is a fair bird for a ladie.
> God of His goodness him framéd and wrought.
> When parrot is dead he doth not putrify,
> Yea, all things mortal shall turn unto nought
> Save mannés soul which Christ so dear bought,
> That never can die, nor never die shall.
> Make much of parrot, that popajay royál.

Machine-gun fire broke up the match. It was not aimed at us; the Germans were shooting at one of our aeroplanes, and the bullets falling from a great height had a penetrative power greater than an ordinary spent bullet.

This is a very idle life, except for night-digging on the reserve line. We can't drill because we are too near the Germans, and no fortification needs doing in the village. Today two spies were shot: a civilian who had hung on in a cellar and was, apparently, flashing news to the Germans; and a German soldier disguised as an R.E. corporal; found tampering with the telephone wires. We officers spend a lot of time revolver-shooting. Jenkins brought out a beautiful target from the only undestroyed living-room in our billet-area: a glass case full of artificial fruit and flowers. We put it up on a post at fifty yards' range. He said: 'I've always wanted to smash one of these damn objects. My aunt has one. It's the sort of thing that *would* survive an intense bombardment.' I smothered a tender impulse to rescue it. So we had five shots each, in turn. Everyone missed. Then we went up to within twenty yards and fired a volley. Someone hit the post and knocked the case off into the grass. Jenkins said: 'Damn the thing, it must be bewitched. Let's take it back.' The glass was unbroken, but some of the fruit had come loose. Walker said: 'No, it's in pain. We must put it out of its suffering.' He gave it the *coup de grâce* from close quarters.

The old Norman church here has been very much broken. What remains of the tower is used as a forward observation-post by the Artillery. I counted eight unexploded shells sticking into it. Jenkins and I went in and found the floor littered with rubbish, broken masonry, smashed chairs, ripped canvas pictures (some of them looked several hundreds of years old), bits of images and crucifixes, muddied church vestments rotting in what was once the vestry. Only a few pieces of stained glass remained fixed in the edges of the windows. I climbed up by way of the altar to the east window, and found a piece about the size of a plate. I gave it to Jenkins. 'Souvenir,' I said. When he held it to the light, it was St Peter's hand with the keys of heaven – medieval glass. 'I'm sending this home,' he said. As we went out, we met two men of the Munsters. Being Irish Catholics, they thought it sacrilegious for Jenkins to be taking the glass away. One of them warned him: 'Shouldn't take that, sir; it will bring you no luck.' (Jenkins got killed not long after.)

Walker was ragging Dunn this evening. 'I believe you'll be sorry when the war's over, skipper. Your occupation will be gone, and you'll have to go back on the square at the depôt for six months, and learn how to form fours regimentally. You missed that little part of the show when you left Sandhurst and came straight here. You'll be a full colonel by then, of course. I'll give the sergeant-major half-a-crown to make you really sweat. I'll be standing in civvies at the barrack-gate laughing at you.'

One of our company commanders here is Captain Furber, whose nerves are in pieces. Somebody played a dirty trick on him the other day – rolling a bomb, undetonated, of course, down the cellar steps to frighten him. This was thought a wonderful joke. Furber is the greatest pessimist in France. He's laid a bet with the adjutant that the trench lines won't be more than a mile from where they are in this sector two years hence.* Everyone laughs at Furber, but they like him because he sings sentimental cockney songs at the brigade gaffs when we are back in Béthune.

14

WITH the advance of summer came new types of bombs and trench-mortars, heavier shelling, improved gas-masks, and a general tightening up of discipline. We met the first battalions of the New Army, and felt like scarecrows by comparison. Our battalion went in and out of the Cambrin and Cuinchy trenches, with billets in Béthune and the neighbouring villages. By this time I had caught the pessimism of the First Division. Its spirit in the trenches was largely defensive; the policy being not to stir the Germans into more than their usual hostility. But casualties remained very heavy for trench warfare. Pessimism made everyone superstitious, and I found myself believing in signs of the most trivial nature.

Sergeant Smith, my second sergeant, told me of the officer who had commanded the platoon before I did. 'He was a nice gentleman, sir, but very wild. Just before the Rue du Bois show, he says to me: "By the way, sergeant, I'm going to get killed tomorrow. I know that. And I know that you're going to be all right. So see that my kit goes back to my people. You'll find their address in my pocket-book. You'll find five hundred francs there too. Now remember

* He won the bet.

101

this, Sergeant Smith, you keep a hundred francs yourself and divide up the rest among the chaps left." He says: "Send my pocket-book back with my other stuff, Sergeant Smith, but for God's sake burn my diary. They mustn't see that. I'm going to get it here!" He points to his forehead. And that's how it was. He got it through the forehead all right. I sent the stuff back to his parents. I divided up the money and I burned the diary.'

One day, walking along a trench at Cambrin, I suddenly dropped flat on my face; two seconds later a whizz-bang struck the back of the trench exactly where my head had been. The sergeant who was with me walking a few steps ahead, turned round: 'Are you killed, sir?' The shell was fired from a battery near Les Brigues Farm, only a thousand yards away, so that I must have reacted simultaneously with the explosion of the gun. How did I know that the shell would be coming my way?

At Béthune, I saw the ghost of a man named Private Challoner, who had been at Lancaster with me, and again in 'F' Company at Wrexham. When he went out with a draft to join the First Battalion, he shook my hand and said: 'I'll meet you again in France, sir.' In June he passed by our 'C' Company billet, where we were just having a special dinner to celebrate our safe return from Cuinchy – new potatoes, fish, green peas, asparagus, mutton chops, strawberries and cream, and three bottles of Pommard. Private Challoner looked in at the window, saluted, and passed on. I could not mistake him, or the cap-badge he wore; yet no Royal Welch battalion was billeted within miles of Béthune at the time. I jumped up, looked out of the window, and saw nothing except a fag-end smoking on the pavement. Challoner had been killed at Festubert in May.

Constant mining went on in this Cambrin-Cuinchy sector. We had the prospect of being blown up at any moment. An officer of the R.E. tunnelling company won the Victoria Cross while we were there. A duel of mining and counter-mining had been going on. When the Germans began to undermine his original boring, he rapidly tunnelled beneath them. It was touch and go who would get ready first. He won. But when he detonated his mine from the trench by an electric lead, nothing happened. So he ran down again, retamped the charge, and got back just in time to set it off before the Germans fired theirs. I had visited the upper boring on the previous day. It ran about twenty feet under the German lines. At the end of the gallery I found a Welsh miner on listening duty, one of our own battalion, who had transferred to the Royal Engineers. He cautioned me to silence. I could distinctly hear the Germans working somewhere below us. He whispered: 'So long as they work, I don't mind. It's when they bloody stop!' He did his two-hour spell by candle-light in the cramped and stuffy dead-end, reading a book. The mining officer had told me that the men were allowed to read; it didn't interfere with their listening. The book was a paper-backed novelette called *From Mill Girl to Duchess*. The tunnelling companies were notorious thieves, by the way. They would snatch things up from the trench and scurry off with them into their borings; just like mice.

After one particularly dangerous spell of trenches, I had bad news in a letter from Charterhouse. Bad news from home might affect a soldier in one of two ways. It might either drive him to suicide (or recklessness amounting to suicide), or else seem trivial by contrast with present experiences and be laughed off. But, unless due for leave, he could do nothing whatever to remedy matters. A year later, in the same sector, an officer of the North Staffordshire Regiment heard from home that his wife was living with another man. He went out on a raid that night and got either killed or captured; so the men with him said. There had been a fight and they came back without him. After two days he was arrested at Béthune, trying to board a leave-train; he had intended to go home and shoot up the wife and her lover. The officers who court-martialled him for deserting in the face of the enemy, were content with a sentence of cashiering. He went as a private soldier to another regiment. I never heard what happened to him afterwards.

The bad news came in a letter from a cousin of mine still at Charterhouse. He said that Dick was not at all the innocent fellow I took him for, but as bad as anyone could be. I remembered that my cousin owed me a grudge, and decided that this must be a very cruel act of spite. Dick's letters had been my greatest stand-by all these months whenever I felt low; he wrote every week, mostly about poetry. They were something solid and clean to set off against the impermanence of trench life and the sordidness of life in billets. I was now back in Béthune. Two officers of another company had just been telling me how they had slept in the same room with a woman and her daughter. They had tossed for the mother, because the daughter was a 'yellow-looking scaly little thing like a lizard'. The Red Lamp, the army brothel, was around the corner in the main street. I had seen a queue of a hundred and fifty men waiting outside the door, each to have his short turn with one of the three women in the house. My servant, who had stood in the queue, told me that the charge was ten francs a man – about eight shillings at that time. Each woman served nearly a battalion of men every week for as long as she lasted. According to the assistant provost-marshal, three weeks was the usual limit: 'after which she retired on her earnings, pale but proud.'

I was always being teased because I would not sleep even with the nicer girls; and I excused myself, not on moral grounds or on grounds of fastidiousness, but in the only way that they could understand: I said that I didn't want a dose. A good deal of talk in billets concerned the peculiar bed-manners of Frenchwomen. 'She was very nice and full of games. But when I said to her: "*S'il vous plaît, ôtes-toi la chemise, ma chérie,*" she wouldn't. She said: "*Oh, no'-non, mon lieutenant. Ce n'est convenable.*"' I was glad when we got back to the trenches. There I had a more or less reassuring letter from Dick. He told me that my cousin did have a spite against him and me, and admitted that he had been ragging about in a silly way, but that nothing bad had happened. He said he was very sorry, and would stop it for the sake of our friendship.

At the end of July, Robertson, one of the other Royal Welch officers attached to the Welsh, and myself had orders to proceed to the Laventie sector. We were to report to the Second Battalion of the Royal Welch Fusiliers. Frank Jones-Bateman and Hanmer Jones, two more of us, went to the First Battalion. The remaining two of the six had already gone back: McLellan sick, and Watkin with bomb wounds that have kept him limping ever since. We were sorry to say goodbye to our men, who all crowded round to shake hands and wish us luck. Nor did we look forward to a fresh start, with a new company and new regimental customs. But it would be worth it, just to serve with our own regiment. Robertson and I agreed to take our journey as leisurely as possible. Laventie lay only seventeen miles off, but our orders were to 'proceed by train'; so a company mess-cart took us down to Béthune. We asked the railway transport officer what trains he had for Laventie. He told us that one would be going in a few minutes; we decided to miss it. No other train ran until the next day; so we stopped the night at the Hôtel de la France, in which the Prince of Wales, then a lieutenant in the Fortieth Siege Battery, was billeted sometimes. We did not find him in. I had spoken to him once – in the public bath at Béthune, where he and I were the only bathers one morning. Dressed in nothing at all, he graciously remarked how bloody cold the water was, and I loyally assented that he was too bloody right. We were very pink and white and did exercises on the horizontal bar afterwards. I joked to Frank Jones-Bateman about it: 'I have just met our future King in a bath.' Frank said: 'I can trump that: two days ago I had a friendly talk with him in the A.S.C. latrines.' The Prince's favourite rendezvous was the 'Globe', a café in the Béthune market square reserved for British officers and French civilians. I once heard him complain indignantly that General French had refused to let him go up into the line.

The next day, Robertson and I caught our train. It took us to a junction, the name of which I forget, where we spent a day botanizing in the fields. No other train arrived until the following day, when we went on to Berguette, a rail-head still a number of miles from Laventie. There a mess-cart was waiting for us in answer to a telegram we had sent. We finally rattled up to battalion headquarters in Laventie High Street, having taken fifty-four hours to come those seventeen miles. We saluted the adjutant smartly, gave our names, and told him that we were Third Battalion officers posted to the regiment. He did not shake hands with us, offer us a drink, or say a word of welcome. 'I see,' he said coldly. 'Well, which of you is senior? Oh, never mind. Give your particulars to the R.S.M. Tell him to post whoever is senior to "A" Company and the other to "B" Company.'

The regimental sergeant-major took our particulars and introduced me to Hilary Drake-Brockman, a young second-lieutenant of 'A' Company, to which I had been posted. He was a special reservist of the East Surrey Regiment, and contemptuously known as 'the Surrey-man'. He took me along to the company billet. When out of earshot of battalion headquarters, I asked him: 'What's wrong with the adjutant? Why didn't he shake hands or give me any sort of decent welcome?'

The Surrey-man said: 'Well, it's your regiment, not mine. They're all like that here. You must realize that this is one of the only four regular infantry battalions in France that has remained still more or less its old self. This is the Nineteenth Brigade, the luckiest in France. It hasn't been permanently attached to any division, but gets used as army reserve, to put in wherever one has been badly knocked. So except for the Retreat, where it lost about a company, and Fromelles, where it lost half of what was left, it's been practically undamaged. More than two hundred of the wounded have rejoined since. All our company commanders are regulars, and so are all our N.C.O.s. The peacetime custom of taking no notice of newly-joined officers is still more or less kept up for the first six months. It's hard enough on the Sandhurst chaps; but worse for special reservists, like you and Rugg and Robertson; and it's worse still for outsiders like me.' We were going down the village street. The men sitting about on the doorsteps jumped up smartly to attention as we passed and saluted with a fixed, stony glare. They were magnificent looking fellows. Their uniforms were spotless, their equipment khaki-blancoed, and their buttons and cap-badges twinkled. We reached company head-quarters, where I reported to my company commander, Captain G. O. Thomas. He was a regular of seventeen years' service, a well-known polo-player, and a fine soldier. This is the descriptive order that he would himself have preferred. He shook hands without a word, waved me to a chair, offered a cigarette, and continued writing his letter. I found later that 'A' was the best company I could have struck.

The Surrey-man asked me to help him censor some company letters before going over to the battalion mess for lunch; they were more literate than the Welsh Regiment ones, but duller. On the way to the mess he asked me whether I had been out in France before. 'I was attached to the Second Welsh Regiment for three months; I commanded a company there for a bit.'

'Oh, did you? Well, I'd advise you to say nothing at all about it, then they'll not expect too much. They treat us like dirt; but it will be worse for you than for me because you're a full lieutenant. They'll resent that with your short service. There's one lieutenant here with six years' service, and several second-lieutenants who have been out since the autumn. Two Special Reserve captains have already been foisted on the battalion; the senior officers are planning to get rid of them somehow. The senior officers are beasts. If you open your mouth or make the slightest noise in the mess, they jump down your throat. Only officers of the rank of captain are allowed to drink whisky or turn on the gramophone. We've got to jolly well keep still and look like furniture. It's just like peacetime. Mess bills are very high; the mess was in debt at Quetta last year, so they're economizing now to pay that back. We get practically nothing for our money but ordinary rations, and we aren't allowed to drink the whisky.

'We've even got a polo-ground here. There was a polo-match between the First and Second Battalions the other day. The First had all their decent ponies pinched last October when they were massacred at Ypres and the cooks and transport men had to come up into the line to prevent a break-through. So the Second won easily. Can you ride? Not decently? Well, subalterns who can't ride like angels have to attend riding-school every afternoon while we're in billets. They give us hell, too. Two of us have been at it for four months and haven't passed out yet. They keep us trotting round the field, with crossed stirrups most of the time, and on pack-saddles instead of riding-saddles. Yesterday we were called up suddenly without being given time to change into breeches. That reminds me, you notice everybody's wearing shorts? It's a regimental order. The battalion thinks it's still in India. The men treat the French civilians just like "niggers", kick them about, talk army Hindustani at them. It makes me laugh sometimes. Well, what with a greasy pack-saddle, bare knees, crossed stirrups, and a wild new transport pony that the transport men had pinched from the French, I got a pretty thin time. The colonel, the adjutant, the second-in-command, and the transport officer stood at the four corners of the ring and slogged at the ponies as they came round. I fell off twice and got so wild with anger, I nearly decided to ride the second-in-command down. The funny thing is that they don't realize how badly they're treating us – it's such an honour to be serving with the regiment. So better pretend you don't care what they do or say.'

I protested: 'But all this is childish. Is there a war on here, or isn't there?'

'The Royal Welch don't recognize it socially,' he answered. 'Still, in trenches I'd rather be with this battalion than with any other I have met. The senior officers do know their job, whatever else one may say about them, and the N.C.O.s are absolutely to be trusted, too.'

The Second Battalion was peculiar in having a battalion mess instead of company messes: another peacetime survival. The Surreyman said grimly: 'It's supposed to be more sociable.'

We went together into the big *château* near the church. About fifteen officers of various ranks were sitting in chairs reading the week's illustrated papers or, the seniors at least, talking quietly. At the door I said: 'Good morning, gentlemen,' the new officer's customary greeting to the mess. No answer. Everybody glanced at me curiously. The silence that my entry had caused was soon broken by the gramophone, which began carolling:

> *We've been married just one year,*
> *And Oh, we've got the sweetest,*
> *We've got the neatest,*
> *We've got the cutest*
> *Little oil stove.*

I found a chair in the background and picked up the *Field*. The door burst open suddenly, and a lieutenant-colonel with a red face and angry eye burst in. 'Who the blazes put that record on?' he shouted to the mess. 'One of the bloody warts, I expect. Take it off, somebody! It makes me sick. Let's have some real music. Put on the "Angelus".'

Two subalterns (in the Royal Welch a subaltern had to answer to the name of 'wart') sprang up, stopped the gramophone, and put on 'When the Angelus is ringing'. The young captain who had put on 'We've been married' shrugged his shoulders and went on reading; the other faces in the room remained blank.

'Who's that?' I whispered to the Surrey-man.

He frowned. 'That's Buzz Off,' he muttered, 'the second-in-command.'

Before the record had finished, the door opened and in came the colonel; Buzz Off reappeared with him. Everybody jumped up and said in unison; 'Good morning, sir,' this being his first appearance that day.

Instead of returning our loyal greeting and asking us to sit down, he turned spitefully to the gramophone: 'Who on earth puts this wretched "Angelus" on every time I come into the mess? For heaven's sake play something cheery for a change!' With his own hands he took off the 'Angelus', wound up the gramophone, and put on 'We've been married just one year'. At that moment a gong rang for lunch, and he abandoned his task.

We filed into the next room, a ball-room with mirrors and a decorated ceiling, and took our places at a long, polished table. The seniors sat at the top, the juniors competed for seats as far away from them as possible. Unluckily I got a seat at the foot of the table, facing the colonel, the adjutant, and Buzz Off. Not a word was spoken down my end, except an occasional whisper for the salt or the beer – very thin French stuff. Robertson, who had not been warned, asked the mess-waiter for whisky. 'Sorry, sir,' said the mess-waiter, 'it's against orders for the young officers.' Robertson was a man of forty-two, a solicitor with a large practice, and had stood for Parliament in the Yarmouth division at the previous election.

I saw Buzz Off glaring at us and busied myself with my meat and potatoes.

He nudged the adjutant. 'Who are those two funny ones down there, Charley?' he asked.

'New this morning from the militia. Answer to the names of Robertson and Graves.'

'Which is which?' asked the colonel.

'I'm Robertson, sir.'

'I wasn't asking you.'

Robertson winced but said nothing. Then Buzz Off noticed something.

'T'other wart's wearing a wind-up tunic.' Then he bent forward and asked me loudly: 'You there, wart! Why the hell are you wearing your stars on your shoulder instead of your sleeve?'

My mouth was full, and everybody had his eyes on me. I swallowed the lump of meat whole and said: 'Shoulder stars were a regimental order in the Welsh Regiment, sir. I understood that it was the same everywhere in France.'

The colonel turned puzzled to the adjutant: 'Why on earth is the man talking about the Welsh Regiment?' And then to me: 'As soon as you have finished your lunch you will visit the master-tailor. Report at the orderly room when you're properly dressed.'

In a severe struggle between resentment and regimental loyalty, resentment for the moment had the better of it. I said under my breath: 'You damned snobs! I'll survive you all. There'll come a time when there won't be one of you left in the battalion to re-member this mess at Laventie.'

We went up to the trenches that night. They were 'high-com-mand' trenches – because water was struck whenever one dug down three feet, the parapet and parados had been built up man-high. I found my platoon curt and reserved. Even on sentry-duty at night my men would never talk confidentially about themselves and their families, like my platoon in the Welsh Regiment. Townsend, the platoon-sergeant, was an ex-policeman who had been on the reserve when war broke out. He used to drive his men rather than lead them. 'A' Company held Red Lamp Corner; the front trench broke off short here and started again farther back on the right, behind a patch of marsh. A red lamp hung at the corner, invisible to the enemy; after dark it warned the company behind us on our right not to fire left of it. Work and duties were done with a silent, soldier-like efficiency quite foreign to the Welsh Regiment.

My first night, Captain Thomas asked whether I would like to go out on patrol. It was the regimental custom to test new officers in this way, and none dared excuse himself. During my whole service with the Welsh I had never once been out in No Man's Land, even to inspect the barbed-wire; the wire being considered the responsibility of the battalion intelligence officer and the Royal Engineers. When Hewitt, the Welsh machine-gun officer, used to go out on patrol sometimes, we regarded this as a mad escapade. But both battalions of the Royal Welch Fusiliers had made it a point of honour to dominate No Man's Land from dusk to dawn. There was never a night at Laventie when a message did not come down the line from sentry to sentry: 'Pass the word; officer's patrol going out.' My orders for this patrol were to see whether a certain German sap-head was occupied by night or not.

Sergeant Townsend and I went out from Red Lamp Corner at about ten o'clock; both carrying revolvers. We had pulled socks, with the toes cut off, over our bare knees, to prevent them showing up in the dark and to make crawling easier. We went ten yards at a time, slowly, not on all fours, but wriggling flat along the ground. After each movement we lay and watched for about ten minutes. We crawled through our own wire entanglements and along a dry ditch; ripping our clothes on more barbed-wire, glaring into the darkness until it began turning round and round. Once I snatched my fingers in horror from where I had planted them on the slimy body of an old corpse. We nudged each other with rapidly beating hearts at the slightest noise or suspicion: crawling, watching, crawling, shamming dead under the blinding light of enemy flares, and again crawling, watching, crawling. A Second Battalion officer, who re-visited these Laventie trenches after the war ended, told me the other day of the ridiculously small area of No Man's Land compared with its seeming immensity on the long, painful journeys that he had made over it. 'It was like the real size of a hollow in one's tooth compared with how it feels to the tongue.'

We found the gap in the German wire and at last came within five yards of the sap-head. We waited quite twenty minutes, listening for any signs of its occupation. Then I nudged Sergeant Townsend and, revolver in hand, we wriggled quickly forward and slid into it. It was about three feet deep and unoccupied. On the floor were a few empty cartridges, and a wicker basket containing something large and smooth and round, twice the size of a football. Very, very carefully I groped and felt all around it in the dark. I was afraid that it might be some sort of infernal machine. Eventually I dared lift it out and carry it back, suspecting that it might be one of the German gas-cylinders we had heard so much about.

We got home after making a journey of perhaps two hundred yards in rather more than two hours. The sentries passed along the word that we were in again. Our prize proved to be a large glass container quarter-filled with some pale yellow liquid. This was sent down to battalion headquarters, and from there to the divisional intelligence officer. Everybody seemed greatly interested in it. The theory was that the vessel contained a chemical for re-damping gas-masks, though it may well have been dregs of country wine mixed with rain water. I never heard the official report. The colonel, however, told Captain Thomas in the hearing of the Surrey-man: 'Your new wart seems to have more guts than the others.'

After this I went on patrol fairly often, finding that the only thing respected in young officers was personal courage. Besides, I had cannily worked it out like this. My best way of lasting through to the end of the war would be to get wounded. The best time to get wounded would be at night and in the open, with rifle fire more or less unaimed and my whole body exposed. Best, also, to get wounded when there was no rush on the dressing-station services, and while the back areas were not being heavily shelled. Best to get wounded, therefore, on a night patrol in a quiet sector. One could usually manage to crawl into a shell hole until help arrived.

Still, patrolling had its peculiar risks. If a German patrol found a wounded man, they were as likely as not to cut his throat. The bowie-knife was a favourite German patrol weapon because of its silence. (We inclined more to the 'cosh', a loaded stick.) The most important information that a patrol could bring back was to what regiment and division the troop opposite belonged. So if it were impossible to get a wounded enemy back without danger to oneself, he had to be stripped of his badges. To do that quickly and silently, it might be necessary first to cut his throat or beat in his skull.

Sir Pyers Mostyn, a Royal Welch lieutenant who often went out patrolling at Laventie, had a feud with a German patrol on the left of the battalion frontage. Our patrols usually consisted of an officer and one, or at the most, two men; German patrols of six or seven men under an N.C.O. German officers did not, as one of our sergeant-majors put it, believe in 'keeping a dog and barking themselves'; so they left as much as they decently could to their N.C.O.s. One night Mostyn caught sight of his opponents; he had raised himself on his knees to throw a percussion bomb, when they fired and wounded him in the arm, which immediately went numb. He caught the bomb before it hit the ground, threw it at them with his left hand, and in the confusion that followed got back to the trench.

Like everyone else, I had a carefully worked out formula for taking risks. In principle, we would all take any risk, even the certainty of death, to save life or to maintain an important position. To take life we would run, say, a one-in-five risk, particularly if there was some wider object than merely reducing the enemy's man-power; for instance, picking off a well-known sniper, or getting fire ascendancy in trenches where the lines came dangerously close. I only once refrained from shooting a German I saw, and that was at Cuinchy, some three weeks after this. While sniping from a knoll in the support line, where we had a concealed loop-hole, I saw a German, perhaps seven hundred yards away, through my telescopic sights. He was taking a bath in the German third line. I disliked the idea of shooting a naked man, so I handed the rifle to the sergeant with me. 'Here, take this. You're a better shot than I am.' He got him; but I had not stayed to watch.

About saving the lives of enemy wounded there was disagreement; the convention varied with the division. Some divisions, like the Canadians and a division of Lowland territorials, who claimed that they had atrocities to avenge, would not only avoid taking risks to rescue enemy wounded, but go out of their way to finish them off. The Royal Welch were gentlemanly: perhaps a one-in-twenty risk to get a wounded German to safety would be considered justifiable. An important factor in calculating risks was our own physical condition. When exhausted and wanting to get quickly from one point in the trenches to another without collapse, we would sometimes take a short cut over the top, if the enemy were not nearer than four or five hundred yards. In a hurry, we would take a one-in-two-hundred risk; when dead tired, a one-in-fifty risk. In battalions where morale was low, one-in-fifty risks were often taken in laziness or despair. The Munsters of the First Division were said by the Welsh to 'waste men wicked', by not keeping properly under cover while in the reserve lines. The Royal Welch never allowed wastage of this sort. At no time in the war did any of us believe that hostilities could possibly continue more than another nine months or a year, so it seemed almost worth while taking care; there might even be a chance of lasting until the end absolutely unhurt.

The Second Royal Welch, unlike the Second Welsh, believed themselves better trench fighters than the Germans. With the Second Welsh it was not cowardice but modesty. With the Second Royal Welch it was not vainglory but courage: as soon as they arrived in a new sector they insisted on getting fire ascendancy. Having found out, from the troops whom they relieved, all possible information as to enemy snipers, machine-guns, and patrols, they set themselves to deal with them one by one. Machine-guns first. As soon as a machine-gun started traversing down a trench by night, the whole platoon farthest removed from its fire would open five rounds rapid at it. The machine-gun would usually stop suddenly, but start again after a minute or two. Again five rounds rapid. Then it gave up.

The Welsh seldom answered a machine-gun. If they did, it was not with organized local fire, beginning and ending in unison, but in ragged confused protest all along the line. The Royal Welch almost never fired at night, except with organized fire at a machine-gun, or a persistent enemy sentry, or a patrol close enough to be distinguished as a German one. With all other battalions I met in France there was a continuous random popping off; the sentries wanted to show their spite against the war. Flares were rarely used in the Royal Welch, except as signals to our patrols that they should be starting back.

When the enemy machine-guns had been discouraged, our patrols would go out with bombs to claim possession of No Man's Land. At dawn next morning came the struggle for sniping ascendancy. The Germans had special regimental snipers, trained in camouflaging themselves. I saw one killed once at Cuinchy, who had been firing all day from a shell-hole between the lines. He wore a sort of cape made of imitation grass, his face was painted green and brown, and his rifle was also green-fringed. A number of empty cartridges lay beside him, and his cap bore the special oak-leaf badge. Few of our battalions attempted to get control of the sniping situation. The Germans had the advantage of having many times more telescopic sights than we did, and bullet-proof steel loop-holes. Also a system by which snipers were kept for months in the same sector until they knew all the loop-holes and shallow places in our trenches, and the tracks that our ration parties used above-ground by night, and where our traverses occurred, and so on, better than most of us did ourselves. British snipers changed their trenches, with their battalions, every week or two, and never had time to study the German trench-geography. But at least we counted on getting rid of the unprofessional sniper. Later we secured an elephant-gun that could send a bullet through enemy loop-holes; and if we failed to locate the loop-hole of a persistent sniper, we tried to dislodge him with a volley of rifle-grenades, or even by ringing up the artillery.

It puzzled us that when a sniper had been spotted and killed, another sniper would often begin operations next day from the same position. The Germans probably underrated us, and regarded their loss as an accident. The willingness of other battalions to allow the Germans sniping ascendancy helped us; enemy snipers, even the professionals, often exposed themselves unnecessarily. There was one advantage of which no progress or retreat of the enemy could rob us, namely that we always more or less faced east. Dawn broke behind the German lines, and they did not realize that for several minutes every morning we could see them, while still invisible ourselves. German night wiring-parties often stayed out too long, and we could get a man or two as they went back; sunsets went against us, of course; but sunset was a less critical time. At night, our sentries had orders to stand with their heads and shoulders above the parapet, and their rifles in position. This surprised me at first, but it implied greater vigilance and self-confidence in the sentry, and also put the top of his head above the level of the parapet. Enemy machine-guns were trained on this level, and it would be safer to get hit in the chest or shoulders than in the forehead. The risk of unaimed fire at night being negligible, this was really the safest plan. It happened in battalions which did not insist on the head-and-shoulder rule, but let their sentries just steal an occasional peep over the top, that an enemy patrol would sneak up unseen to the British wire, throw a few bombs, and get safely back. With the Royal Welch, the barbed-wire entanglement became the responsibility of the company it protected. One of our first acts on taking over trenches was to inspect and repair it. We did a lot of work on our wire.

Captain Thomas kept extremely silent; but from shyness, not sullenness. 'Yes' and 'no' were the limit of his usual conversation. He never took us subalterns into his confidence about company affairs, and we did not like asking him too much. He proved most conscientious in taking his watch at night, which the other company commanders did not always do. We enjoyed his food-hampers, sent every week from Fortnum & Mason – we messed by companies when in trenches. Our one complaint was that Buzz Off, who had a good nose for a hamper, used to spend longer than he would otherwise have done in the company mess. His presence embarrassed us. Thomas went on leave to England about this time. I heard of his doings there accidentally. He had walked through the West End in mufti, astonished at the amateur militariness that he met everywhere. To be more in keeping with it, he gave elaborate awkward salutes to newly-joined second-lieutenants, and raised his hat to dug-out colonels and generals – a private joke at the expense of the war.

At Laventie, I used to look forward to our spells in trenches. Billet life spelt battalion mess, also riding-school, which turned out to be rather worse than the Surrey-man had described. Parades were carried out with peacetime punctiliousness and smartness, especially the daily battalion guard-changing which, every now and then, it was my duty to supervise as orderly officer. On one occasion, after the guard-changing had ended and I was about to dismiss the old guard, I saw Buzz Off cross the village street from one company headquarters to another. As he went by I called the guard to attention and saluted. After waiting for half a minute, I dismissed the guard. But Buzz Off had not really gone into the billet; he was hiding in the doorway. Now he dashed out with a great show of anger. 'As you were, as you were, stand fast!' he shouted to the guard. And then to me: 'Why in hell's name, Mr Graves, didn't you ask my permission to dismiss the parade? You've read the King's Regulations, haven't you? And where the devil are your manners, anyhow?'

I apologized, explaining that I thought he had gone into the billet. This made matters worse. He bellowed at me for arguing; then asked where I had learned to salute. 'At the depôt, sir,' I answered.

'Then, by heaven, Mr Graves, you'll have to learn to salute as the battalion does! You'll parade every morning before breakfast for a month under staff-sergeant Evans and do an hour's saluting drill.'

He turned to the guard and dismissed them himself. This was not a particular act of spite against me, but an incident in the general game of 'chasing the warts', at which all conscientious senior officers played, and honestly intended to make us better soldiers.

I had been with the Royal Welch about three weeks, when the Nineteenth Brigade moved south to the Béthune sector to fill a gap in the Second Division; the gap had been made by taking out the Brigade of Guards to include in a Guards division then being formed. On the way down, we marched past Lord Kitchener. Kitchener, we were told, commented to the brigadier on the soldier-like appearance of the leading battalion – which was ourselves – but said cynically: 'Wait until they've been a week or two in the trenches; they'll soon lose some of that high polish.' He apparently mistook us for a New Army formation.

The first trenches we went into on arrival were the Cuinchy brick-stacks. My company held the canal-bank frontage, a few hundred yards to the left of where I had been with the Welsh Regiment at the end of May. The Germans opposite wanted to be sociable. They sent messages over to us in undetonated rifle-grenades. One of these was evidently addressed to the Irish battalion we had relieved:

We all German korporals wish you English korporals a good day and invite you to a good German dinner tonight with beer (ale) and cakes. Your little dog ran over to us and we keep it safe; it became no food with you so it run to us. Answer in the same way, if you please.

Another grenade contained a copy of the *Neueste Nachrichten*, a German Army newspaper printed at Lille, giving sensational details of Russian defeats around Warsaw, with immense captures of prisoners and guns. But what interested us far more was a full account in another column of the destruction of a German submarine by British armed trawlers; no details of the sinking of German submarines had been allowed to appear in any English papers. The battalion cared as little about the successes or reverses of our Allies as about the origins of the war. It never allowed itself to have any political feelings about the Germans. A professional soldier's duty was simply to fight whomever the King ordered him to fight. With the King as colonel-in-chief of the regiment it became even simpler. The Christmas 1914 fraternization, in which the battalion was among the first to participate, had had the same professional simplicity: no emotional hiatus, this, but a common-place of military tradition – an exchange of courtesies between officers of opposing armies.

Cuinchy bred rats. They came up from the canal, fed on the plentiful corpses, and multiplied exceedingly. While I stayed here with the Welsh, a new officer joined the company and, in token of welcome, was given a dug-out containing a spring-bed. When he turned in that night, he heard a scuffling, shone his torch on the bed, and found two rats on his blanket tussling for the possession of a severed hand. This story circulated as a great joke.

The colonel called for a patrol to visit the side of the tow-path, where we had heard suspicious sounds on the previous night, and see whether they came from a working-party. I volunteered to go at dark. But that night the moon shone so bright and full that it dazzled the eyes. Between us and the Germans lay a flat stretch of about two hundred yards, broken only by shell craters and an occasional patch of coarse grass. I was not with my own company, but lent to 'B', which had two officers away on leave. Childe-Freeman, the company-commander, asked: 'You're not going out on patrol tonight, Graves, are you? It's almost as bright as day.'

'All the more reason for going,' I answered. 'They won't be expecting me. Will you please keep everything as usual? Let the men fire an occasional rifle, and send up a flare every half-hour. If I go carefully, the Germans won't see me.'

While we were having supper, I nervously knocked over a cup of tea, and after that a plate. Freeman said: 'Look here, I'll phone through to battalion and tell them it's too bright for your patrol.' But I knew that, if he did, Buzz Off would accuse me of cold feet.

So one Sergeant Williams and I put on our crawlers, and went out by way of a mine-crater at the side of the tow-path. We had no need to stare that night. We could see only too clearly. Our plan was to wait for an opportunity to move quickly, to stop dead and trust to luck, then move on quickly again. We planned our rushes from shell-hole to shell-hole, the opportunities being provided by artillery or machine-gun fire, which would distract the sentries. Many of the craters contained the corpses of men who had been wounded and crept in there to die. Some were skeletons, picked clean by the rats.

We got to within thirty yards of a big German working-party, who were digging a trench ahead of their front line. Between them and us we counted a covering party of ten men lying on the grass in their greatcoats. We had gone far enough. A German lay on his back about twelve yards off, humming a tune. It was the 'Merry Widow' waltz. The sergeant, from behind me, pressed my foot with his hand and showed me the revolver he was carrying. He raised his eyebrows inquiringly. I signalled 'no'. We turned to go back; finding it hard not to move too quickly. We had got about half-way, when a German machine-gun opened traversing fire along the top of our trenches. We immediately jumped to our feet; the bullets were brushing the grass, so to stand up was safer. We walked the rest of the way home, but moving irregularly to distract the aim of the covering party if they saw us. Back in the trench, I rang up brigade artillery, and asked for as much shrapnel as they could spare, fifty yards short of where the German front trench touched the tow-path; I knew that one of the night-lines of the battery supporting us was trained near enough to this point. A minute and a quarter later the shells started coming over. Hearing the clash of downed tools and distant shouts and cries, we reckoned the probable casualties.

The next morning, at stand-to, Buzz Off came up to me: 'I hear you were on patrol last night?'

'Yes, sir.'

He asked for particulars. When I told him about the covering party, he cursed me for not 'scuppering them with that revolver of yours.' As he turned away, he snorted: 'Cold feet!'

One night at Cuinchy we had orders from divisional headquarters to shout across No Man's Land and make the enemy take part in a conversation. The object was to find out how strongly the German front trenches were manned after dark. A German-speaking officer in the company among the brick-stacks shouted through a mega-phone: '*Wie geht's Ihnen, Kameraden?*'

Somebody shouted back in delight: '*Ach, Tommee, hast du denn deutsch gelernt?*'

Firing stopped, and a conversation began across the fifty yards or so of No Man's Land. The Germans refused to disclose what regiment they were, or talk any military shop.

One of them shouted out: '*Les sheunes madamoiselles de La Bassée bonnes pour coucher avec. Les madamoiselles de Béthune bonnes aussi, hein?*'

Our spokesman refused to discuss sex. In the pause that followed he asked after the Kaiser. They replied respectfully that he was in excellent health, thank you.

'And how is the Crown Prince?' he asked them.

'Oh, b—r the Crown Prince,' shouted somebody in English, and was immediately suppressed by his comrades. After a confusion of angry voices and laughter, they all began singing '*Die Wacht am Rhein*'. That trench was evidently very well held indeed.

I now had a trench periscope, a little rod-shaped metal one, sent me from home. When I poked it above the parapet, it offered only an inch-square target to the German snipers; yet a sniper at Cuinchy, in May, drilled it through, exactly central, at four hundred yards range. I sent it back as a souvenir; but my mother, practical as usual, returned it to the makers and made them change it for a new one.

My dug-out at Cuinchy was a rat-riddled culvert beside the tow-path; when we went back to support billets, I dossed in the cellar of a ruined house at Cambrin village, lit by a couple of shell-holes through the floor above; but when back in reserve billets at Béthune, I had a beautiful Louis XVI bedroom at the Château Montmorency with mirrors and tapestries, found the bed too soft for comfort, and laid my mattress on the parquet floor.

15

By the end of August 1915, particulars of the coming offensive against La Bassée were beginning to leak through the young staff officers. The French civilians knew about it; and so, naturally, did the Germans. Every night now new batteries and lorry-trains of shells came rumbling up the Béthune–La Bassée road. Other signs of movement included sapping forward at Vermelles and Cambrin, where the lines lay too far apart for a quick rush across, and the joining up of the sap-heads to make a new front line. Also, orders for evacuation of hospitals; the appearance of cavalry and New Army divisions; issue of new types of weapons. Then Royal Engineer officers supervised the digging of pits at intervals along the front line. They were sworn not to reveal what these were for, but we knew that it would be gas-cylinders. Ladders for climbing quickly out of the trenches were brought up by the lorry-load and dumped at Cambrin village. As early as September 3rd I had a bet with Robertson that our division would attack from the Cambrin–Cuinchy line. When I went home on leave six days later, the sense of impending events had become so strong that I almost hated to go.

Leave came round for officers about every six or eight months in ordinary times; heavy casualties shortened the period, general offensives cut leave altogether. Only one officer in France ever refused to go on leave when his turn came – Cross of the Fifty-second Light Infantry (the Second Battalion of the Oxford and Bucks Light Infantry, which insisted on its original style as jealously as we kept our *c* in Welch). Cross is alleged to have refused leave on the following grounds: 'My father fought with the regiment in the South African War, and had no leave; my grandfather fought in the Crimea with the regiment, and had no leave. I do not regard it in the regimental tradition to take home-leave when on active service.' Cross, a professional survivor, was commanding the battalion in 1917 when I last heard of him.

London seemed unreally itself. Despite the number of uniforms in the streets, the general indifference to, and ignorance about, the war surprised me. Enlistment remained voluntary. The universal catchword was 'Business as usual'. My family were living in London now at the house formerly occupied by my uncle Robert von Ranke, the German Consul-General. He had been forced to leave in a hurry on August 4th, 1914, and my mother undertook to look after the house for him while the war lasted. So when Edward Marsh rang me up from the Prime Minister's office at Downing Street to arrange a meal, someone intervened and cut him off – the telephone of the German Consul-General's sister was, of course, closely watched by the anti-espionage section of Scotland Yard. The Zeppelin scare had just begun. Some friends of the family came in one night, and began telling me of the Zeppelin air-raids, of bombs dropped only three streets off.

'Well, do you know,' I said, 'the other day I was asleep in a house and in the early morning a bomb dropped next door and killed three soldiers who were billeted there, a woman, and a child.'

'Good gracious,' they cried, 'what did you do then?'

'It was at a place called Beuvry, about four miles behind the trenches,' I explained, 'and I was tired out, so I went to sleep again.' 'Oh,' they said, 'but that happened in France!' and the look of interest faded from their faces as though I had taken them in with a stupid catch. 'Yes,' I agreed, 'and it was only an aeroplane that dropped the bomb.'

I went up to Harlech for the rest of my leave, and walked about on the hills in an old shirt and a pair of shorts. When I got back to France, 'The Actor', a regular officer in 'A' Company, asked me: 'Had a good time on leave?'

'Yes.'

'Go to many dances?'

'Not one.'

'What shows did you go to?'

'I didn't go to any shows.'

'Hunt?'

'No.'

'Slept with any nice girls?'

'No, I didn't. Sorry to disappoint you.'

'What the hell *did* you do, then?'

'Oh, I just walked about on some hills.'

'Good God,' he said, 'chaps like you don't deserve leave!'

On September 19th we relieved the Middlesex Regiment at Cambrin, and were told that these would be the trenches from which we attacked. The preliminary bombardment had already started, a week in advance. As I led my platoon into the line, I recognized with some disgust the same machine-gun shelter where I had seen the suicide on my first night in trenches. It seemed ominous. This was by far the heaviest bombardment from our own guns we had yet seen. The trenches shook properly, and a great cloud of drifting shell-smoke obscured the German lines. Shells went over our heads in a steady stream; we had to shout to make our neighbours hear. Dying down a little at night, the racket began again every morning at dawn, a little louder each time. 'Damn it,' we said, 'there can't be a living soul left in those trenches.' But still it went on. The Germans retaliated, though not very vigorously. Most of their heavy artillery had been withdrawn from this sector, we were told, and sent across to the Russian front. More casualties came from our own shorts and blow-backs than from German shells. Much of the ammunition that our batteries were using came from the United States and contained a high percentage of duds; the driving bands were always coming off. We had fifty casualties in the ranks and three officer casualties, including Buzz Off – badly wounded in the head. This happened before steel helmets were issued; we would not have lost nearly so many with those. I got two insignificant wounds on the hand, which I took as a favourable omen.

On the morning of the 23rd, Thomas came back from battalion headquarters carrying a notebook and six maps, one for each of us company officers. 'Listen,' he said, 'and copy out all this skite on the back of your maps. You'll have to explain it to your platoons this afternoon. Tomorrow morning we go back to dump our blankets, packs, and greatcoats in Béthune. The next day, that's Saturday the

25th, we attack.' This being the first definitive news we had been given, we looked up half startled, half relieved. I still have the map, and these are the orders as I copied them down:

FIRST OBJECTIVE – *Les Briques Farm* – The big house plainly visible to our front, surrounded by trees. To get this it is necessary to cross three lines of enemy trenches. The first is three hundred yards distant, the second four hundred, and the third about six hundred. We then cross two railways. Behind the second railway line is a German trench called the Brick Trench. Then comes the Farm, a strong place with moat and cellars and a kitchen garden strongly staked and wired.

SECOND OBJECTIVE – *The Town of Auchy* – This is also plainly visible from our trenches. It is four hundred yards beyond the Farm and defended by a first line of trench half way across, and a second line immediately in front of the town. When we have occupied the first line our direction is half-right, with the left of the battalion directed on Tall Chimney.

THIRD OBJECTIVE – *Village of Haisnes* – Conspicuous by high-spired church. Our eventual line will be taken up on the railway behind this village, where we will dig in and await reinforcements.

When Thomas had reached this point, The Actor's shoulders were shaking with laughter.

'What's up?' asked Thomas irritably.

The Actor giggled: 'Who in God's name is responsible for this little effort?'

'Don't know,' Thomas said. 'Probably Paul the Pimp, or someone like that.' (Paul the Pimp was a captain on the divisional staff, young, inexperienced, and much disliked. He 'wore red tabs upon his chest And even on his undervest.') 'Between the six of us, but you young-sters must be careful not to let the men know, this is what they call a "subsidiary attack". There will be no troops in support. We've just got to go over and keep the enemy busy while the folk on our right do the real work. You notice that the bombardment is much heavier over there. They've knocked the Hohenzollern Redoubt to bits. Personally, I don't give a damn either way. We'll get killed whatever happens.'

We all laughed.

'All right, laugh now, but by God, on Saturday we've got to carry out this funny scheme.' I had never heard Thomas so talkative before.

'Sorry,' The Actor apologized, 'carry on with the dictation.'

Thomas went on:

The attack will be preceded by forty minutes' discharge of the accessory,* which will clear the path for a thousand yards, so that the two railway lines will be occupied without difficulty. Our advance will follow closely behind the accessory. Behind us are three fresh divisions and the Cavalry Corps. It is expected we shall have no difficulty in breaking through. All men will parade with their platoons; pioneers, servants, etc., to be warned. All platoons to be properly told off under N.C.O.s. Every N.C.O. is to know exactly what is expected of him, and when to take over command in case of casualties. Men who lose touch must join up with the nearest company or regiment and push on. Owing to the strength of the accessory, men should be warned against remaining too long in captured trenches where the accessory is likely to collect, but to keep to the open and above all to push on. It is important that if smoke-helmets have to be pulled down they must be tucked in under the shirt.

The Actor interrupted again. 'Tell me, Thomas, do you believe in this funny accessory?'

Thomas said: 'It's damnable. It's not soldiering to use stuff like that, even though the Germans did start it. It's dirty, and it'll bring us bad luck. We're sure to bungle it. Take those new gas-companies – sorry, excuse me this once, I mean accessory-companies – their very look makes me tremble. Chemistry-dons from London University, a few lads straight from school, one or two N.C.O.s of the old-soldier type, trained together for three weeks, then given a job as responsible as this. Of course they'll bungle it. How could they do anything else? But let's be merry. I'm going on again:

Men of company: what they are to carry:

Two hundred rounds of ammunition (bomb-throwers fifty, and signallers one hundred and fifty rounds).

Heavy tools carried in sling by the strongest men.

Waterproof sheet in belt.

Sandbag in right tunic-pocket.

Field dressing and iodine.

Emergency ration, including biscuit.

One tube-helmet, to be worn when we advance, rolled up on the head. It must be quite secure and the top part turned down. If possible each man will be provided with an elastic band.

* The gas-cylinders had by this time been put into position on the front line. A special order came round imposing severe penalties on anyone who used any word but 'accessory' in speaking of the gas. This was to keep it secret, but the French civilians knew all about the scheme long before this.

One smoke helmet, old pattern, to be carried for preference behind the back where it is least likely to be damaged by stray bullets, etc.

Wire-cutters, as many as possible, by wiring party and others; hedging gloves by wire party.

Platoon screens, for artillery observation, to be carried by a man in each platoon who is not carrying a tool.

Packs, capes, greatcoats, blankets will be dumped, not carried.

No one is to carry sketches of our position or anything to be likely of service to the enemy.

That's all. I believe we're going over first with the Middlesex in support. If we get through the German wire I'll be satisfied. Our guns don't seem to be cutting it. Perhaps they're putting that off until the intense bombardment. Any questions?'

That afternoon I repeated the whole rigmarole to the platoon, and told them of the inevitable success attending our assault. They seemed to believe it. All except Sergeant Townsend. 'Do you say, sir, that we have three divisions and the Cavalry Corps behind us?' he asked.

'Yes,' I answered.

'Well, excuse me, sir, I'm thinking it's only those chaps on the right that'll get reinforcements. If we get half a platoon of Mons Angels,* that's about all we will get.'

'Sergeant Townsend,' I said, 'you're a well-known pessimist. This is going to be a really good show.'

We spent the night repairing damaged trenches.

When morning came we were relieved by the Middlesex, and marched back to Béthune, where we dumped our spare kit at the Montmorency Barracks. The battalion officers messed together in a *château* near by. This billet was claimed at the same time by the staff of a New Army division, due to take part in the fighting next day. The argument ended amicably with the division and battalion messing together. It was, someone pointed out, like a brutal caricature of The Last Supper in duplicate. In the middle of the long table sat the two pseudo-Christs, our colonel and the divisional general. Everybody was drinking a lot; the subalterns, allowed whisky for a treat, grew rowdy. They raised their glasses with: 'Cheerio, we will be messing together tomorrow night in La Bassée!' Only the company commanders were looking worried. I remember 'C' Company commander especially,

---

* According to the newspapers, a vision of angels had been seen by the British Army at Mons; but it was not vouchsafed to Sergeant Townsend, who was there, with most of 'A' Company.

Captain A. L. Samson, biting his thumb and refusing to join in the excitement. I think it was Childe-Freeman of 'B' Company who said that night: 'The last time the regiment visited these parts we were under decent leadership. Old Marlborough had more sense than to attack the La Bassée lines; he masked them and went around.'

The G.S.O.1 of the New Army division, a staff-colonel, knew the adjutant well. They had played polo together in India. I happened to be sitting opposite them. The G.S.O.1 said, rather drunkenly: 'Charley, see that silly old woman over there? Calls himself General Commanding! Doesn't know where he is; doesn't know where his division is; can't even read a map properly. He's marched the poor sods off their feet and left his supplies behind, God knows how far back. They've had to use their iron rations and what they could pick up in the villages. And tomorrow he's going to fight a battle. Doesn't know anything about battles; the men have never been in trenches before, and tomorrow's going to be a glorious balls-up, and the day after tomorrow he'll be sent home.' Then he ended, quite seriously: 'Really, Charley, it's just like that, no exaggeration. You mark my words!'

That night we marched back again to Cambrin. The men were singing. Being mostly from the Midlands, they sang comic songs rather than Welsh hymns: *Slippery Sam*, *When we've Wound up the Watch on the Rhine*, and *I do like a S'nice S'mince Pie*, to concertina accompaniment. The tune of *S'nice S'mince Pie* ran in my head all next day, and for the week following I could not get rid of it. The Second Welsh would never have sung a song like *When we've Wound up the Watch on the Rhine*. Their only songs about the war were defeatist:

> *I want to go home,*
> *I want to go home.*
> *The coal-box and shrapnel they whistle and roar,*
> *I don't want to go to the trenches no more,*
> *I want to go over the sea*
> *Where the Kayser can't shoot bombs at me.*
> *Oh, I*
> *Don't want to die,*
> *I want to go home.*

There were several more verses in the same strain. Hewitt, the Welsh machine-gun officer, had written one in a more offensive spirit:

> *I want to go home,*
> *I want to go home.*
> *One day at Givenchy the week before last*
> *The Allmands attacked and they nearly got past.*
> *They pushed their way up to the Keep,*
> *Through our maxim-gun sights we did peep,*
> *Oh, my!*
> *They let out a cry,*
> *They never got home.*

But the men would not sing it, though they all admired Hewitt.

The Béthune–La Bassée road was choked with troops, guns, and transport, and we had to march miles north out of our way to circle round to Cambrin. Even so, we were held up two or three times by massed cavalry. Everything radiated confusion. A casualty clearing-station had been planted astride one of the principal cross-roads, and was already being shelled. By the time we reached Cambrin, the battalion had marched about twenty miles that day. Then we heard that the Middlesex would go over first, with us in support; and to their left the Second Argyll and Sutherland Highlanders, with the Cameronians in support. The young Royal Welch officers complained loudly at our not being given the honour of leading the attack. As the senior regiment, they protested, we were entitled to the 'Right of the Line'. An hour or so past midnight we moved into trench sidings just in front of the village. Half a mile of communication trench, known as 'Maison Rouge Alley', separated us from the firing line. At half-past five the gas would be discharged. We were cold, tired, sick, and not at all in the mood for a battle, but tried to snatch an hour or two of sleep squatting in the trench. It had been raining for some time.

A grey, watery dawn broke at last behind the German lines; the bombardment, surprisingly slack all night, brisked up a little. 'Why the devil don't they send them over quicker?' The Actor complained. 'This isn't my idea of a bombardment. We're getting nothing opposite us. What little there seems to be, is going into the Hohenzollern.'

'Shell shortage. Expected it,' was Thomas's laconic reply.

We were told afterwards that on the 23rd a German aeroplane had bombed the Army Reserve shell-dump and sent it up. The bombardment on the 24th, and on the day of the battle itself, compared very poorly with that of the previous days. Thomas looked strained and ill. 'It's time they were sending that damned accessory off. I wonder what's doing.'

The events of the next few minutes are difficult for me now to sort out. I found it more difficult still at the time. All we heard back there in the sidings was a distant cheer, confused crackle of rifle fire, yells, heavy shelling on our front line, more shouts and yells, and a continuous rattle of machine-guns. After a few minutes, lightly wounded men of the Middlesex came stumbling down Maison Rouge Alley to the dressing-station. I stood at the junction of the siding and the Alley.

'What's happened? What's happened?' I asked.

'Bloody balls-up,' was the most detailed answer I could get.

Among the wounded were a number of men yellow-faced and choking, their buttons tarnished green – gas cases. Then came the badly wounded. Maison Rouge Alley being narrow, the stretchers had difficulty in getting down. The Germans started shelling it with five-point-nines.

Thomas went back to battalion headquarters through the shelling to ask for orders. It was the same place that I had visited on my first night in the trenches. This cluster of dug-outs in the reserve line showed very plainly from the air as battalion headquarters, and should never have been occupied during a battle. Just before Thomas arrived, the Germans put five shells into it. The adjutant jumped one way, the colonel another, the R.S.M. a third. One shell went into the signals dug-out, killed some signallers, and destroyed the telephone. The colonel, slightly cut on the hand, joined the stream of wounded and was carried back as far as the Base with it. The adjutant took command.

Meanwhile 'A' Company had been waiting in the siding for the rum to arrive; the tradition of every attack being a double tot of rum beforehand. All the other companies got theirs. The Actor began cursing: 'Where the bloody hell's that storeman gone?' We fixed bayonets in readiness to go up and attack as soon as Captain Thomas returned with orders. Hundreds of wounded streamed by. At last Thomas's orderly appeared. 'Captain's orders, sir: "A" Company to move up to the front line.' At that moment the storeman arrived, without rifle or equipment, hugging the rum-bottle, red-faced and retching. He staggered up to The Actor and said: 'There you are, sir!', then fell on his face in the thick mud of a sump-pit at the junction of the trench and the siding. The stopper of the bottle flew out and what remained of the three gallons bubbled on the ground.

127

The Actor made no reply. This was a crime that deserved the death penalty. He put one foot on the storeman's neck, the other in the small of his back, and trod him into the mud. Then he gave the order 'Company forward!' The company advanced with a clatter of steel, and that was the last I ever heard of the storeman.

It seems that at half past four an R.E. captain commanding the gas-company in the front line phoned through to divisional headquarters: 'Dead calm. Impossible discharge accessory.' The answer he got was: 'Accessory to be discharged at all costs.' Thomas had not over-estimated the gas-company's efficiency. The spanners for unscrewing the cocks of the cylinders proved, with two or three exceptions, to be misfits. The gas-men rushed about shouting for the loan of an adjustable spanner. They managed to discharge one or two cylinders; the gas went whistling out, formed a thick cloud a few yards off in No Man's Land, and then gradually spread back into our trenches. The Germans, who had been expecting gas, immediately put on their gas-helmets: semi-rigid ones, better than ours. Bundles of oily cotton-waste were strewn along the German parapet and set alight as a barrier to the gas. Then their batteries opened on our lines. The confusion in the front trench must have been horrible; direct hits broke several of the gas-cylinders, the trench filled with gas, the gas-company stampeded.

No orders could come through because the shell in the signals dug-out at battalion headquarters had cut communication not only be-tween companies and battalion, but between battalion and division. The officers in the front trench had to decide on immediate action; so two companies of the Middlesex, instead of waiting for the intense bombardment which would follow the advertised forty minutes of gas, charged at once and got as far as the German wire – which our artillery had not yet cut. So far it had been treated only with shrapnel, which had no effect on it; the barbed-wire needed high-explosive, and plenty of it. The Germans shot the Middlesex men down. One platoon is said to have found a gap and got into the German trench. But there were no survivors of the platoon to confirm this. The Argyll and Sutherland Highlanders went over, also, on the Middlesex left; but two companies, instead of charging at once, rushed back out of the gas-filled assault trench to the support line, and attacked from there. It will be recalled that the trench system had been pushed forward nearer the enemy in preparation for the battle. These companies were therefore attacking from the old front line, but the barbed-wire entanglements protecting it had not been removed, so that the High-landers got caught and machine-gunned between their own assault and support lines. The other two companies were equally unsuccessful. When the attack started, the German N.C.O.s had jumped up on the parapet to encourage their men. These were Jäger, famous for their musketry.

The survivors of the two leading Middlesex companies now lay in shell-craters close to the German wire, sniping and making the Germans keep their heads down. They had bombs to throw, but these were nearly all of a new type issued for the battle. The fuses were lighted on the match-box principle, and the rain had made them useless. The other two companies of the Middlesex soon followed in support. Machine-gun fire stopped them half-way. Only one German machine-gun remained in action, the others having been knocked out by rifle or trench-mortar fire. Why the single gun survived is a story in itself.

It starts with the privilege granted British colonial governors and high-commissioners of nominating one or two officers from their countries for attachment in wartime to the regular Army. Under this scheme, the officers began as full lieutenants. The Captain-General of Jamaica (if that is his correct style) nominated the eighteen-year-old son of a rich planter, who went straight from Kingston to the First Middlesex. He was good-hearted enough, but of little use as an officer, having never been out of the island in his life or, except for a short service with the West India militia, seen any soldiering. His company commander took a fatherly interest in 'Young Jamaica', and tried to teach him his duties. This company commander was known as 'The Boy'. He had twenty years' service with the Middlesex, and the unusual boast of having held every rank from 'boy' to captain in the same company. His father, I believe, had been the regimental sergeant-major. But 'Jamaica', as a full lieutenant, ranked senior to the other experienced subalterns in the company, who were only second-lieutenants.

The Middlesex colonel decided to shift Jamaica off on some course of extra-regimental appointment at the earliest opportunity. Somewhere about May or June, when instructed to supply an officer for the brigade trench-mortar company, he had sent Jamaica. Trench-mortars being then both dangerous and ineffective, the appointment seemed suitable. At the same time, the Royal Welch had also been asked to detail an officer, and the colonel selected Tiley, an ex-planter from Malaya, and what is called a 'fine natural soldier'. Tiley had been chosen because, when attached to us from a Lancashire regiment, he showed his resentment at the manner of his welcome somewhat too plainly. But, by September, mortars had improved in design and become an important infantry arm; so Jamaica, being senior to Tiley, held the responsible position of brigade mortar officer.

When the Middlesex charged, The Boy fell mortally wounded as he climbed over the parapet. He tumbled back and began crawling down the trench to the stretcher-bearers' dug-out, past Jamaica's trench-mortar emplacement. Jamaica had lost his gun-team, and was boldly serving the trench-mortars himself. On seeing The Boy, however, he deserted his post and ran off to fetch a stretcher-party. Tiley, meanwhile, on the other flank opposite Mine Point, had knocked out all the machine-guns within range. He went on until his mortar burst. Only one machine-gun in the Pope's Nose, a small salient facing Jamaica, remained active.

At this point the Royal Welch Fusiliers came up Maison Rouge Alley. The Germans were shelling it with five-nines (called 'Jack Johnsons' because of their black smoke) and lachrymatory shells. This caused a continual scramble backwards and forwards, to cries of: 'Come on!' 'Get back you bastards!' 'Gas turning on us!' 'Keep your heads, you men!' 'Back like hell, boys!' 'Whose orders?' 'What's happening?' 'Gas!' 'Back!' 'Come on!' 'Gas!' 'Back!' Wounded men and stretcher-bearers kept trying to squeeze past. We were alternately putting on and taking off our gas-helmets, which made things worse. In many places the trench had caved in, obliging us to scramble over the top. Childe-Freeman reached the front line with only fifty men of 'B' Company; the rest had lost their way in some abandoned trenches half-way up.

The adjutant met him in the support line. 'Ready to go over, Freeman?' he asked.

Freeman had to admit that he had lost most of his company. He felt this disgrace keenly; it was the first time that he had commanded a company in battle. Deciding to go over with his fifty men in support of the Middlesex, he blew his whistle and the company charged. They were stopped by machine-gun fire before they had got through our own entanglements. Freeman himself died – oddly enough, of heart-failure – as he stood on the parapet.

A few minutes later, Captain Samson, with 'C' Company and the remainder of 'B', reached our front line. Finding the gas-cylinders still whistling and the trench full of dying men, he decided to go over too – he could not have it said that the Royal Welch had let down the Middlesex. A strong, comradely feeling bound the Middlesex and the Royal Welch, intensified by the accident that the other three battalions in the brigade were Scottish, and that our Scottish brigadier was, unjustly no doubt, accused of favouring them. Our adjutant voiced the extreme non-Scottish view 'The Jocks are all the same; both the trousered kind and the bare-arsed kind: they're dirty in trenches, they skite too much, and they charge like hell – both ways.' The First Middlesex, who were the original 'Diehards', had more than once, with the Royal Welch, considered themselves let down by the Jocks. So Samson charged with 'C' and the remainder of 'B' Company.

One of 'C' officers told me later what happened. It had been agreed to advance by platoon rushes with supporting fire. When his platoon had gone about twenty yards, he signalled them to lie down and open covering fire. The din was tremendous. He saw the platoon on his left flopping down too, so he whistled the advance again. Nobody seemed to hear. He jumped up from his shell-hole, waved, and signalled 'Forward!'

Nobody stirred.

He shouted: 'You bloody cowards, are you leaving me to go on alone?'

His platoon-sergeant, groaning with a broken shoulder, gasped· 'Not cowards, sir. Willing enough. But they're all f—ing dead.' The Pope's Nose machine-gun, traversing, had caught them as they rose to the whistle.

'A' Company, too, had become separated by the shelling. I was with the leading platoon. The Surrey-man got a touch of gas and went coughing back. The Actor accused him of scrimshanking. This I thought unfair; the Surrey-man looked properly sick. I don't know what happened to him, but I heard that the gas-poisoning was not serious and that he managed, a few months later, to get back to his own regiment in France. I found myself with The Actor in a narrow communication trench between the front and support lines. This trench had not been built wide enough for a stretcher to pass the bends. We came on The Boy lying on his stretcher, wounded in the lungs and stomach. Jamaica was standing over him in tears, blubbering: 'Poor old Boy, poor old Boy, he's going to die; I'm sure he is. He's the only one who treated me decently.'

The Actor, finding that we could not get by, said to Jamaica: 'Take that poor sod out of the way, will you? I've got to get my company up. Put him into a dug-out, or somewhere.'

Jamaica made no answer; he seemed paralysed by the horror of the occasion and kept repeating: 'Poor old Boy, poor old Boy!'

'Look here,' said The Actor, 'if you can't shift him into a dug-out we'll have to lift him on top of the trench. He can't live now, and we're late getting up.'

'No, no,' Jamaica shouted wildly.

The Actor lost his temper and shook Jamaica roughly by the shoulders. 'You're the bloody trench-mortar wallah, aren't you?' he shouted.

Jamaica nodded miserably.

'Well, your battery is a hundred yards from here. Why the hell aren't you using your gas-pipes to some purpose? Buzz off back to them!' And he kicked him down the trench. Then he called over his shoulder: 'Sergeant Rose and Corporal Jennings! Lift this stretcher up across the top of the trench. We've got to pass.'

Jamaica leaned against a traverse. 'I do think you're the most heartless beast I've ever met,' he said weakly.

We went up to the corpse-strewn front line. The captain of the gas-company, who was keeping his head and wore a special oxygen respirator, had by now turned off the gas-cocks. Vermorel-sprayers had cleared out most of the gas, but we were still warned to wear our masks. We climbed up and crouched on the fire-step, where the gas was not so thick – gas, being heavy stuff, kept low. Then Thomas brought up the remainder of 'A' Company and, with 'D', we waited for the whistle to follow the other two companies over. Fortunately at this moment the adjutant appeared. He was now left in command of the battalion, and told Thomas that he didn't care a damn about orders; he was going to cut his losses and not send 'A' and 'D' over to their deaths until he got definite orders from brigade. He had sent a runner back, and we must wait.

Meanwhile, the intense bombardment that was to follow the forty minutes' discharge of gas began. It concentrated on the German front trench and wire. A good many shells fell short, and we had further casualties from them. In No Man's Land, the survivors of the Middlesex and of our 'B' and 'C' Companies suffered heavily.

My mouth was dry, my eyes out of focus, and my legs quaking under me. I found a water-bottle full of rum and drank about half a pint; it quieted me, and my head remained clear. Samson lay groaning about twenty yards beyond the front trench. Several attempts were made to rescue him. He had been very badly hit. Three men got killed in these attempts; two officers and two men, wounded. In the end his own orderly managed to crawl out to him. Samson waved him back, saying that he was riddled through and not worth rescuing; he sent his apologies to the company for making such a noise.

We waited a couple of hours for the order to charge. The men were silent and depressed; only Sergeant Townsend was making feeble, bitter jokes about the good old British Army muddling through, and how he thanked God we still had a Navy. I shared the rest of my rum with him, and he cheered up a little. Finally a runner arrived with a message that the attack had been postponed.

Rumours came down the trench of a disaster similar to our own in the brick-stack sector, where the Fifth Brigade had gone over; and again at Givenchy, where men of the Sixth Brigade at the Duck's Bill salient had fought their way into the enemy trenches, but been repulsed, their supply of bombs failing. It was said, however, that things were better on the right, where there had been a slight wind to take the gas over. According to one rumour, the First, Seventh, and Forty-seventh Divisions had broken through.

My memory of that day is hazy. We spent it getting the wounded down to the dressing-station, spraying the trenches and dug-outs to get rid of the gas, and clearing away the earth where trenches were blocked. The trenches stank with a gas-blood-lyddite-latrine smell. Late in the afternoon we watched through our field-glasses the advance of reserves under heavy shell-fire towards Loos and Hill 70; it looked like a real break-through. They were troops of the New Army division, whose staff we had messed with the night before. Immediately to the right of us we had the Highland Division, whose exploits on that day Ian Hay has celebrated in *The First Hundred Thousand*; I suppose that we were 'the flat caps on the left' who 'let down' his comrades-in-arms.

At dusk, we all went out to get in the wounded, leaving only sentries in the line. The first dead body I came upon was Samson's, hit in seventeen places. I found that he had forced his knuckles into his mouth to stop himself crying out and attracting any more men to their death. Major Swainson, the second-in-command of the Middlesex, came crawling in from the German wire. He seemed to be wounded in lungs, stomach, and one leg. Choate, a

Middlesex second-lieutenant, came back unhurt; together we bandaged Swainson and got him into the trench and on a stretcher. He begged me to loosen his belt; I cut it with a bowie-knife I had bought at Béthune for use during the battle. He said: 'I'm about done for.'*
We spent all that night getting in the wounded of the Royal Welch, the Middlesex, and those Argyll and Sutherland Highlanders who had attacked from the front trench. The Germans behaved generously. I do not remember hearing a shot fired that night, though we kept on until it was nearly dawn and we could see plainly; then they fired a few warning shots, and we gave it up. By this time we had recovered all the wounded, and most of the Royal Welch dead. I was surprised at some of the attitudes in which the dead stiffened – bandaging friends' wounds, crawling, cutting wire. The Argyll and Sutherland had seven hundred casualties, including fourteen officers killed out of the sixteen who went over; the Middlesex, five hundred and fifty casualties, including eleven officers killed.

Two other Middlesex officers besides Choate came back unwounded; their names were Henry and Hill, recently commissioned second-lieutenants, who had been lying out in shell-holes all day under the rain, sniping and being sniped at. Henry, according to Hill, had dragged five wounded men into a shell-hole and thrown up a sort of parapet with his hands and the bowie-knife which he carried. Hill had his platoon-sergeant beside him, screaming with a stomach wound, begging for morphia; he was done for, so Hill gave him five pellets. We always carried morphia for emergencies like that.

Choate, Henry, and Hill, returning to the trenches with a few stragglers, reported at the Middlesex headquarters. Hill told me the story. The colonel and the adjutant were sitting down to a meat pie when he and Henry arrived. Henry said: 'Come to report, sir. Ourselves and about ninety men of all companies. Mr Choate is back, unwounded, too.'

They looked up dully. 'So you've survived, have you?' the colonel said. 'Well, all the rest are dead. I suppose Mr Choate had better command what's left of "A" Company: the bombing officer will command what's left of "B" [the bombing officer had not gone over, but remained with headquarters]; Mr Henry goes to "C" Company.

* Major Swainson recovered, and was back at the Middlesex Depôt after a few weeks. On the other hand, Lawrie, a Royal Welch quartermaster-sergeant back at Cambrin, was hit in the neck that day by a spent machine-gun bullet which just pierced the skin, and died of shock a few hours later.

Mr Hill to "D". The Royal Welch are holding the front line. We are here in support. Let me know where to find you if you're needed. Good night.'

Not having been offered a piece of meat pie or a drink of whisky, they saluted and went miserably out.

The adjutant called them back. 'Mr Hill! Mr Henry!'

'Sir?'

Hill said that he expected a change of mind as to the propriety with which hospitality could be offered by a regular colonel and adjutant to temporary second-lieutenants in distress. But it was only: 'Mr Hill, Mr Henry, I saw some men in the trench just now with their shoulder-straps unbuttoned and their equipment fastened anyhow. See that this does not occur in future. That's all.'

Henry heard the colonel from his bunk complaining that he had only two blankets and that it was a deucedly cold night.

Choate, in peacetime a journalist, arrived a few minutes later; the others had told him of their reception. After he had saluted and reported that Major Swainson, hitherto thought killed, was wounded on the way down to the dressing-station, he boldly leaned over the table, cut a large piece of meat pie and began eating it. This caused such a surprise that no further conversation took place. Choate finished his meat pie and drank a glass of whisky; saluted, and joined the others.

Meanwhile, I took command of what remained of 'B' Company. Only six company officers survived in the Royal Welch. Next morning we were only five. Thomas was killed by a sniper while despondently watching through field-glasses the return of the New Army troops on the right. Pushed blindly into the gap made by the advance of the Seventh and Forty-seventh Divisions on the previous afternoon, they did not know where they were or what they were supposed to do. Their ration supply broke down, so they flocked back, not in panic, but stupidly, like a crowd returning from a cup final, with shrapnel bursting above them. We could scarcely believe our eyes, it was so odd.

Thomas need not have been killed; but everything had gone so wrong that he seemed not to care one way or the other. The Actor took command of 'A' Company. We lumped 'A' and 'B' Companies together after a couple of days, for the sake of relieving each other on night watch and getting some sleep. I agreed to take the first watch, waking him up at midnight. When the time came, I shook him, shouted in his ear, poured water over him, banged his head against the side of the bed. Finally I threw him on the floor. I was desperate for a lie-down myself, but he had attained a depth of sleep from which nothing could rouse him; so I heaved him back on the bunk, and had to finish the night without relief. Even 'Stand-to!' failed to wake him. In the end I got him out of bed at nine o'clock in the morning, and he was furious with me for not having called him at midnight.

We had spent the day after the attack carrying the dead down for burial and cleaning the trench up as best we could. That night the Middlesex held the line, while the Royal Welch carried all the unbroken gas-cylinders along to a position on the left flank of the brigade, where they were to be used on the following night, September 27th. This was worse than carrying the dead; the cylinders were cast-iron, heavy and hateful. The men cursed and sulked. Only the officers knew of the proposed attack; the men must not be told until just beforehand. I felt like screaming. Rain was still pouring down, harder than ever. We knew definitely, this time, that ours would be only a diversion to help troops on our right make the real attack.

The scheme was the same as before: at 4 p.m. gas would be discharged for forty minutes, and after a quarter of an hour's bombardment we should attack. I broke the news to the men about three o'clock. They took it well. The relations of officers and men, and of senior and junior officers, had been very different in the excitement of battle. There had been no insubordination, but a greater freedom of speech, as though we were all drunk together. I found myself calling the adjutant 'Charley' on one occasion; he appeared not to mind in the least. For the next ten days my relations with my men were like those I had in the Welsh Regiment; later, discipline reasserted itself, and it was only occasionally that I found them intimate.

At 4 p.m. then, the gas went off again with a strong wind; the gas-men had brought enough spanners this time. The Germans stayed absolutely silent. Flares went up from the reserve lines, and it looked as though all the men in the front trench were dead. The brigadier decided not to take too much for granted; after the bombardment he sent out a Cameronian officer and twenty-five men as a feeling-patrol. The patrol reached the German wire; there came a burst of machine-gun and rifle fire, and only two wounded men regained the trench.

We waited on the fire-step from four to nine o'clock, with fixed bayonets, for the order to go over. My mind was a blank, except for the recurrence of *S'nice S'mince S'pie, S'nice S'mince S'pie* ... *I don't like ham, lamb or jam, and I don't like roley-poley* ...

The men laughed at my singing. The acting C.S.M. said: 'It's murder, sir.'

'Of course it's murder, you bloody fool,' I agreed. 'But there's nothing else for it, is there?' It was still raining. *But when I sees a s'nice s'mince s'pie, I asks for a helping twice* ...

At nine o'clock brigade called off the attack; we were told to hold ourselves in readiness to go over at dawn.

No order came at dawn, and no more attacks were promised us after this. From the morning of September 24th to the night of October 3rd, I had in all eight hours of sleep. I kept myself awake and alive by drinking about a bottle of whisky a day. I had never drunk it before, and have seldom drunk it since; it certainly helped me then. We had no blankets, greatcoats, or waterproof sheets, nor any time or material to build new shelters. The rain poured down. Every night we went out to fetch in the dead of the other battalions. The Germans continued indulgent and we had few casualties. After the first day or two the corpses swelled and stank. I vomited more than once while superintending the carrying. Those we could not get in from the German wire continued to swell until the wall of the stomach collapsed, either naturally or when punctured by a bullet; a disgusting smell would float across. The colour of the dead faces changed from white to yellow-grey, to red, to purple, to green, to black, to slimy.

On the morning of the 27th a cry arose from No Man's Land. A wounded soldier of the Middlesex had recovered consciousness after two days. He lay close to the German wire. Our men heard it and looked at each other. We had a tender-hearted lance-corporal named Baxter. He was the man to boil up a special dixie for the sentries of his section when they came off duty. As soon as he heard the wounded Middlesex man, he ran along the trench calling for a volunteer to help fetch him in. Of course, no one would go; it was death to put one's head over the parapet. When he came running to ask me I excused myself as being the only officer in the company. I would come out with him at dusk, I said – not now. So he went alone. He jumped quickly over the parapet, then strolled across No Man's Land, waving a handkerchief; the Germans fired to frighten him, but since he persisted they let him come up close. Baxter continued towards them and, when he got to the Middlesex man, stopped and pointed to show the Germans what he was at. Then he dressed the man's wounds, gave him a drink of rum and some biscuit that he had with him, and promised to be back again at nightfall. He did come back, with a stretcher-party, and the man eventually recovered. I recommended Baxter for the Victoria Cross, being the only officer who had witnessed the action, but the authorities thought it worth no more than a Distinguished Conduct Medal.

The Actor and I had decided to get in touch with the battalion on our right. It was the Tenth Highland Light Infantry. I went down their trench some time in the morning of the 26th and walked nearly a quarter of a mile without seeing either a sentry or an officer. There were dead men, sleeping men, wounded men, gassed men, all lying anyhow. The trench had been used as a latrine. Finally I met a Royal Engineer officer who said: 'If the Boche knew what an easy job he had, he'd just walk over and take this trench.'

So I reported to The Actor that we might find our flank in the air at any moment. We converted the communication trench which made the boundary between the two battalions into a fire-trench facing right; and mounted a machine-gun to put up a barrage in case the Highlanders ran. On the night of the 27th they mistook some of our men, who were out in No Man's Land getting in the dead, for the enemy, and began firing wildly. The Germans retaliated. Our men caught the infection, but were at once ordered to cease fire. 'Cease fire!' went along the trench until it reached the H.L.I., who misheard it as 'Retire!' A panic seized them and they went rushing away, fortunately down the trench, instead of over the top. They were stopped by Sergeant McDonald of the Fifth Scottish Rifles, a pretty reliable territorial battalion now in support to ourselves and the Middlesex. He chased them back at the point of the bayonet; and was decorated for this feat.

On October 3rd we were relieved by a composite battalion consisting of about a hundred men of the Second Warwickshire Regiment and about seventy Royal Welch Fusiliers – all that was left of our own First Battalion. Hanmer Jones and Frank Jones-Bateman had both been wounded. Frank had his thigh broken with a rifle bullet while stripping the equipment off a wounded man in No Man's Land; the cartridges in the man's pouches had been set on fire by a shot and were exploding.* We went back to Sailly la Bourse for

* He was recommended for a Victoria Cross, but got nothing because no officer evidence, which is a condition of award, was available.

a couple of days, where the colonel rejoined us with his bandaged hand; and then farther back to Annezin, a little village near Béthune, where I lodged in a two-roomed cottage with a withered old woman called Adelphine Heu.

16

At Annezin we reorganized. Some of the lightly wounded rejoined for duty, and a big draft from the Third Battalion arrived, so that within a week we were nearly seven hundred strong, with a full supply of officers. Old Adelphine made me comfortable. She used to come into my room in the morning while I shaved and tell me the local gossip – about her stingy daughter-in-law and the unscrupulous Maire and the woman at Fouquières who had just been delivered of black twins. She called the Kaiser a bitch, and spat on the floor to confirm it. Her favourite subject was the shamelessness of modern girls. Yet she herself had been gay and beautiful and much sought after when young, she said. As lady's maid to a rich draper's wife at Béthune, she had travelled widely in the surrounding country, and even over the border into Belgium. She told me scandal about the important families who once lived in the various villages we were now using as billets. Once she innocently asked whether I knew La Bassée. I said that I had tried to visit it recently but been detained.

'Do you know Auchy, then?'

'I have seen it often from a distance.'

'Well, perhaps you know a big farm-house between Auchy and Cambrin, called Les Briques Farm?'

I answered, startled, that I knew it very well as a strong place with moat and cellars, and a kitchen garden now full of barbed wire.

'In that case I shall tell you a story,' she said. 'I was staying there in 1870, the year of the other war, and we had with us at the house a handsome *petit-caporal* who loved me. So, because he was a nice boy and because of the war, we slept together and I had a baby. But God punished me, and the baby died. That's a long time ago.'

She told me that all the girls in Annezin prayed every night for the war to end, and for the English to go away – as soon as their money was spent. And that the clause about the money was always repeated in case God should miss it.

On the whole, troops serving in the Pas de Calais loathed the French and found it difficult to sympathize with their misfortunes. They had all the shortcomings of a border people. Also, we were shocked at the severity of French national accountancy; when we were told, for instance, that every British hospital train, the locomotive and carriages of which had been imported from England, had to pay a £200 fee for use of the rails on each journey they made from railhead to base.

I wrote home about this time: 'I find it very difficult to like the French here, except occasional members of the official class. Even when billeted in villages where no troops have been before, I have not met a single case of the hospitality that one meets among the peasants of other countries. It is worse than inhospitality here, for after all we are fighting for their dirty little lives. They suck enormous quantities of money out of us, too. Calculate how much has flowed into the villages around Béthune, which for many months now have been housing about a hundred thousand men. Apart from what they get paid directly as billeting allowance, there is the pay that troops spend. Every private soldier gets his five-franc note (nearly four shillings) every ten days, and spends it at once on eggs, coffee, and beer in the local *estaminets*; the prices are ridiculous and the stuff bad. In the brewery at Béthune, the other day, I saw barrels of already thin beer being watered from the canal with a hose-pipe. The *estaminet*-keepers water it further.'*

It was surprising that there were so few clashes between the British and the local French – who returned our loathing and were convinced that, when the war ended, we would stay and hold the Channel ports. We failed to realize that the peasants did not much care whether they were on the German or the British side of the line. They just had no use for foreign soldiers, and were not at all interested in the sacrifices that we might be making for 'their dirty little lives'.

Fighting still continued around Loos. We could hear the guns in the distance, but the main thrust had clearly failed, and we were now skirmishing for local advantages. On October 13th, there came a final flare-up; the noise of the guns increased until even the inhabitants

* The fortunes made in the War were consolidated after the Versailles Treaty, when peasants in the devastated areas staked preposterous compensation claims for the loss of possessions they never had.

of Annezin, accustomed to these alarms, were properly scared, and began packing up in case the Germans broke through. Old Adelphine wept for fright. In Béthune, early that afternoon, as I sat at the *Globe* drinking champagne-cocktails with some friends who had joined from the Third Battalion, the assistant provost-marshal put his head in the door and called out: 'Any officers of the Fifth, Sixth, or Nineteenth Brigades here?'

We jumped up.

'You are to return at once to your units.'

'Oh, God,' said Robertson, 'that means another show!' He had been with 'D' Company during the battle, and so escaped the charge. 'We'll be pushed over the top tonight to reinforce someone, and that'll be the end of us!'

At Annezin, we found everything in confusion. 'We're standing-to – at half an hour's notice for the trenches,' they told us. We packed up hastily, and in a few minutes the whole battalion was out on the road in fighting order. Our destination was the Hohenzollern Redoubt, new trench maps of which were now issued to us. The men seemed in high spirits, even the survivors of the show: singing to the accompaniment of an accordion and a penny-whistle. But once, when a 'mad-minute' of artillery noise began, they stopped and looked at each other.

'That's the charge,' Sergeant Townsend said sententiously. 'Many good fellows going west at this moment; maybe chums of ours.'

Gradually the noise died down, and at last a message came from brigade that we would not be needed. It had been another dud show, chiefly notorious for the death of Charles Sorley, a twenty-year-old captain in the Suffolks, one of the three poets of importance killed during the war. (The other two were Isaac Rosenberg and Wilfred Owen.)

So ended the operations for 1915. Tension relaxed. We returned to battalion mess, to company drill, and to riding-school for the young officers. There might have been no Battle of Loos, except that the senior officers were fewer, and the Special Reserve element larger. Two or three days later we went back to trenches in the same sector. On October 15th, I was gazetted a Special Reserve captain. Promotion was rapid for Special Reserve subalterns who had joined early, because the battalion had trebled its strength and become entitled to three times as many captains as before. Though pleased to see my pay go up several shillings a day, with an increase of War Bonus and possibly gratuity and pension if I were wounded, I realized with disquiet that my new rank was effective overseas. And now I had been promoted captain, at the age of just twenty, over the heads of elder officers who had longer trench service and were better trained than myself. A Special Reserve major and a captain had recently been sent home from the First Battalion, with a confidential report of inefficiency. Being anxious to avoid any such disgrace, I went to the adjutant and offered not to wear my badges of rank while serving with the battalion. 'No, put your stars up,' he said, not unkindly. 'It can't be helped.'

This proved to have been a wise move. Pretty soon afterwards, two other Special Reserve captains, one of them promoted at the same time as myself, and certainly far more efficient, were sent back as 'likely to be of more service in the training of troops at home'.

Had I returned to the trenches as a company officer, I should probably have modified my formula for taking risks; because a black depression held me. However, I got attached to the brigade sappers. Hill of the Middlesex was also enjoying this relief. He told me that the Middlesex colonel had addressed the survivors of his battalion as soon as they were back in billets, promising them that they would soon be given an opportunity of avenging their dead and making a fresh, and, this time, he hoped, successful attack upon La Bassée. 'I know you, Diehards! You will go like lions over the top!' Hill's servant had whispered confidentially: 'Not on purpose I don't, sir!' The sapping company specialized in the repair and maintenance of communication and reserve trenches. The adjutant recalled me, a month later, to ordinary company duty; as a punishment for failing, one day in billets, to observe a paragraph in Orders requiring us sappers to attend battalion parade.

My remaining trench service with the Second Battalion that autumn proved uneventful; I found no excitement in patrolling, no horror in the continual experience of death. The single memorable event was one of purely technical interest: a new method that an officer named Owen and myself discovered for silencing machine-guns firing at night. We gave each sentry a piece of string about a yard long, with a cartridge tied at each end. When the machine-gun began traversing, sentries farthest from the line of fire would stretch their string towards it and peg them down with cartridge points; so we got a pretty accurate line on the machine-gun. When we had about thirty or more of these lines taken on a single machine-gun, we fixed rifles as carefully as possible along them and waited; as soon as it started again we opened five rounds rapid. This gave a close concentration of fire, and no element of nervousness could disturb the aim, the rifles being secured between sandbags. Divisional headquarters asked us for a report of the method. There was a daily exchange of courtesies between our machine-guns and the Germans' at stand-to; by removing cartridges from the ammunition-belt one could rap out the rhythm of the familiar prostitutes' call: 'MEET me DOWN in PICC-a-DILL-y', to which the Germans would reply, though in slower tempo, because our guns were faster than theirs: 'YES, with-OUT my DRAWERS ON!'

Late this October a press-cutting from *John Bull* reached me. Horatio Bottomley, the editor, was protesting against the unequal treatment for criminal offences meted out to commoners and aristo-crats. A young man, he said, convicted in the police court of sexual delinquency had merely been bound over and placed in the care of a physician – because he happened to be the grandson of an earl! An offender not belonging to the influential classes would have been given three months, without the option of a fine. The article de-scribed in some detail how Dick, a sixteen-year-old boy, had made 'a certain proposal' to a corporal in a Canadian regiment stationed near 'Charterhouse College', and how the corporal had very properly given him in charge of the police. This news nearly finished me. I decided that Dick had been driven out of his mind by the war. There was madness in the family, I knew; he had once shown me a letter from his grandfather, scrawled in circles all over the page. Well, with so much slaughter about, it would be easy to think of him as dead.

Having now been in the trenches for five months, I had passed my prime. For the first three weeks, an officer was of little use in the front line; he did not know his way about, had not learned the rules of health and safety, or grown accustomed to recognizing degrees of danger. Between three weeks and four weeks he was at his best, unless he happened to have any particular bad shock or sequence of shocks. Then his usefulness gradually declined as neurasthenia de-veloped. At six months he was still more or less all right; but by nine or ten months, unless he had been given a few weeks' rest on a technical course, or in hospital, he usually became a drag on the other company officers. After a year or fifteen months he was often worse than useless. Dr W. H. R. Rivers told me later that the action of one of the ductless glands – I think the thyroid – caused this slow general decline in military usefulness, by failing at a certain point to pump its sedative chemical into the blood. Without its continued assistance the man went about his tasks in an apathetic and doped condition, cheated into further endurance. It has taken some ten years for my blood to recover.

Officers had a less laborious but a more nervous time than the men. There were proportionately twice as many neurasthenic cases among officers as among men, though a man's average expectancy of trench service before getting killed or wounded was twice as long as an officer's. Officers between the ages of twenty-three and thirty-three could count on a longer useful life than those older or younger. I was too young. Men over forty, though not suffering from want of sleep so much as those under twenty, had less resistance to sudden alarms and shocks. The unfortunates were officers who had endured two years or more of continuous trench service. In many cases they became dipsomaniacs. I knew three or four who had worked up to the point of two bottles of whisky a day before being lucky enough to get wounded or sent home in some other way. A two-bottle company commander of one of our line battalions is still alive who, in three shows running, got his company needlessly destroyed because he was no longer capable of taking clear decisions.

Apart from wounds, gas, and the accidents of war, the life of the trench soldier could not be called unhealthy while his ductless glands still functioned well. Plentiful food and hard work in the open air made up for the discomfort of wet feet, wet clothes, and draughty billets. A continual need for alertness discouraged minor illnesses: a cold vanished in a few hours, an attack of indigestion passed almost unnoticed. This was true, at least, in a good battalion, where the men were bent on going home either with an honourable wound or not at all. In an inferior battalion, the men would prefer a wound to bronchitis, but not mind the bronchitis. In a bad battalion, they did not care 'whether', in the trench phrase, 'the cow calved or the bull broke its bloody neck'. In a really good battalion, like the Second when I first joined it, the question of getting wounded and going home was not allowed to be raised. Such a battalion had a very small sick list. During the winter of 1914-15, the Second reported no more than four or five casualties from 'trench feet', and in the following winter no more than eight or nine; the don't care battalions lost very heavily indeed.

'Trench feet' seemed to be almost entirely a matter of morale,

1. Robert Graves in Majorca

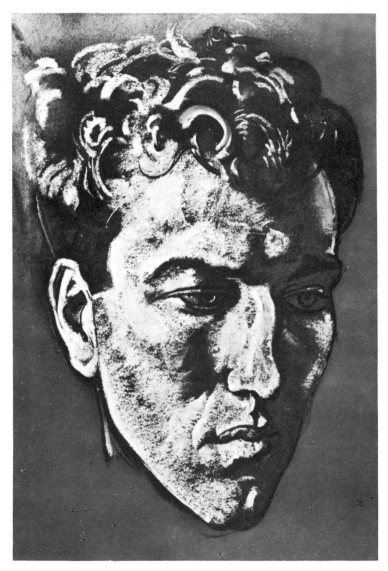

2. Robert Graves, from a portrait by Eric Kennington

3a. Charterhouse School in 1914

3b. Béthune before the shelling, 1915

4a. The brickstacks at Cuinchy

4b. Somme Battle. First Royal Welch Fusiliers attacking near Mametz, 1 July 1916

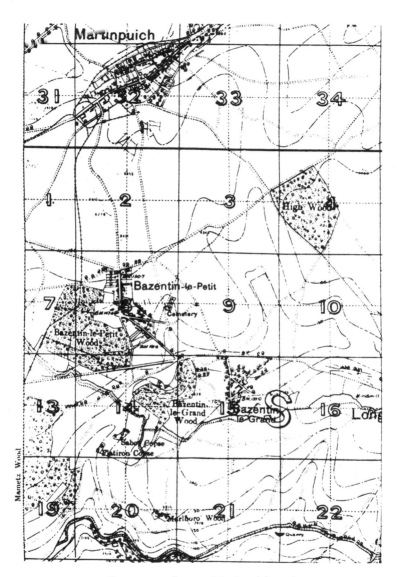

5. Somme trench map: Martinpuich section

6a. Waterlogged mine crater

6b. Somme Battle. Scene in a communication trench before an attack

7a. Royal Welch Fusiliers at rest, 28 June 1916

7b. Mametz village, July 1916

8. The Second Royal Welch Fusilier Goat and Band at the 33rd Division Horse Show, July 1917

in spite of the lecture formula that N.C.O.s and officers used to repeat time after time to the men: '"Trench feet" is caused by tight boots, tight puttees, or any other clothing calculated to interfere with the circulation of blood in the legs.' Trench feet was caused, rather, by going to sleep with wet boots, cold feet, and depression. Wet boots, by themselves, did not matter. If a man warmed his feet at a brazier, or stamped until they were warm, and then went off to sleep with a sandbag tied around them, he took no harm: He might even fall asleep with cold, wet feet, and find that they had swelled slightly owing to the pressure of his boots or puttees; but trench feet came only if he did not mind getting trench feet, or anything else – because his battalion had lost the power of sticking things out. At Bouchavesnes, on the Somme, in the winter of 1916-17, a battalion of dismounted cavalry lost half its strength in two days from trench feet; our Second Battalion had just completed ten days in the same trenches with no cases at all.

Autumn brought melancholy to the Béthune–La Bassée sector; in the big poplar forests the leaves had turned French-yellow, the dykes were overflowing, and the ground utterly sodden. Béthune had lost some of its charm; the Canadians billeted there drew two or three times as much pay as our own troops and had sent the prices up. But it was still more or less intact, and one could still buy cream buns and fish dinners.

In November, much to my delight, I had orders to join the First Battalion, now reorganizing after the Loos fighting. I found it in billets at Locon, only a mile or so north of Cambrin. The difference between the two battalions continued markedly throughout the war, however many times each got broken. The difference was that, in August 1914, the Second Battalion had just finished its eighteen years overseas tour, whereas the First Battalion had not left England since the South African War and was, therefore, less old-fashioned in its militarism and more humane. Livers were better; the men had dealings with white women and not with brown; it would have been impossible there to see what I once saw in the Second – a senior officer pursuing a private soldier down the street, kicking his bottom because he had given a slack salute. The First Battalion was as efficient and regimental, on the whole even more successful in its fighting, and a much easier battalion to live in.

The battalion already had its complement of company commanders, so I went as second-captain to young Richardson of 'A' – one of the best companies I ever served with. He came from Sandhurst, and his men were largely Welshmen of 1915 enlistment. No officer in the company was more than twenty-two or twenty-three years old. A day or two after I arrived I went to visit 'C' Company mess, where I got a friendly welcome. I noticed *The Essays of Lionel Johnson* lying on the table. It was the first book I had seen in France (except my own Keats and Blake) that was neither a military textbook nor a rubbishy novel. I stole a look at the fly-leaf, and the name was Siegfried Sassoon. Then I looked around to see who could possibly be called Siegfried Sassoon and bring *Lionel Johnson* with him to the First Battalion. The answer being obvious, I got into conversation with him, and a few minutes later we set out for Béthune, being off duty until dusk, and talked about poetry.

Siegfried Sassoon had, at the time, published only a few privately-printed pastoral pieces of eighteen-ninetyish flavour, and a satire on Masefield which, half-way through, had forgotten to be a satire and turned into rather good Masefield. We went to the cake shop and ate cream buns. At this time I was getting my first book of poems, *Over the Brazier*, ready for the press; I had one or two drafts in my pocket-book and showed them to Siegfried. He frowned and said that war should not be written about in such a realistic way. In return, he showed me some of his own poems. One of them began:

> Return to greet me, colours that were my joy,
> Not in the woeful crimson of men slain . . .

Siegfried had not yet been in the trenches. I told him, in my old-soldier manner, that he would soon change his style.

That night, the whole battalion went up to work on a new defence scheme at Festubert. Festubert had been a nightmare ever since the first fighting there in 1914 when the inmates of its lunatic asylum, caught between two fires, broke out and ran all over the countryside. The British trench line, which crossed a stretch of ground marked on the map as 'Marsh, sometimes dry in the summer', consisted of islands of high-command trench, with no communication between them except at night. The battalion had been nearly wiped out here six months previously. We were set to build up a strong reserve line, and came night after night. The temperature being ten degrees below zero, and the ground frozen a foot deep, we managed only to raise some two hundred yards of trench about knee-high, at the cost of several men wounded by casual shot skimming the trench in front of us. Other troops resumed work when the thaw came and built a thick, seven-foot-high ramp which, little by little, sank down into the marsh, and in the end was completely engulfed.

When I left the Second Battalion, the adjutant let me take my admirable servant, Private Fahy (known as 'Tottie Fay', after the actress), with me. Tottie, a reservist from Birmingham, had been called up when war broke out, and fought with the Second Battalion ever since. By trade a silversmith, he had recently gone on leave, and brought me back a gift cigarette-case, all his own work, engraved with my name. On arrival at the First Battalion, however, he met one Sergeant Dickens. They had been boozing chums in India seven or eight years ago, and joyfully celebrated the reunion. The next morning I was surprised and annoyed to find my buttons unpolished and only cold water for shaving; it made me late for breakfast. I could get no news of Tottie, but on my way to rifle inspection at nine o'clock at the company billet, noticed Field Punishment No. 1 being carried out in a corner of the farmyard. Tottie had just been awarded twenty-eight days of it for 'drunkenness in the field', and stood spread-eagled to the wheel of a company limber, tied by the ankles and wrists in the form of an X. He was obliged to stay in this position – 'Crucifixion' they called it – for several hours every day so long as the battalion remained in billets, and then again after the next spell of trenches. I shall never forget the look that my quiet, respectful, devoted Tottie gave me. He wanted to tell me that he regretted having let me down, and his immediate reaction was an attempt to salute. I could see him vainly trying to lift his hand to his forehead, and bring his heels together. The battalion police-sergeant, a fierce-looking man, had just finished knotting him up when I arrived. I told Tottie, for what that might be worth, that I was sorry to see him in trouble.

The spree, as it proved, did him good in the end. I had to find another servant, and Old Joe Cotterell, the quartermaster, aware that Tottie was the only trained officer's servant left in the battalion, took him from me when his sentence expired; even inducing the colonel to remit a few days of it. I bore no grudge to Old Joe. Tottie would be safer in billets with him than in trenches with me. A few weeks later his seven years' contract as a reservist expired. When their 'buckshee seven' came to an end, reservists were sent home for a few days, but then 'deemed to have re-enlisted under the Military Service Act' and recalled to the battalion. Tottie made good use of his leave. His brother-in-law, the director of a munitions factory, took him in as a skilled metal-worker. He became a starred man – one whose work was so important to industry that he could not be spared for military service – so Tottie is, I hope, still alive.

Sergeant Dickens was a different case: a born fighter, and one of the best N.C.O.s in either battalion of the regiment. He had won the Distinguished Conduct Medal and Bar, the Military Medal, and the French Médaille Militaire; been two or three times promoted to sergeant's rank, and each time reduced for drunkenness. He always escaped the Field Punishment awarded for this crime, because it was considered sufficient disgrace if he merely lost his stripes; and as soon as a battle started would distinguish himself so conspicuously by his leadership that he would be given them back again.

Early in December a rumour came that we were going for divisional training to the distant countryside. I refused to believe it, having heard stories of this kind too often; yet it turned out to be true. Siegfried Sassoon, in his *Memoirs of a Fox-hunting Man*, has described this battalion move. Our 'A' Company had an even more laborious experience than his 'C' Company. We got up at five o'clock one morning, breakfasted hastily, packed our kits, and marched down to the railhead three miles away. Here we entrained all the battalion stores, transport, and transport animals. This took us to the middle of the morning. We then entrained ourselves for a ten-hour journey to a Somme junction, about twenty miles behind the front line. The officers travelled in third-class compartments, the men in closed trucks marked '*Hommes 40, chevaux 8*' – they were very stiff when they arrived. 'A' Company was then ordered to do the detraining job too. When we had finished, the dixies of tea prepared for us were cold. The other companies got a couple of hours' rest; we had only a few minutes.

The march took us along *pavé* roads and rough chalk tracks of Picardy downland. It started about midnight and finished at six o'clock next morning, the men carrying their packs and rifles. There was a competition between the companies as to which would have the fewest stragglers; 'A' won. The village we finally arrived at was named Montagne le Fayel. No troops had been billeted here before, and its inhabitants were pardonably annoyed at being knocked up in the middle of the night by our advance party to provide accommodation for eight hundred men at two hours' notice. We found these Picard peasants much more likeable than the Pas de Calais folk. I was billeted with an old man called Monsieur Élie Caron, a kindly retired schoolmaster with a bright eye and white hair, who lived entirely on vegetables, and gave me a vegetarian pamphlet entitled *Comment Vivre Cent Ans.* (We already knew of the coming Somme offensive, so this seemed a good joke.) He also gave me Longfellow's *Evangeline* in English. Since I have always been sorry for English books stranded in France, whatever their demerits, I accepted it and later brought it home.

We stayed at Montagne for six weeks. Colonel Ford, known in the regiment as 'Scatter' (short for 'Scatter-cash' because, when he first joined, he had spent his allowance so lavishly), put the battalion through its paces with peacetime severity. He ordered us to forget the trenches and to prepare ourselves for the open warfare that was bound to follow once the Somme defences had been pierced. Every other day was field-day; we were back, in spirit, to General Haking's *Company Training.* Even those of us who did not believe in the breakthrough thoroughly enjoyed our exercises over quite unspoiled country. The guns could only just be heard in the distance, and every man in the battalion was fit. Days other than field-days were spent on battalion drill and musketry. The training seemed entirely unrelated to war as we had experienced it. Games included inter-battalion rugger; I played full-back for the battalion. Three other officers were members of the team: Richardson, a front-row scrum-man; Pritchard, another Sandhurst boy, the fly-half; and David Thomas, a Third Battalion second-lieutenant, an inside three-quarter. David came from South Wales: simple, gentle, fond of reading. He, Siegfried Sassoon, and I always went about together.

One day David stopped me in the village street. 'Did you hear the bugle? There's a hell of a row brewing. All officers and warrant-officers are to meet at the village school-room at once. Scatter's looking as black as thunder. No one knows yet what the axe is.'

We went along to the school-room and squeezed into one of the desk-benches.

When Scatter entered, the room was called to attention by the senior major; David and I hurt ourselves attempting to stand up, bench and all. Scatter told us to be seated. The officers were in one class, the warrant-officers and N.C.O.s in another. Scatter glared at us from the teacher's desk. He began his lecture with general accusations, saying that he had lately noticed many signs of slovenliness in the battalion – men with their pocket-flaps undone, and actually walking along the village street with hands in trouser-pockets and boots unpolished; sentries strolling about on their beats at company billets, instead of marching up and down in a soldier-like way – rowdiness at the *estaminets* – slackness in saluting – and many other grave indications of lowered discipline. He threatened to stop all leave to the United Kingdom unless matters improved, and promised us a saluting parade every morning before breakfast which he would attend in person.

All this was general axe-ing; we knew that he had not yet reached the particular axe. It was this: 'I have here principally to tell you of a very disagreeable occurrence. As I left my orderly-room this morning, I came upon a group of soldiers; I will not particularize their company. One of these soldiers was in conversation with a lance-corporal. You may not believe me, but it is a fact that he addressed the corporal by his Christian name: *he called him Jack!* And the corporal made no protest! To think that the First Battalion has sunk to a level where it is possible for such familiarity to exist between N.C.O.s and the men under their command! Naturally, I put the corporal under arrest, and he appeared before me at once on the charge of "conduct unbecoming to an N.C.O." I reduced him to the ranks, and awarded the man Field Punishment for using insubordinate language to an N.C.O. But I warn you, if any further case of this sort comes to my notice – and I expect you officers to report the slightest instance to me at once – instead of dealing with it as a company matter ...'

I tried to catch Siegfried's eye, but he was obviously avoiding it, so I caught David's instead. This is one of those caricature scenes that now seem to sum up the various stages of my life. Myself in faultless khaki with highly polished buttons and belt, revolver at hip, whistle on cord, delicate moustache on upper lip, and stern endeavour a-glint in either eye, pretending to be a Regular Army captain; but crushed into that inky desk-bench like an over-grown school-boy. A fresco ran around the walls of the class-room illustrating the evils of alcoholism. It started with the innocent boy being offered a drink by his mate, and then showed his downward path of degradation, culminating in wife-beating, murder, and *delirium tremens*; but, at least, he never went so far as to call his *petit-caporal* 'Jacquot'!

The battalion's sole complaint against Montagne was that women were not so complaisant in that part of the country as around Béthune.

The officers had the unfair advantage of being able to borrow horses and ride into Amiens. There was a 'Blue Lamp' at Amiens, as at Abbeville, Le Havre, Rouen, and all the large towns behind the lines: the Blue Lamp reserved for officers, the Red Lamp for men. Whether, in this careful maintenance of discipline, the authorities made any special provision for warrant-officers, and whether the Blue Lamp women had to show any particular qualifications for their higher social ranking, are questions I cannot answer. I remained puritanical, except in language, throughout my overseas service.

At New Year, the Seventh Division sent two company officers from each brigade to instruct troops at the Base. I and a Queen's captain happened to be the two who had been out longest, so we were given this gift of eight weeks' additional life.

17

THERE were about thirty instructors at the Harfleur 'Bull Ring', where newly-arrived drafts now went for technical instruction before going up the line. Most of my colleagues specialized on musketry, machine-guns, gas, or bombs. Having no specialist training, but only general experience, I taught troops trench relief and trench discipline in a model system of trenches. My principal other business was arms-drill. One day it rained, and the terrifying Major Currie, the Bull Ring commandant, suddenly ordered me to lecture in the big concert hall. 'You'll find three thousand men there waiting for you, Graves, and you're the only available officer with a loud enough voice to make himself heard.' They were Canadians, so instead of giving my usual semi-facetious lecture on 'How to be Happy, Though in the Trenches', I paid them the compliment of telling the real story of Loos, and what a balls-up it had been, and why – more or less as it has been given here. This was the only audience I have ever held for an hour with real attention. I expected Major Currie to be furious, because the principal object of the Bull Ring was to inculcate the offensive spirit; but he took it well and put several other concert-hall lectures on me after this.

In the instructors' mess, the chief subjects of conversation, besides local and technical talk, were the reliability of various divisions in battle, the value of different training methods, and war morality, with particular reference to atrocities. We talked more freely than would have been possible in England or in the trenches. It seemed to be agreed that about a third of the troops forming the British Expeditionary Force were dependable on all occasions: those always called on for important tasks. About a third were variable: divisions that contained one or two weak battalions but could usually be trusted. The remainder were more or less untrustworthy: being put in places of comparative safety, they lost about a quarter of the men that the best troops did. It was a matter of pride to belong to one of the recognized top-notch divisions – the Second, Seventh, Twenty-ninth, Guards', First Canadian, for instance. These were not pampered when in reserve, as the German storm-troops were; but promotion, leave, and the chance of a wound came quicker in them.

The mess agreed dispassionately that the most dependable British troops were the midland county regiments, industrial Yorkshire and Lancashire troops, and Londoners. The Ulstermen, Lowland Scots, and Northern English ranked pretty high. The Catholic Irish and Highland Scots took unnecessary risks in trenches and had unnecessary casualties; and in battle, though they usually reached their objective, too often lost it in the counter-attack; without officers they became useless. English southern county regiments varied from good to very bad. All overseas troops seemed to be good. The dependability of divisions also varied with their seniority in date of formation. The latest New Army divisions and the second-line territorial divisions, whatever their recruiting area, ranked low because of inefficient officers and warrant-officers.

We once discussed which were the cleanest troops in trenches, taken by nationalities. We agreed on a descending-order list like this: English and German Protestants; Northern Irish, Welsh, and Canadians; Irish and German Catholics; Scots, with certain higher-ranking exceptions; Mohammedan Indians; Algerians; Portuguese; Belgians; French. We put the Belgians and French there for spite; they could not have been dirtier than the Algerians and the Portuguese.

Propaganda reports of atrocities were, it was agreed, ridiculous. We remembered that while the Germans *could* commit atrocities against enemy civilians, Germany itself, except for an early Russian cavalry raid, had never had the enemy on her soil. We no longer believed the highly-coloured accounts of German atrocities in Belgium; knowing the Belgians now at first-hand. By atrocities we meant, specifically, rape, mutilation, and torture – not summary shootings of suspected spies, harbourers of spies, *francs-tireurs*, or disobedient local officials. If the atrocity-list had to include the accidental-on-purpose bombing or machine-gunning of civilians from the air, the Allies were now committing as many atrocities as the Germans. French and Belgian civilians had often tried to win our sympathy by exhibiting mutilations of children – stumps of hands and feet, for instance – representing them as deliberate, fiendish atrocities when, as likely as not, they were merely the result of shell-fire. We did not believe rape to be any more common on the German side of the line than on the Allied side. And since a bully-beef diet, fear of death, and absence of wives made ample provision of women necessary in the occupied areas, no doubt the German army authorities provided brothels in the principal French towns behind the line, as the French did on the Allied side. We did not believe stories of women's forcible enlistment in these establishments. 'What's wrong with the voluntary system?' we asked cynically.

As for atrocities against soldiers – where should one draw the line? The British soldier, at first, regarded as atrocious the use of bowie-knives by German patrols. After a time, he learned to use them himself; they were cleaner killing weapons than revolvers or bombs. The Germans regarded as equally atrocious the British Mark VII rifle bullet, which was more apt to turn on striking than the German bullet. For true atrocities, meaning personal rather than military violations of the code of war, few opportunities occurred – except in the interval between the surrender of prisoners and their arrival (or non-arrival) at headquarters. Advantage was only too often taken of this opportunity. Nearly every instructor in the mess could quote specific instances of prisoners having been murdered on the way back. The commonest motives were, it seems, revenge for the death of friends or relatives, jealousy of the prisoner's trip to a comfortable prison camp in England, military enthusiasm, fear of being suddenly overpowered by the prisoners, or, more simply, impatience with the escorting job. In any of these cases the conductors would report on arrival at headquarters that a German shell had killed the prisoners; and no questions would be asked. We had every reason to believe that the same thing happened on the German side, where prisoners, as useless mouths to feed in a country already short of rations, would be even less welcome. None of us had heard of German prisoners being more than threatened at headquarters to get military information from them. The sort that they could give was not of sufficient importance to make torture worth while; and anyhow, it had been found that, when treated kindly, prisoners were anxious in gratitude to tell as much as they knew. German intelligence officers had probably discovered that too.

The troops with the worst reputation for acts of violence against prisoners were the Canadians (and later the Australians). The Canadians' motive was said to be revenge for a Canadian found crucified with bayonets through his hands and feet in a German trench. This atrocity had never been substantiated; nor did we believe the story, freely circulated, that the Canadians crucified a German officer in revenge shortly afterwards. How far this reputation for atrocities was deserved, and how far it could be ascribed to the overseas habit of bragging and leg-pulling, we could not decide. At all events, most overseas men, and some British troops, made atrocities against prisoners a boast, not a confession.

Later in the war, I heard two first-hand accounts.

A Canadian-Scot: 'They sent me back with three bloody prisoners, you see, and one started limping and groaning, so I had to keep on kicking the sod down the trench. He was an officer. It was getting dark and I felt fed up, so I thought: "I'll have a bit of a game." I had them covered with the officer's revolver and made 'em open their pockets without turning round. Then I dropped a Mills bomb in each, with the pin out, and ducked behind a traverse. Bang, bang, bang! No more bloody prisoners. No good Fritzes but dead 'uns.'

An Australian: 'Well, the biggest lark I had was at Morlancourt, when we took it the first time. There were a lot of Jerries in a cellar, and I said to 'em: "Come out, you Camarades!" So out they came, a dozen of 'em, with their hands up. "Turn out your pockets," I told 'em. They turned 'em out. Watches and gold and stuff, all dinkum. Then I said: "Now back to your cellar, you sons of bitches!" For I couldn't be bothered with 'em. When they were all safely down I threw half a dozen Mills bombs in after 'em. I'd got the stuff all right, and we weren't taking prisoners that day.'

An old woman at Cardonette on the Somme gave me my firsthand account of large-scale atrocities. I was billeted with her in July 1916. Close to her home, a battalion of French Turcos overtook the rear-guard of a German division retreating from the Marne in September 1914. The Turcos surprised the dead-weary Germans while still marching in column. The old woman went, with gestures, through the pantomime of slaughter, and ended: '*Et enfin, ces animaux leur ont arraché les oreilles et les ont mises à la poche!*'

The presence of semi-civilized coloured troops in Europe was, from the German point of view, we knew, one of the chief Allied atrocities. We sympathized. Recently, at Flixécourt, one of the instructors told us, the cook of a corps headquarters mess used to be visited at the *château* every morning by a Turco – the orderly to a French liaison officer. The Turco used to say: 'Tommy, give Johnny pozzy,' and got his tin of plum-and-apple jam.

One day the corps had orders to shift by the afternoon, so the cook told the Turco, giving him his farewell tin: 'Oh la, la, Johnny, napoo pozzy tomorrow!'

The Turco would not believe it. 'Yes, Tommy, mate,' he insisted, 'pozzy for Johnny tomorrow, tomorrow, tomorrow!'

To get rid of him, the cook said: 'Fetch me the head of a Fritz, Johnny, tonight. I'll ask the general to give you pozzy tomorrow, tomorrow, tomorrow.'

'Right, mate,' said the Turco, 'me get Fritz head tonight, general give me pozzy tomorrow.'

That evening the mess cook of the new corps that had taken over the *château* found a Turco asking for him and swinging a bloody head in a sandbag. 'Here Fritz head, mate,' said the Turco, 'general give me pozzy tomorrow, tomorrow, tomorrow.'

As Flixécourt lay more than twenty miles behind the line . . .

We discussed the continuity of regimental morale. A captain in a line battalion of a Surrey regiment said: 'Our battalion has never recovered from the first battle of Ypres. What's wrong is that we have a rotten depôt. The drafts are bad, and so we get a constant re-infection.' He told me one night in our sleeping hut: 'In both the last two shows I had to shoot a man of my company to get the rest out of the trench. It was so bloody awful, I couldn't stand it. That's why I applied to be sent down here.' This was the truth, not the usual loose talk that one heard at the Base. I felt sorrier for him than for any other man I met in France. He deserved a better regiment.

The boast of every good battalion was that it had never lost a trench; both our line battalions made it – meaning, that they had never been forced out of a trench without recapturing it before the action ended. Capturing a German trench and being unable to hold it for lack of reinforcements did not count; nor did retirement by order from headquarters, or when the battalion next door had broken and left a flank in the air. And, towards the end of the war, trenches could be honourably abandoned as being wholly obliterated by bombardment, or because not really trenches at all, but a line of selected shell-craters.

We all agreed on the value of arms-drill as a factor in morale. 'Arms-drill as it should be done,' someone said, 'is beautiful, especially when the company feels itself as a single being, and each movement is not a synchronized movement of every man together, but the single movement of one large creature.' I used to get big bunches of Canadians to drill: four or five hundred at a time. Spokesmen stepped forward once and asked what sense there was in sloping and ordering arms, and fixing and unfixing bayonets. They said they had come across to fight, and not to guard Buckingham Palace. I told them that in every division of the four in which I had served – the First, Second, Seventh, and Eighth – there were three different kinds of troops. Those that had guts but were no good at drill; those that were good at drill but had no guts; and those that had guts and were good at drill. These last, for some reason or other, fought by far the best when it came to a show – I didn't know why, and I didn't care. I told them that when they were better at fighting than the Guards they could perhaps afford to neglect their arms-drill.

We often theorized in the mess about drill. I held that the best drill never resulted from being bawled at by a sergeant-major: that there must be perfect respect between the man who gives the order and the men that carry it out. The test of drill came, I said, when the officer gave an incorrect word of command. If the company could, without hesitation, carry out the order intended or, if the order happened to be impossible, could stand absolutely still, or continue marching, without confusion in the ranks, that was good drill ... Some instructors regarded the corporate spirit that resulted from drilling together as leading to loss of initiative in the men drilled.

Others argued that it acted just the other way round: 'Suppose a section of men with rifles get isolated from the rest of the company, without an N.C.O. in charge, and meet a machine-gun. Under the stress of danger this section will have that all-one-body feeling of drill, and obey an imaginary word of command. There may be no communication between its members, but there will be a drill movement, with two men naturally opening fire on the machine-gun while the remainder work round, part on the left flank and part on the right; and the final rush will be simultaneous. Leadership is supposed to be the perfection for which drill has been instituted. That's wrong. Leadership is only the first stage. Perfection of drill is communal action. Though drill may seem to be antiquated parade-ground stuff, it's the foundation of tactics and musketry. Parade-ground musketry won all the battles in our regimental histories; this war, which is unlikely to open out, and must almost certainly end with the collapse, by "attrition", of one side or the other, will be won by parade-ground tactics – by the simple drill tactics of small units fighting in limited spaces, and in noise and confusion so great that leadership is quite impossible.' Despite variance on this point we all agreed that regimental pride remained the strongest moral force that kept a battalion going as an effective fighting unit; contrasting it particularly with patriotism and religion.

Patriotism, in the trenches, was too remote a sentiment, and at once rejected as fit only for civilians, or prisoners. A new arrival who talked patriotism would soon be told to cut it out. As 'Blighty', a geographical concept, Great Britain was a quiet, easy place for getting back to out of the present foreign misery; but as a nation it included not only the trench-soldiers themselves and those who had gone home wounded, but the staff, Army Service Corps, lines of communication troops, base units, home-service units, and all civilians down to the detested grades of journalists, profiteers, 'starred' men exempted from enlistment, conscientious objectors, and members of the Goverment. The trench-soldier, with this carefully graded caste-system of honour, never considered that the Germans opposite might have built up exactly the same system themselves. He thought of Germany as a nation in arms, a unified nation inspired with the sort of patriotism that he himself despised. He believed most newspaper reports on conditions and sentiments in Germany, though believing little or nothing of what he read about similar conditions and sentiments in England. Yet he never underrated the German as a soldier. Newspaper libels on Fritz's courage and efficiency were resented by all trench-soldiers of experience.

Hardly one soldier in a hundred was inspired by religious feeling of even the crudest kind. It would have been difficult to remain religious in the trenches even if one survived the irreligion of the training battalion at home. A regular sergeant at Montagne, a

Second Battalion man, had recently told me that he did not hold with religion in time of war. He said that the niggers (meaning the Indians) were right in officially relaxing their religious rules while fighting. 'And all this damn nonsense, sir – excuse me, sir – that we read in the papers, sir, about how miraculous it is that the way-side crucifixes are always getting shot at, but the figure of our Lord Jesus somehow don't get hurt, it fairly makes me sick, sir.' This was his explanation why, when giving practice fire-orders from the hill-top, he had shouted, unaware that I stood behind him: 'Seven hundred, half left, bloke on cross, five rounds, concentrate, FIRE!' And why, for 'concentrate', he had humorously substituted 'consecrate'. His platoon, including the two unusual 'bible-wallahs' whose letters home always began in the same formal way: 'Dear Sister in Christ', or 'Dear Brother in Christ', blazed away.

The troops, while ready to believe in the Kaiser as a comic personal devil, knew the German soldier to be, on the whole, more devout than himself. In the instructors' mess we spoke freely of God and Gott as opposed tribal deities. For Anglican regimental chaplains we had little respect. If they had shown one-tenth the courage, endur-ance, and other human qualities that the regimental doctors showed, we agreed, the British Expeditionary Force might well have started a religious revival. But they had not, being under orders to avoid getting mixed up with the fighting and to stay behind with the transport. Soldiers could hardly respect a chaplain who obeyed these orders, and yet not one in fifty seemed sorry to obey them. Occasion-ally, on a quiet day in a quiet sector, the chaplain would make a daring afternoon visit to the support line and distribute a few cigar-ettes, before hurrying back. But he was always much to the fore in rest-billets. Sometimes the colonel would summon him to come up with the rations and bury the day's dead; he would arrive, speak his lines, and shoot off again. The position was complicated by the respect that most commanding officers had for the cloth – though not all. The colonel in one battalion I served with got rid of four new Anglican chaplains in four months; finally he applied for a Roman Catholic, alleging a change of faith in the men under his command. For the Roman Catholic chaplains were not only per-mitted to visit posts of danger, but definitely enjoyed to be wherever fighting was, so that they could give extreme unction to the dying. And we had never heard of one who failed to do all that was expected of him and more. Jovial Father Gleeson of the Munsters, when all the officers were killed or wounded at the first battle of Ypres, had stripped off his black badges and, taking command of the survivors, held the line.

Anglican chaplains were remarkably out of touch with their troops. The Second Battalion chaplain, just before the Loos fighting, had preached a violent sermon on the Battle against Sin, at which one old soldier behind me grumbled: 'Christ, as if one bloody push wasn't enough to worry about at a time!' A Roman Catholic padre, on the other hand, had given his men his blessing and told them that if they died fighting for the good cause they would go straight to Heaven or, at any rate, be excused a great many years in Purgatory. When I told this story to the mess, someone else said that on the eve of a battle in Mesopotamia the Anglican chaplain of his battalion had preached a sermon on the commutation of tithes. 'Much more sensible than that Battle against Sin. Quite up in the air, and took the men's minds off the fighting.'

I felt better after a few weeks at Harfleur, though the knowledge that this was merely a temporary relief haunted me all the time. One day I left the mess to begin the afternoon's work on the drill-ground, and passed the place at which bombing instruction went on. A group of men stood around a table where the various types of bombs were set out for demonstration. I heard a sudden crash. A sergeant of the Royal Irish Rifles had been giving a little unofficial instruction before the proper instructor arrived. He picked up a No. 1 percussion-grenade and said: 'Now lads, you've got to be careful here! Remember that if you touch anything while you're swinging this chap, it'll go off.' To illustrate the point, he rapped the grenade against the table edge. It killed him and the man next to him and wounded twelve others more or less severely.

18

In March I rejoined the First Battalion on the Somme. It was the primrose season. We went in and out of the Fricourt trenches, with billets at Morlancourt, a country village still untouched by shell-fire. (Later it got knocked to pieces; the Australians and the Germans captured and recaptured it from each other several times, until only the site remained.) 'A' Company headquarters were a farmhouse kitchen, where we slept in our valises on the red-brick floor. An old lady and her daughter stayed to safeguard their possessions. The old lady was senile and paralysed; almost all she could do was to shake her head and say: *'Triste, la guerre!'* We called her 'Triste la Guerre'. The daughter used to carry her about like a child.

At Fricourt, the trenches were cut in chalk, which we found more tolerable in wet weather than La Bassée clay. Division had given us a brigade-frontage where the lines came closer to each other than at any other point for miles. The British had only recently extended their line down to the Somme, and the French had been content, as they usually were, unless definitely contemplating a battle, to be at peace with the Germans and not dig in too near. But here a slight ridge occurred, and neither side could afford to let the other hold the crest, so they shared it, after a prolonged dispute. This area was used by both the Germans and ourselves as an experimental station for new types of bombs and grenades. The trenches were wide and tumble-down, too shallow in many places, and without sufficient traverses. The French had left relics both of their nonchalance – corpses buried too near the surface; and of their love of security – a number of deep though lousy dug-outs. We busied ourselves raising the front-line parapet and building traverses to limit the damage of the trench-mortar shells that fell continually. Every night not only the companies in the front line, but both support companies, kept hard at work all the time. It was an even worse place than Cuinchy for rats; they scuttled about 'A' Company mess at meal-times. We always ate with revolvers beside our plates, and punctuated our conversation with sudden volleys at a rat rummaging at somebody's valise or crawling along the timber support of the roof above our heads. 'A' Company officers were gay. We had all been in our school choirs, except Edmund Dadd, who sang like a crow, and used to chant anthems and bits of cantatas whenever things went well. Edmund insisted on taking his part.

At dinner one day a Welsh boy came rushing in, hysterical from terror. He shouted to Richardson: 'Sirr, sirr, there is a trenss-mortar in my dug-out!'

His sing-song Welsh made us all shout with laughter. 'Cheer up, 33 Williams,' Richardson said, 'how did a big thing like a trench-mortar happen to occur in your dug-out?'

But 33 Williams could not explain. He went on again and again: 'Sirr, sirr, there is a trenss-mortar in my dug-out!'

Edmund Dadd went out to investigate. He reported that a mortar-shell had fallen into the trench, bounced down the dug-out steps, exploded, and killed five men. 33 Williams, the only survivor, had been lying asleep, protected by the body of another man.

Our greatest trial was the German canister – a two gallon drum with a cylinder containing about two pounds of an explosive called ammonal that looked like salmon paste, smelled like marzipan, and, when it went off, sounded like the Day of Judgement. The hollow around the cylinder contained scrap metal, apparently collected by French villagers behind the German lines: rusty nails, fragments of British and French shells, spent bullets, and the screws, nuts, and bolts that heavy lorries leave behind on the road. We dissected one unexploded canister, and found in it, among other things, the cog-wheels of a clock and half a set of false teeth. The canister could easily be heard approaching and looked harmless in the air, but its shock was as shattering as the very heaviest shell. It would blow in any but the very deepest dug-outs; and the false teeth, rusty nails, cog-wheels, and so on went flying all over the place. We could not agree how the Germans fired a weapon of that size. The problem remained unsolved until July 1st, when the battalion attacked from these same trenches and discovered a wooden cannon buried in the earth and discharged with a time-fuse. The crew offered to surrender, but our men had sworn for months to get them.

One evening (near 'Trafalgar Square', should any reader remember that trench-junction), Richardson, David Thomas, and I met Pritchard and the adjutant. We stopped to talk. Richardson complained what a devil of a place this was for trench-mortars.

'That's where I come in,' said Pritchard. As battalion trench-mortar officer he had just been given two Stokes mortar-guns. 'They're beauties,' Pritchard went on. 'I've been trying them out, and tomorrow I'm going to get some of my own back. I can put four or five shells in the air at once.'

'About time, too,' the adjutant said. 'We've had three hundred casualties in the last month here. It doesn't seem so many as that because, curiously enough, none of them have been officers. In fact, we've had about five hundred casualties in the ranks since Loos, and not a single officer.'

Then he suddenly realized that his words were unlucky.

'Touch wood!' David shouted.

Everybody jumped to touch wood, but it was a French trench and unrevetted. I pulled a pencil out of my pocket; that was wood enough for me.

Richardson said: 'I'm not superstitious, anyway.'

The following evening I led 'A' Company forward as a working-party. 'B' and 'D' Companies were in the line, and we overtook 'C' also going to work. David, bringing up the rear of 'C', looked worried about something. 'What's wrong?' I asked.

'Oh, I'm fed up,' he answered, 'and I've got a cold.'

'C' Company filed along to the right of the battalion frontage; and we went to the left. It was a weird kind of night, with a bright moon. Germans occupied a sap only forty or fifty yards away. We stood on the parapet piling the sandbags, with the moon at our backs, but the German sentries ignored us – probably because they had work on hand themselves. It happened at times, when both sides were busy putting up proper defences, that they turned a blind eye to each other's work. Occasionally, it was said, the rival wiring-parties 'as good as used the same mallets' for hammering in the pickets. The Germans seemed much more ready than we were to live and let live. (Only once, so far as I know, apart from Christmas 1914, did both sides show themselves in daylight without firing at each other: one February at Ypres, when the trenches got so flooded that everyone had to crawl out on top to avoid drowning.) Nevertheless, a continuous exchange of grenades and trench-mortars had begun. Several canisters went over, and the men found it difficult to get out of their way in the dark; but for the first time we were giving the enemy as good as they gave us. Pritchard had been using his Stokes mortars all day, and sent over hundreds of rounds; twice the Germans had located his emplacement and forced him to shift hurriedly.

'A' Company worked from seven in the evening until midnight. We must have put three thousand sandbags into position, and fifty yards of front trench were already looking presentable. About half past ten, rifle fire broke out on the right, and the sentries passed along the news: 'Officer hit.'

Richardson hurried away to investigate. He came back to say: 'It's young Thomas. A bullet through the neck; but I think he's all right. It can't have hit his spine or an artery, because he's walking to the dressing-station.'

I was delighted: David should now be away long enough to escape the coming offensive, and perhaps even the rest of the war.

At twelve o'clock we finished for the night. Richardson said: 'Von Ranke,' (only he pronounced it 'von Runicke' – which was my regimental nickname) 'take the company down for their rum and tea, will you? They've certainly earned it tonight. I'll be back in a few minutes. I'm going out with Corporal Chamberlen to see what the wiring-party's been at.' As I took the men back, I heard a couple of shells fall somewhere behind us. I noticed them, because they were the only shells fired that night: five-nines by the noise. We had hardly reached the support line on the reverse side of the hill, when we heard the cry: 'Stretcher-bearers!' and presently a man ran up to say: 'Captain Graves is hit!'

That raised a general laugh, and we walked on; but all the same I sent a stretcher-party to investigate. It was Richardson: the shells had caught him and Corporal Chamberlen among the wire. Chamberlen lost his leg and died of wounds a day or two later. Richardson, blown into a shell-hole full of water, lay there stunned for some minutes before the sentries heard the corporal's cries and realized what had happened. The stretcher-bearers brought him down semi-conscious; he recognized us, said he wouldn't be long away from the company, and gave me instructions about it. The doctor found no wound in any vital spot, though the skin of his left side had been riddled, as we saw, with the chalky soil blown against it. We felt the same relief in his case as in David's: that he would be out of it for a while.

Then news came that David was dead. The regimental doctor, a throat specialist in civil life, had told him at the dressing-station: 'You'll be all right, only don't raise your head for a bit.' David then took a letter from his pocket, gave it to an orderly, and said: 'Post this!' It had been written to a girl in Glamorgan, for delivery if he got killed. The doctor saw that he was choking and tried tracheotomy; but too late.

Edmund and I were talking together in 'A' Company headquarters at about one o'clock when the adjutant entered. He looked ghastly. Richardson was dead: the explosion and the cold water had over-strained his heart, weakened by rowing in the Eight at Radley. The adjutant said nervously: 'You know, somehow I feel – responsible in a way for this; what I said yesterday at Trafalgar Square. Of course, really, I don't believe in superstition, but . . .'

Just at that moment three or four whizz-bang shells burst about twenty yards off. A cry of alarm went up, followed by: 'Stretcher-bearers!'

The adjutant turned white, and we did not have to be told what had happened. Pritchard, having fought his duel all night and finally silenced the enemy, was coming off duty. A whizz-bang had caught him at the point where the communication trench reached Maple Redoubt – a direct hit. The total casualties were three officers and one corporal.

It seemed ridiculous, when we returned without Richardson to 'A' Company billets in Morlancourt to find the old lady still alive, and to hear her once more quaver: '*Triste, la guerre!*', when her daughter explained that *le jeune capitaine* had been killed. The old woman had taken a fancy to *le jeune capitaine*; we used to chaff him about it.

I felt David's death worse than any other since I had been in France, but it did not anger me as it did Siegfried. He was acting transport-officer and every evening now, when he came up with the rations, went out on patrol looking for Germans to kill. I just felt empty and lost.

One of the anthems that we used to sing in the mess was: 'He that shall endure to the end, shall be savèd.' The words repeated themselves in my head, like a charm, whenever things went wrong. 'Though thousands languish and fall beside thee, And tens of thousands around thee perish, Yet still it shall not come nigh thee.' And there was another bit: 'To an inheritance incorruptible . . . Through faith unto salvation, Ready to be revealèd at the last trump.' For 'trump' we always used to sing 'crump'. A crump was a German five-point-nine shell, and 'the last crump' would be the end of the war. Should we ever live to hear it burst safely behind us? I wondered whether I could endure to the end with faith unto salvation . . . My breaking-point was near now, unless something happened to stave it off. Not that I felt frightened. I had never yet lost my head and turned tail through fright, and knew that I never would. Nor would the breakdown come as insanity; I did not have it in me. It would be a general nervous collapse, with tears and twitchings and dirtied trousers; I had seen cases like that.

We were issued with a new gas-helmet, popularly known as 'the goggle-eyed booger with the tit'. It differed from the previous models. One breathed in through the nose from inside the helmet, and breathed out through a special valve held in the mouth; but I could not manage this. Boxing with an already broken nose had recently displaced the septum, which forced me to breathe through my mouth. In a gas-attack, I would be unable to use the helmet – the only type claimed to be proof against the newest German gas. The battalion doctor advised a nose-operation as soon as possible.

I took his advice, and missed being with the First Battalion when the expected offensive started. Three out of five of my fellow-officers were killed in it. Scatter's dream of open warfare failed to materialize. He himself got very badly wounded. Of 'A' Company choir, there is one survivor besides myself: C. D. Morgan, who had his thigh smashed, and was still in hospital some months after the war ended.

19

I WENT on leave in April 1916. That Good Friday was the last occasion on which I ever attended a church service, apart from subsequent weddings, church parades, and so on. I remember the date, because the choir boys wore no surplices, and the psalms were read, not sung. My father wanted me to attend the early morning service, and even tried to bully me into it, but I was owed thirteen months' sleep; and though he came hobbling along to my bedroom door at half past six, banging loudly and saying that my mother counted on my accompanying her, this day of all days, I did not turn out. I pleaded a bad toothache; and it wasn't an excuse. A rear molar had flared up. So they had a grievance at breakfast and, having won the first trick, I knew that I must lose the second and attend the morning service. Not wanting to face a religious argument, I decided to humour my parents; if they believed that God stood squarely behind the British Expeditionary Force, it would be unkind to dissent.

I smelt no rat, beyond a slight suspicion that they were anxious to show me off in church wearing my battle-stained officer's uniform. But my toothache got the better of me and arguments arose at the breakfast-table, during which I said things that angered my father and grieved my mother. At last, on her account alone – because she took no active part in the argument, just looking sad and only officially siding with my father – I consented to come with them.

At nine o'clock they went upstairs to dress. The service was to be at half past nine. I thought this unusually early for matins, but attributed it to the new wartime principle of getting things over quickly. Then a ring came at the door. The proprietor of a neighbouring bath-chair business had arrived with a bath-chair. He explained that, as he had previously told my mother, they could not spare a man to take it to church, being seriously under-staffed because of the war – his sole remaining employee, in fact, had a job pulling the aged Countess of I-forget-what to the parish church, a mile or so in the opposite direction. For the moment I thought that it had been a very generous thought of my mother's on my behalf but, ill as I felt, I could surely manage to reach the church, about half a mile away, without such a parade of infirmity. I forgot my father's gout, and also forgot that passage in Herodotus about the two dutiful sons who yoked themselves to an ox-cart to pull their mother, the priestess, to the Temple and were oddly used by Solon, in a conversation with King Croesus, as a symbol of ultimate happiness.

When I realized what I was in for, I could only laugh. Then down came my mother with her prayer-book, veil, and deep religious look, and I could not spoil the day for her. I took hold of the beastly vehicle without a word; my father appeared in a top-hat and his better carpet-slippers and hoisted himself in; and we set off. The bath-chair needed oiling badly; also, one tyre kept coming unstuck and winding itself around the axle. There was an appreciable slope down towards the church, and so the going, though heavy, was easier than the returning. By half past ten the service did not seem to be getting on so fast as it should have, and I grew dreadfully bored, longing to sneak outside for – well, anyhow, I wanted to sneak outside.

I whispered to my mother: 'Isn't it nearly over?'

She answered: 'My dear, didn't your father tell you that it would be a three-hour service? And, of course, since you couldn't get up to pull him to church for the early service, he'll want to stay for Holy Communion at the end. That will make it a little longer.'

So I stayed and tried to compose Latin epigrams, which was, in those days, my way of killing time – on ceremonial parades, for instance, or in the dentist's chair, or at night in the trenches when things were quiet. I composed a maledictory epigram on the strapping young curate – besides myself, my father, the verger, and an old, old man with a palsied hand sitting just in front of me, the only male in the congregation, though there were sixty or seventy women present. I tried to remember whether the *i* of *clericus* was long or short, and couldn't; but it did not matter, because I could make alternative versions to suit either case:

> *O si bracchipotens qui fulminat ore clericus* ...

and:

> *O si bracchipotens clericus qui fulminat ore* ...*

For he was now preaching a sermon about Divine Sacrifice, and bellowing about the Glurious Perfurmances of our Surns and Brethren in Frurnce today. I decided to ask him afterwards why, if he felt like that, he wasn't himself either in Frurnce or in khurki.

To please my mother I took the Sacrament, though by no means in the required mood of spiritual resignation. That ends the story, except the being introduced at the church door to new family friends – 'Your father has showed us your very interesting letters from the trenches. Do tell me, etc., etc.' – and the dreary push up-hill, my mother helping me, my father holding her prayer-book, myself sweating like a bull.

The next day I went first to a dentist, and then to the Milbank Military Hospital in London, where I had my nose operated on free by an Army surgeon. In peacetime this would have cost me sixty guineas, and another twenty guineas in nursing-home fees. On the other hand, I should have been able to pick my specialist; this one bungled the job, and I still cannot breathe properly through one nostril.

After a stay in hospital, I went up to Harlech and walked the hills. The verse of a psalm: 'I will lift up mine eyes unto the hills, from whence cometh my help', had been another charm against trouble; though I have since learned that the last five words of the original Hebrew are really a question, not a relative clause. I bought a small two-roomed cottage from my mother, who owned considerable house-property at Harlech. This was done in defiance of the war: something to look forward to when the guns stopped. We always thought of the end of the war as 'when the guns stop'. I whitewashed the cottage, which stood at some distance from the village, and furnished it with a table, a chair, a bed, a few dishes, and cooking

* 'O, if the powerful cleric who fulminates with his mouth ...'

utensils. I had decided to live there one day on bread and butter, bacon and eggs, lettuce in season, cabbage and coffee; and to write poetry. My war-bonus would keep me for a year or two at least. Having put in a big window to look out over the wood below and across the broad plain to the sea, I wrote two or three poems here as a foretaste of the good life to come; but have suppressed them all since.

Later, in London, my father took me to a dinner of the Honourable Cymmrodorion Society – a Welsh literary club – where Lloyd George, then Secretary for War, and W. M. Hughes, the Australian Prime Minister, both spoke. Hughes was perky, dry, and to the point; Lloyd George was up in the air on one of his 'glory of the Welsh hills' speeches. The power of his rhetoric amazed me. The substance of the speech might be commonplace, idle, and false, but I had to fight hard against abandoning myself with the rest of his audience. He sucked power from his listeners and spurted it back at them. Afterwards, my father introduced me to Lloyd George, and when I looked closely at his eyes they seemed like those of a sleep-walker.

I rejoined the Third Battalion at Litherland, near Liverpool, where it had been shifted from Wrexham as part of the Mersey defence force. The senior officers generously put no more work on me than I wished to undertake, and I met again three of my Wrexham contemporaries who had been severely wounded (all of them, by a coincidence, in the left thigh), and seemed to be out of it for the rest of the war – Frank Jones-Bateman and 'Father' Watkin, who had been in the Welsh Regiment with me, and Aubrey Attwater, the assistant-adjutant, who had gone to the Second Battalion early in 1915, and been badly hit when out on patrol. Attwater came from Cambridge at the outbreak of the war and was known as 'Brains' in the battalion. The militia majors, for the most part country gentlemen with estates in Wales and no thoughts in peacetime beyond hunting, shooting, fishing, and the control of their tenantry, were delighted with Attwater's informative talk over the port at mess. Sergeant Malley, the mess-sergeant, would go round with his 'Light or vintage, sir?', and the old majors would prompt Attwater: 'Now, Brains! Tell us about Shakespeare. Is it true that Bacon wrote him?' Or: 'Well, Brains! What do you think about this chap Hilaire Belloc? Does he really know when the war's going to end?' Attwater would humorously accept his position as combined encyclopedia and almanac. Sergeant Malley, another friend whom I was always pleased to see again, could pour more wine into a glass than any other waiter in the world: it bulged up over the top like a cap, and he never spilled a drop.

Wednesdays were guest-nights in the mess, when the colonel expected the married officers, who usually dined at home, to attend. The band played Gilbert and Sullivan music behind a curtain. In the intervals, the regimental harper gave solos – Welsh melodies picked out rather uncertainly on a hand-harp. Afterwards the bandmaster was invited to the senior officers' table for his complimentary glass of Light or Vintage. When he and the junior officers had retired, the port went round and round, and the conversation, at first very formal, became rambling and intimate. Once, I remember, an old major laid it down axiomatically that every so-called sportsman had at some time or other committed a sin against sportsmanship. When challenged to make good this slander, he cross-examined each of his neighbours in turn, putting them on their honour to tell the truth.

One of them, blushing, admitted that he had once shot grouse two days before the Twelfth: 'I was sailing next day to rejoin the battalion in India and this was my last chance.' Another said that when a public-school boy, and old enough to know better, he had killed a sitting pheasant with a stone. Another had gone out with a poacher – in his Sandhurst days – and crumbled poison-berry into a trout-stream. An even more scandalous confession came from a New Army major, a gentleman-farmer: that his estate had been over-run by foxes one year and, the headquarters of the nearest hunt being thirty miles away, he had permitted his bailiff to protect the hen roosts with a gun. Then came the turn of the medical officer, who said: 'Well, once while I was a student at St Andrews, a friend asked me to put ten bob for him on a horse in the Lincolnshire. I couldn't find my bookmaker in time. The horse lost, but I never returned the ten bob.' At this, one of the guests, an officer in the King's Own Scottish Borderers, suddenly grew excited, jumped up, and leaned over the table, doubling his fists, 'And was not the name of the horse Strathspey? And will you not pay me my ten shillings now immediately?'

Only the bombing-field separated the camp from Brotherton's factory, which made an especially sensitive explosive for detonators. The munition workers had permanently yellow faces and hands, and drew appropriately high wages. Attwater used to argue at mess sometimes what would happen when Brotherton's blew up. Most of us held that the explosion would immediately kill all the three thousand men of the camp, besides destroying Litherland and a large part of Bootle. Attwater maintained that the very closeness of the camp would save it; that the vibrations would go over and strike a large munition camp about a mile away and probably set that off too. One Sunday afternoon, Attwater limped out of the mess and saw smoke rising from Brotherton's. Part of the factory was on fire. He immediately had the camp fire-brigade bugled for, and they managed to smother the fire before it reached a vital spot; so the argument was never decided.

As much Welsh as English was now talked in the huts, the chapels having put their full manpower at Lloyd George's disposal. A deputation of soldiers from Harlech and the neighbourhood came to me one morning and said solemnly: 'Captain Graves, sir, we do not like our sergeant-major. He do curse, and he do swear, and he do drink, and he do smoke, and he is a man of lowly origin too.'

I told them to make their complaint in proper form, under the escort of an N.C.O. They did not return.

A deputation of Welsh chapel ministers went to Attwater and complained of the blasphemous language used by the N.C.O.s. Attwater agreed that swearing on parade, at least, was contrary to King's Regulations; but called the ministers' attention to a rise of nearly two hundred per cent in affiliation orders since their innocent flocks had come to Litherland for training.

I stayed at Litherland a few weeks only. On July 1st, 1916, the Somme offensive began, and all available trained men and officers went out to replace casualties. I had the pleasure of riding up the line on a locomotive and helping the French stoker, thus fulfilling a childhood dream; though bitterly disappointed at finding myself posted to the Second Battalion, not the First.

The Second Battalion was in trenches at Givenchy, on the other side of the canal from the Cuinchy brick-stacks. I arrived on July 5th, to find one of our raids in progress. Prisoners were already coming down the trench, scared and chattering to each other: Saxons, just back from a divisional rest and a week's leave to Germany, with new uniforms and their packs full of good lootable stuff. One prisoner got a stern talking-to from 'C' Company sergeant-major, a Birmingham man, shocked at a packet of indecent photographs found in the man's haversack.

It was a retaliatory raid. Only a few days before, the Germans had sent up the biggest mine blown on the Western front so far.

It caught our 'B' Company – the 'B's were proverbially unlucky. The crater, afterwards named 'Red Dragon Crater' after the Royal Welch Regimental badge, must have been about thirty yards across. There were few survivors of 'B' Company. The Germans immediately came over in force to catch the other companies in confusion. Stanway, who had been a company sergeant-major during the retreat, and was now a major, rallied some men on the flank and drove the Germans back. Blair, 'B' Company commander, buried by the mine up to his neck, remained for the rest of the day under constant fire. Though a Boer War veteran, he survived this experience, recovered from his wounds, and returned to the battalion a few months later.

This raid had been Stanway's revenge. He and Colonel 'Tibs' Crawshay – the depôt adjutant who had originally sent me out to France – planned it most elaborately, with bombardments and smoke-screen diversion on the flanks. A barrage of shrapnel would shift forward and back from the German front line to the supports. The intention was that the Germans should go down into the shell-proof dug-outs at the first bombardment, leaving only sentries in the trench, and reappear as soon as the barrage lifted. When it started again, they would make another dash for the dug-outs. After this had happened two or three times they would be slow in emerging. Then, under cover of a smoke-screen, the raid would be made and the barrage put down uninterruptedly on the support and reserve lines, to prevent reinforcements from coming up.

My only part in the raid, which proved very successful, was to make a detailed report of it at Crawshay's request – not the report for divisional headquarters, but a page of history to be sent to the depôt for filing in regimental records. I noted that for the first time since the eighteenth century the regiment had reverted to the pike: instead of rifle and bayonet, some of the raiders had used butchers' knives secured with medical plaster to the ends of broomsticks. This pike, a lighter weapon than rifle and bayonet, was a useful addition to bombs and revolvers.

An official journalist at headquarters also wrote an account of the raid. The battalion enjoyed the bit about how they had gone over the top shouting: 'Remember Kitchener!' and 'Avenge the *Lusitania*!' 'What a damn silly thing to shout,' said someone. 'Old Kitchener served his purpose as a figure-head, but nobody wants him back at the War Office, that I've heard. As for the *Lusitania*, the Germans gave the Yanks full warning; and if her sinking brings them into the war, that's all to the good.'

Few officers in the Second Battalion had been with it when I went away after Loos; and not a single one – except Yates, the quarter-master, and Robertson, now adjutant (but killed soon afterwards) – remembered the battalion mess at Laventie. So I expected a friendlier welcome than on my first arrival. However, as Captain Dunn, the battalion doctor (I have since heard), recorded in his diary: 'Graves had a chilly reception, which surprised me.' The reason was simple. One of the officers who had joined the Third Battalion in August 1914, and been sent out to France ahead of me as the more efficient, had now achieved his ambition of a regular commission. But this made him only a second-lieutenant, and jealousy of my two extra stars embittered him. When he made a nasty remark in public about 'jumped-up captains', I refrained from putting him under arrest, as I should have done, and instead quoted at him the consoling lines:

> *O deem it pride, not lack of skill,*
> *That will not let my sleeves increase.*
> *The morning and the evening still*
> *Have but one star apiece.*

We had not met in France hitherto, and he now most unethically revived the suspicion raised by my German name on my first arrival at Wrexham: that I was a German spy. As a result, I found myself treated with great reserve by all officers who had not known me in trenches before. Unluckily, the most notorious German spy caught in England had assumed the name of Carl Graves. My enemy put it out that Carl and I were brothers. I consoled myself by thinking that a battle was obviously due soon, and would put an end either to me or to the suspicion – 'So long as no N.C.O. is told off to shoot me on the slightest appearance of treachery.' Such things were known.

As a matter of fact, though I myself had no traffic with the Germans, my mother and her sisters in Germany kept up a desultory corres-pondence through my aunt, Clara von Faber du Faur, whose husband was German Consul at Zürich: a register of the deaths of relatives, and discreet references to the war service of the survivors. My aunts wrote, as their Government had ordered every German with relatives or friends abroad to do, pointing out the righteousness of the German cause, and presenting Germany as the innocent party in a war engineered by France and Russia. My mother, equally strong for the Allied cause, wrote back that they were deluded, but that she forgave them.

The officers I liked best in the battalion, besides Robertson, were Colonel Crawshay and Doctor Dunn. Dunn, a hard-bitten Scot, had served as a trooper in the South African War, and there won the Distinguished Conduct Medal. Now he was far more than a doctor: living at battalion headquarters, he became the right-hand man of three or four colonels in succession. Whoever failed to take his advice usually regretted it afterwards. Once, in the autumn fighting of 1917, a shell burst among the headquarters staff, knocking out colonel, adjutant, and signal officer. Dunn had no hesitation in becoming a temporary combatant officer of the Royal Welch, resigning his medical duties to the stretcher-bearer sergeant. The men had immense respect for him, and he earned his D.S.O. many times over.

20

FOUR days after the raid we marched through Béthune, now much knocked about and nearly deserted, to Fouquières, and there entrained for the Somme. The Somme railhead was near Amiens, and we proceeded by easy stages through Cardonette, Daours, and Buire until, on the afternoon of July 14th, we came to the original front line, close to where David Thomas, Richardson, and Pritchard had been killed. The fighting had moved two miles on. At 4 a.m. on July 15th, we struck the Méaulte–Fricourt–Bazentin road, which ran through 'Happy Valley', and reached the more recent battle area. Wounded and prisoners came streaming past in the half-light. I was shocked by the dead horses and mules; human corpses were all very well, but it seemed wrong for animals to be dragged into the war like this. We marched by platoons, at fifty yards' distance. Just beyond Fricourt a German shell-barrage made the road impassable; so we left it and moved forward over thickly shell-pitted ground until 8 a.m., when we found ourselves on the fringe of Mametz Wood, among the dead of our own New Army battalions who had helped to capture it. There we halted in thick mist. The Germans had been using lachrymatory shell, and the mist held the fumes, making us cough. We tried to smoke, but our cigarettes tasted of gas, so we threw them away. Later, we cursed ourselves for fools, because it was our throats, not the cigarettes, that were affected.

When the mist cleared, we saw a German gun with 'First Battalion Royal Welch Fusiliers' chalked on it – evidently a trophy. I wondered what had happened to Siegfried and my friends of 'A' Company. We found the battalion quite close in bivouacs; Siegfried was still alive, so were Edmund Dadd, and two other 'A' Company officers. The battalion had seen heavy fighting: in their first attack at Fricourt they overran our opposite number in the German Army, the Twenty-third Infantry Regiment, who were undergoing a special disciplinary spell in the trenches because an inspecting staff-officer, coming round, discovered all the officers ensconced in a deep dug-out at Mametz village, instead of being up in the trenches with their men. (Edmund Dadd told me that throughout the bad time in March there were no German soldiers of higher rank opposite us than corporals.) The battalion's next objective was 'The Quadrangle', a small copse this side of Mametz Wood, where Siegfried distinguished himself by taking, single-handed, a battalion frontage which the Royal Irish Regiment had failed to take the day before. He went over with bombs in daylight, under covering fire from a couple of rifles, and scared away the occupants. A pointless feat, since instead of signalling for reinforcements, he sat down in the German trench and began reading a book of poems which he had brought with him. When he finally went back he did not even report. Colonel Stockwell, then in command, raged at him. The attack on Mametz Wood had been delayed for two hours because British patrols were still reported to be out. 'British patrols' were Siegfried and his book of poems. 'I'd have got you a D.S.O., if you'd only shown more sense,' stormed Stockwell. Siegfried had been doing heroic things ever since I left the battalion. His nickname in the Seventh Division was 'Mad Jack'. He won a Military Cross for bringing in a wounded lance-corporal from a mine-crater close to the German lines, under heavy fire. I missed him this time; he was down with the transport, having a rest. But I sent him, by one of our own transport men, a rhymed letter about the times that we were going to have together when the war ended; how, after a rest at Harlech, we were going for a visit to the Caucasus and Persia and China; and what good poetry we would write. This was in answer to a rhymed letter he had written to me from the Army School at Flixécourt a few weeks previously. (It appears in *The Old Huntsman*.)

I went for a stroll with Edmund Dadd, who now commanded 'A' Company. 'It's not fair, Robert,' Edmund began, plaintively. 'You remember that "A" Company under Richardson was always the best in the battalion? Well, it's kept up its reputation, and Stockpot shoves us in as the leading company at every show. We get our objectives and hold them, and so we've always got to do the same again. The worst of it is, he thinks I'm indispensable; and makes me go over each time, instead of giving me a rest and letting my second-in-command take his turn. I've had five shows in just over a fortnight, and I can't go on being lucky much longer. Stockpot's about due for his C.B. Apparently "A" Company is making sure he gets it.'

The next two days we spent in bivouacs outside Mametz Wood. We were in fighting kit and felt cold at night, so I went into the wood to find German overcoats to use as blankets. It was full of dead Prussian Guards Reserve, big men, and dead Royal Welch and South Wales Borderers of the New Army battalions, little men. Not a single tree in the wood remained unbroken. I collected my overcoats, and came away as quickly as I could, climbing through the wreckage of green branches. Going and coming, by the only possible route, I passed by the bloated and stinking corpse of a German with his back propped against a tree. He had a green face, spectacles, close-shaven hair; black blood was dripping from the nose and beard. I came across two other unforgettable corpses: a man of the South Wales Borderers and one of the Lehr Regiment had succeeded in bayoneting each other simultaneously. A survivor of the fighting told me later that he had seen a young soldier of the Fourteenth Royal Welch bayoneting a German in parade-ground style, automatically exclaiming: 'In, out, on guard!'

I was still superstitious about looting or collecting souvenirs. 'These greatcoats are only a loan,' I told myself. Our brigade, the Nineteenth, was the reserve brigade of the Thirty-third Division; the other brigades, the Ninety-ninth and Hundredth, had attacked Martinpuich two days previously, but been halted with heavy losses as soon as they started. We were left to sit about in shell-holes and watch our massed artillery blazing away, almost wheel to wheel. On the 18th, we advanced to a position just north of Bazentin-le-Petit, and relieved the Tyneside Irish. I had been posted to 'D' Company. Our Irish guide was hysterical and had forgotten the way; we put him under arrest and found it ourselves. On the way up through the ruins of Bazentin-le-Petit, we were shelled with gas-shells. The standing order with regard to gas-shells was not to bother about respirators, but push on. Hitherto, they had all been lachrymatory ones; these were the first of the deadly kind, so we lost half a dozen men.

When at last 'D' Company reached the trenches, scooped beside a road and not more than three feet deep, the badly shaken Tyneside company we were relieving hurried off, without any of the usual formalities. I asked their officers where the Germans were. He said he didn't know, but pointed vaguely towards Martinpuich, a mile to our front. Then I asked him who held our left flank, and how far off they were. He didn't know. I damned his soul to Hell as he went away. Having got into touch with 'C' Company behind us on the right, and the Fourth Suffolks fifty yards to the left, we began deepening the trenches and presently located the Germans – in a trench system some five hundred yards to our front, keeping fairly quiet.

The next day, at dinnertime, very heavy shelling started: shells bracketed along the trench about five yards short and five yards over, but never quite got it. Three times running, my cup of tea was spilled by the concussion and filled with dirt. I happened to be in a cheerful mood, and just laughed. My parcel of kippers from home seemed far more important than any bombardment – I recalled with appreciation one of my mother's sayings: 'Children, remember this when you eat your kippers; kippers are cheap, yet if they cost a hundred guineas each they would still find buyers among the million-aires.' A tame magpie had come into the trench; apparently be-longing to the Germans driven out of the village by the Gordon Highlanders a day or two before. It looked very bedraggled. 'That's one for sorrow,' I said. The men swore that it made some remark in German as it joined us, and talked of wringing its neck.

Being now off duty, I fell asleep in the trench without waiting for the bombardment to stop. It would be no worse getting killed asleep than awake. There were no dug-outs, of course. I found it quite easy to sleep through bombardments; though vaguely conscious of the noise, I let it go by. Yet if anybody came to wake me for my watch, or shouted 'Stand-to!', I was always alert in a second. I could fall asleep sitting down, standing, marching, lying on a stone floor, or in any other position, at a moment's notice at any time of day or night. But on this occasion I had a fearful nightmare: of somebody handling me secretly, choosing the place to drive a knife into me. Finally, he gripped me in the small of the back. I woke up with a start, shouting, punched at the assassin's hand – and found I had killed a mouse which had run down my neck for fear of the shells.

That afternoon the company got an order from brigade to build two cruciform strong-points at such-and-such a map reference. Moodie, the company commander, and I looked at our map and laughed. Moodie sent back a message that he would be glad to obey, but would first need an artillery bombardment and considerable reinforcements; because the points selected, half-way to Martinpuich, were occupied by the enemy. Colonel Crawshay came up and verified this. He told us to build the strong-points about three hundred yards forward and two hundred yards apart. So one platoon stayed behind in the trench, and the others went out and began digging. A cruciform strong-point consisted of two trenches, each some thirty yards long, crossing at right angles in the middle; being wired all round, it looked, in diagram, like a hot-cross bun. The defenders could bring fire to bear against attacks from any direction. We were to hold these points with a Lewis gun and a platoon of men apiece.

I had the first watch that night, and periodically visited both strong-points. My way to the right-hand one took me in bright moonlight along the Bazentin–High Wood road. A dead German sergeant-major, wearing a pack and full equipment, lay supine in the middle of the sunken cart-track, his arms stretched out wide. He was a short, powerful man with a full black beard. I needed a charm to get myself past this sinister figure. The simplest way, I found, was to cross myself. Evidently a brigade of the Seventh Division had captured the road, whereupon the Germans shelled it heavily. The defenders, who were Gordon Highlanders, had begun to scrape fire-positions in the north bank, facing the Germans, a task apparently interrupted by a counter-attack. Wounded men had crawled to a number of these small hollows, thrust their heads and shoulders inside, and died there. They looked as if hiding from the black beard.

On my second visit to the strong-point, I found the trench already dug two or three feet down, and a party of Royal Engineers waiting with coils of barbed-wire for the entanglement. But work had stopped. The whisper went round: 'Get your rifles ready. Here comes Fritz!' I lay flat on my face to see better, and some seventy yards away in the moonlight, made out massed figures. I restrained the men, who were itching to fire, and sent a runner back to company headquarters asking Moodie for a Lewis gun and a flare-pistol at once. I said: 'They probably don't know we're here, and we'll get more of them if we let them come closer. They may even surrender.' The men seemed to be under no proper command: we wondered why. There had been a number of German surrenders recently at night, and this might be one on a big scale. Then Moodie arrived with the Lewis gun, the flare-pistol, and a few more men carrying rifle-grenades. Deciding to give the enemy a chance, he sent up a flare and fired the Lewis gun over their heads. The tall officer who came running towards us, his hands lifted in surrender, seemed surprised to find that we were not Germans. He claimed that he belonged to the Public Schools Battalion in our own brigade. When asked what the hell the game was, he explained that he commanded a patrol. So Moodie sent him back for a few more of his men, to make sure it was not a trick. The patrol consisted of fifty men, wandering about aimlessly between the lines, their rifles slung, and, it seemed, without the faintest idea where they were, or what information they were supposed to secure. This Public Schools Battalion was one of four or five similar ones formed in 1914. Their training had been continually interrupted by the large withdrawal of men needed to officer other regiments. The only men left, in fact, appeared to be those unfitted to hold commissions; or even to make good private soldiers. The other battalions remained in England as training corps: this alone was sent out, and proved a constant embarrassment to the brigade.

I picked up a souvenir that night. A German gun-team had been shelled while galloping out of Bazentin towards Martinpuich. The horses and driver lay dead on the road. At the back of the limber were the gunners' treasures, among them a large lump of chalk wrapped in a piece of cloth – carved and decorated in colours with military mottoes, the flags of the Central Powers, and the names of the various battles in which the gunner had served. I sent it to headquarters as a present to Dr Dunn. Both he and it survived the war; he is practising at Glasgow again, and the lump of chalk reposes under a glass case in his consulting room.

Next evening, July 19th, we were relieved and told that we would be attacking High Wood, which could be seen a thousand yards away to the right at the top of a slope. High Wood, which the

French called 'Raven Wood', formed part of the main German battle-line that ran along the ridge, with Delville Wood not far off on the German left. Two British brigades had already attempted it; in both cases a counter-attack drove them out again. The Royal Welch were now reduced by casualties to about four hundred strong, including transport, stretcher-bearers, cooks, and other non-combatants. I took command of 'B' Company.

I have kept a Battalion Order issued at midnight:

To O.C. 'B' Co. 2nd R.W.F. 20.7.16.

Companies	will	move	as	under
to	same	positions	in	S14b
as	were	to	have	been
taken	over	from	Cameronians	aaa
	A Coy.	12.30 a.m.		
	B Coy.	12.45 a.m.		
	C Coy.	1 a.m.		
	D Coy.	1.15 a.m.	aaa	
	At	2 A.M.	Company	Commanders
will	meet	C.O.	at	X
Roads	S14b 99	aaa		
Men	will	lie	down	and
get	under	cover	but	equipment
will	not	be	taken	off
aaa				

S14b 99 was the map reference for Bazentin churchyard. We lay here on the reverse slope of a slight ridge, about half a mile from the wood. I attended the meeting of company commanders; Colonel Crawshay told us the plan. 'Look here, you fellows,' he said, 'we're in reserve for this attack. The Cameronians and the Fifth Scottish Rifles are going up to the wood first; that's at 5 a.m. The Public Schools Battalion are in support, should anything go wrong. I don't know whether we shall be called on; if we are, it will mean that the Jocks have legged it.' He added: 'As usual.' This was an appeal to prejudice. 'The Public Schools Battalion is, well, what we know it is; so if we're called for, that will be the end of us.' He said this with a laugh, and we all laughed.

We were sitting on the ground, protected by a road-bank; a battery of French 75's began firing rapid over our heads from about twenty yards away. There was an even greater concentration of guns in Happy Valley now. We could hardly hear the colonel's words, but understood that if we did get orders to reinforce, we were to shake out in artillery formation; once in the wood, we were to hang on like death. Then he said goodbye and good luck, and we rejoined our companies.

At this juncture the usual inappropriate message came through from division. Division could always be trusted to send a warning about verdigris on vermorel-sprayers, or the keeping of pets in trenches, or being polite to our allies, or some other triviality, exactly when an attack was in progress. This time orders came for a private in 'C' Company to report immediately, under escort of a lance-corporal, to the assistant provost-marshal back at Albert, where a court-martial had been convened. A sergeant of the company must also report as a witness in the case. The private was charged with the murder of a French civilian in an *estaminet* at Béthune a month previously. It seems that a good deal of cognac had been going round, and the French civilian, who bore a grudge against the British because of his faithless wife, began to insult the private. He was reported, somewhat improbably, as having said: '*Anglais no bon, Allmand très bon. War fineesh, napoo les Anglais. Allmand win.*' The private had thereupon drawn his bayonet and run the man through. At the court-martial the private was exonerated; the French civil representative commending him for having 'energetically repressed local defeatism'. So he and two N.C.O.s missed the battle.

What sort of a battle they missed I pieced together afterwards. The Jocks did get into the wood, and the Royal Welch were not called on to reinforce until eleven o'clock in the morning. The Germans put down a barrage along our ridge where we were lying, and we lost a third of the battalion before the show started. I was one of the casualties.

The German batteries were handing out heavy stuff, six- and eight-inch, and so much of it that we decided to move back fifty yards at a rush. As we did so, an eight-inch shell burst three paces behind me. I heard the explosion, and felt as though I had been punched rather hard between the shoulder-blades, but without any pain. I took the punch merely for the shock of the explosion; but blood trickled into my eye and, turning faint, I called to Moodie: 'I've been hit.' Then I fell. A minute or two before I had got two very small wounds on my left hand; and in exactly the same position as the two that drew blood from my right hand during the preliminary bombardment at Loos. This I took as a lucky sign, and for further security repeated to myself a line of Nietzsche's, in French translation:

Non, tu ne me peux pas tuer!

It was the poem about a man on the scaffold with the red-bearded executioner standing over him. (My copy of Nietzsche's poems, by the way, had contributed to the suspicions of my spying activities. Nietzsche, execrated in the newspapers as the philosopher of German militarism, was more properly interpreted as a William le Queux mystery-man – the sinister figure behind the Kaiser.)

One piece of shell went through my left thigh, high up, near the groin; I must have been at the full stretch of my stride to escape emasculation. The wound over the eye was made by a little chip of marble, possibly from one of the Bazentin cemetery headstones. (Later. I had it cut out, but a smaller piece has since risen to the surface under my right eyebrow, where I keep it for a souvenir.) This, and a finger-wound which split the bone, probably came from another shell bursting in front of me. But a piece of shell had also gone in two inches below the point of my right shoulder-blade and came out through my chest two inches above the right nipple.

My memory of what happened then is vague. Apparently Dr Dunn came up through the barrage with a stretcher-party, dressed my wound, and got me down to the old German dressing-station at the north end of Mametz Wood. I remember being put on the stretcher, and winking at the stretcher-bearer sergeant who had just said: 'Old Gravy's got it, all right!' They laid my stretcher in a corner of the dressing-station, where I remained unconscious for more than twenty-four hours.

Late that night, Colonel Crawshay came back from High Wood and visited the dressing-station; he saw me lying in the corner, and they told him I was done for. The next morning, July 21st, clearing away the dead, they found me still breathing and put me on an ambulance for Heilly, the nearest field hospital. The pain of being jolted down the Happy Valley, with a shell hole at every three or four yards of the road, woke me up. I remember screaming. But back on the better roads I became unconscious again. That morning, Crawshay wrote the usual formal letters of condolence to the next-of-kin of the six or seven officers who had been killed. This was his letter to my mother:

Dear Mrs Graves,   22.7.16

I very much regret to have to write and tell you your son has died of wounds. He was very gallant, and was doing so well and is a great loss.

He was hit by a shell and very badly wounded, and died on the way down to the base I believe. He was not in bad pain, and our doctor managed to get across and attend to him at once.

We have had a very hard time, and our casualties have been large. Believe me you have all our sympathy in your loss, and we have lost a very gallant soldier.

Please write to me if I can tell you or do anything.

Yours sincerely,
C. Crawshay, Lt-Col.

Then he made out the official casualty list – a long one, because only eighty men were left in the battalion – and reported me 'died of wounds'. Heilly lay on the railway; close to the station stood the hospital tents with the red cross prominently painted on the roofs, to discourage air-bombing. Fine July weather made the tents insufferably hot. I was semi-conscious now, and aware of my lung-wound through a shortness of breath. It amused me to watch the little bubbles of blood, like scarlet soap-bubbles, which my breath made in escaping through the opening of the wound. The doctor came over to my bed. I felt sorry for him; he looked as though he had not slept for days.

I asked him: 'Can I have a drink?'

'Would you like some tea?'

I whispered: 'Not with condensed milk.'

He said, most apologetically: 'I'm afraid there's no fresh milk.'

Tears of disappointment pricked my eyes; I expected better of a hospital behind the lines.

'Will you have some water?'

'Not if it's boiled.'

'It is boiled. And I'm afraid I can't give you anything alcoholic in your present condition.'

'Some fruit then?'

'I have seen no fruit for days.'

Yet a few minutes later he returned with two rather unripe green-gages. In whispers I promised him a whole orchard when I recovered.

The nights of the 22nd and 23rd were horrible. Early on the morning of the 24th, when the doctor came round the ward, I said: 'You must send me away from here. This heat will kill me.' It was beating on my head through the canvas.

'Stick it out. Your best chance is to lie here and not to be moved. You'd not reach the Base alive.'

'Let me risk the move. I'll be all right, you'll see.'

Half an hour later he returned. 'Well, you're having it your way. I've just got orders to evacuate every case in the hospital. Apparently the Guards have been in it up at Delville Wood, and they'll all be coming down tonight.' I did not fear that I would die, now – it was enough to be honourably wounded and bound for home.

A brigade-major, wounded in the leg, who lay in the next bed, gave me news of the battalion. He looked at my label and said: 'I see you're in the Second Royal Welch. I watched your High Wood show through field-glasses. The way your battalion shook out into artillery formation, company by company – with each section of four or five men in file at fifty yards interval and distance – going down into the hollow and up the slope through the barrage, was the most beautiful bit of parade-ground drill I've ever seen. Your company officers must have been superb.' Yet one company at least had started without a single officer. When I asked whether they had held the wood, he told me: 'They hung on to near the end. I believe what happened was that the Public Schools Battalion came away at dark; and so did most of the Scotsmen. Your chaps were left there more or less alone for some time. They steadied themselves by singing. Afterwards the chaplain – R.C. of course – Father McCabe, brought the Scotsmen back. Being Glasgow Catholics, they would follow a priest where they wouldn't follow an officer. The centre of the wood was impossible for either the Germans or your fellows to hold – a terrific concentration of artillery on it. The trees were splintered to matchwood. Late that night a brigade of the Seventh Division relieved the survivors; it included your First Battalion.'

This was not altogether accurate. I know now that some men of the Public Schools Battalion, without officers or N.C.O.s, maintained their positions in the left centre of the wood, where they stayed until relieved by a brigade of the Seventh Division twenty-two hours later.

Nor did the Scots all behave badly, though I have since substantiated the flight from the wood of a great many Cameronians, and their return under Father McShane (not McCabe). Captain Colbart of the Fifth Scottish Rifles has recently written to me:

We attacked on the right; the Cameronians on the left, taking our objectives and sundry Germans. After midday I was the only officer left in our battalion. At about 9 a.m., the troops on the left fell back before a counter-attack – they didn't try to fight, as far as I saw. They were all mixed up – Cameronians, Scottish Rifles, Public Schools Battalion. The debacle was stopped in mid-wood, and my company on the right retook our objective. I was holding a strong-point at the east corner of the wood, which we had built according to orders, when the Royal Welch came up under Moodie. They attacked North-west and took the whole wood. Colonel Crawshay had his headquarters at the south corner; I reported to him there, and then rejoined my troops when the Germans counter-attacked with heavy artillery support at about 5 p.m. under heavy shell-fire.

Crawshay reported to Brigade that he had captured the wood but would not be responsible for holding it unless reinforcements came up at once. By the time these arrived, the Germans had got a footing in the North-west corner. We were relieved by the Ninety-eighth Brigade of our own Division.

That evening, the R.A.M.C. orderlies dared not lift me from the stretcher into a hospital train bunk, for fear of starting haemorrhage in the lung. So they laid the stretcher above it, with the handles resting on the head-rail and foot-rail. I had now been on the same stretcher for five days. I remember the journey as a nightmare. My back was sagging, and I could not raise my knees to relieve the cramp, the bunk above me being only a few inches away. A German flying-officer, on the other side of the carriage, with a compound fracture of the leg from an aeroplane crash, groaned and wept without a pause. Though the other wounded men cursed him, telling him to stow it and be a man, he continued pitiably, keeping everyone awake. He was not delirious – just frightened and in great pain. An orderly gave me a pencil and paper, and I wrote home to my mother: 'I am wounded, but all right.' This was July 24th, my twenty-first birthday, and also the official date of my death. She got the letter two days after that written by the colonel; mine was dated 'July 23rd', because I had lost count of days; his, the 22nd.* They could

* I cannot explain the discrepancy between his dating of my death and that of the published casualty list.

not decide whether my letter had been written just before I died and misdated, or whether I had died just after writing it. 'Died of wounds', however, seemed so much more circumstantial than 'killed' that, on receipt of a long telegram from the Army Council confirming my death, they gave me up. I found myself in No. 8 Hospital at Rouen – an ex-*château* high above the town. The next day my Aunt Susan came from the South of France to visit a South Wales Borderer nephew in the same hospital, whose leg had just been amputated. Happening to see my name listed on the door of the ward, she gave me some of the nectarines intended for him, and wrote to reassure my mother. On the 30th, Colonel Crawshay sent me a letter:

Dear von Runicke, 30.7.16

I cannot tell you how pleased I am you are alive. I was told your number was up for certain, and a letter was supposed to have come in from Field Ambulance saying you had gone under.

Well, it's good work. We had a rotten time, and after succeeding in doing practically the impossible we collected that rotten crowd and put them in their places, but directly dark came they legged it. It was too sad.

We lost heavily. It is not fair putting brave men like ours alongside that crowd. I also wish to thank you for your good work and bravery, and only wish you could have been with them. I have read of bravery but I have never seen such magnificent and wonderful disregard for death as I saw that day. It was almost uncanny – it was so great. I once heard an old officer in the Royal Welch say the men would follow you to Hell; but these chaps would bring you back and put you in a dug-out in Heaven.

Good luck and a quick recovery. I shall drink your health tonight.

'Tibs.'

I had much discomfort from the shortness of my breath; but no pain except from the finger wound, which was festering because nobody could be bothered with a slight thing like that; and from the thigh, where the sticky medical plaster, used to hold down the dressing, pulled out the hair each time it was taken off to let the wound be sterilized. I contrasted the pain and discomfort favourably with that of the operation on my nose two months previously; for which I had won no sympathy at all, because it was not a war injury. The R.A.M.C. bugling outraged me. The 'Rob All My Comrades', I complained petulantly, had taken everything I possessed, except for a few papers in my tunic-pocket, and a ring which was too tight on my finger to be pulled off; and now they mis-blew the Last Post – flatly and windily, and with the pauses in the wrong places – just to annoy me. I told an orderly to put the bugler under arrest and jump to it, or I'd report him to the senior medical officer.

Next to me lay a Royal Welch second-lieutenant named O. M. Roberts, who had joined the battalion only a few days before the show. He told me about High Wood; he had reached the fringe when he got wounded in the groin and fell into a shell-hole. Some time during the afternoon he recovered consciousness and saw a German staff officer working round the edge of the wood, killing off the wounded with an automatic pistol. Some of the Royal Welch were, apparently, not lying as still as wounded men should, but sniping. They owed the enemy a grudge: a section of Germans had pretended to surrender but, when within range, started throwing stick-bombs. The officer worked nearer. He saw Roberts move, came towards him, fired, and hit him in the arm. Roberts, very weak, tugged at his Webley. He had great difficulty in getting it out of the holster. The German fired again and missed. Roberts rested the Webley against the lip of the shell-hole and tried to pull the trigger, but lacked the strength. The German had come quite close now, to make certain of him. Roberts just managed to pull the trigger with the fingers of both hands when the German was only five paces off. The shot took the top of his head off. Roberts fainted.

The doctors had been anxiously watching my lung, as it filled with blood and pressed my heart too far away to the left of my body; the railway journey had restarted the haemorrhage. They marked its gradual progress with an indelible pencil on my skin, and said that when it reached a certain point they would have to aspirate me. This sounded a serious operation, but it simply consisted in pushing a hollow needle into my lung from the back, and drawing the blood off with a vacuum flask. They gave me a local anaesthetic; the prick hurt no worse than a vaccination, and I was reading the *Gazette de Rouen* as the blood hissed into the flask. It did not look more than half a pint.

That evening, I heard a sudden burst of lovely singing in the court-yard where the ambulances pulled up. I recognized the quality of the voices. 'The First Battalion have been in it again,' I said to Roberts; and the nurse verified this for me. It must have been their Delville Wood show.

A day or two later I sailed back to England by hospital ship.

21

I HAD wired my parents that I should be arriving at Waterloo Station the next morning. The roadway from the hospital train to a row of waiting ambulances had been roped off; as each stretcher case was lifted from the train, a huge hysterical crowd surged up to the barrier and uttered a new roar. Flags were being waved. The Somme battle seemed to be regarded at home as the beginning of the end of the war. As I looked idly at the crowd, one figure detached itself: to my embarrassment – I recognized my father, hopping about on one leg, waving an umbrella, and cheering with the best of them.

The ambulance took me to Queen Alexandra's Hospital at Highgate: Sir Alfred Mond's big house, lent for the duration of the War, and reputedly the best hospital in London. Having a private room to myself came as an unexpected luxury. What I most disliked in the Army was never being alone, forced to live and sleep with men whose company, in many cases, I would have run miles to avoid.

At Highgate, the lung healed up easily, and the doctors saved my finger. I heard here for the first time of my supposed death; the joke contributed greatly to my recovery. People with whom I had been on the worst terms during my life, wrote the most enthusiastic condolences to my mother: 'Gosh' Parry, my horrible housemaster, for instance. I have kept a letter from *The Times* advertising manager, dated August 5th, 1916:

Captain Robert Graves.
Dear Sir,
We have to acknowledge receipt of your letter with reference to the announcement contradicting the report of your death from wounds. Having regard, however, to the fact that we had previously published some biographical details, we inserted your announcement in our issue of today (Saturday) under 'Court Circular' without charge, and we have much pleasure in enclosing herewith cutting of same.

Yours, etc.

The cutting read:
Captain Robert Graves, Royal Welch Fusiliers, officially reported died of wounds, wishes to inform his friends that he is recovering from his wounds at Queen Alexandra's Hospital, Highgate, N.
Mrs Lloyd George has left London for Criccieth.

I never saw the biographical details supplied by my father; they might have been helpful here. Some letters written to me in France were returned to him, as my next-of-kin, surcharged: 'Died of wounds – present location uncertain – P. Down, Post-corporal.'

The only inconvenience caused by this death was that Cox's Bank stopped my pay, and I had difficulty in persuading it to honour my cheques. Siegfried wrote of his joy to hear I was alive again. He had been sent back to England with suspected lung trouble and felt nine parts dead from the horror of the Somme fighting. We agreed to take our leave together at Harlech when I got well enough to travel. I was able to travel in September. We met on Paddington Station. Siegfried bought a copy of *The Times* at the book-stall. As usual, we turned to the casualty list first; and found there the names of practically every officer in the First Battalion, listed as either killed or wounded. Edmund Dadd, killed; his brother Julian, in Siegfried's Company, wounded – shot through the throat, as we learned later, only able to talk in a whisper, and for months utterly prostrated. It had happened at Ale Alley near Ginchy, on September 3rd. A dud show, with the battalion out-flanked by a counter-attack. News like this in England was far more upsetting than in France. Still feeling very weak, I could not help crying all the way up to Wales. Siegfried complained bitterly: 'Well, old Stockpot got his C.B. at any rate!'

England looked strange to us returned soldiers. We could not understand the war-madness that ran wild everywhere, looking for a pseudo-military outlet. The civilians talked a foreign language; and it was newspaper language. I found serious conversation with my parents all but impossible. Quotations from a single typical document of this time will be enough to show what we were facing:

A MOTHER'S ANSWER TO
'A COMMON SOLDIER'
By A Little Mother

A Message to the Pacifists.   *A Message to the Bereaved.*
A Message to the Trenches.

Owing to the immense demand from home and from the trenches for this letter, which appeared in *The Morning Post*, the Editor found it necessary to place it in the hands of London publishers to be reprinted in pamphlet form, seventy-five thousand copies of which were sold in less than a week direct from the publishers.

'The Queen was deeply touched at the "Little Mother's" beautiful letter, and Her Majesty fully realizes what her words must mean to our soldiers in the trenches and in hospitals.'

*

To the Editor of 'The Morning Post'

Sir, – As a mother of an only child – a son who was early and eager to do his duty – may I be permitted to reply to Tommy Atkins, whose letter appeared in your issue of the 9th inst.? Perhaps he will kindly convey to his friends in the trenches, not what the Government thinks, not what the Pacifists think, but what the mothers of the British race think of our fighting men. It is a voice which demands to be heard, seeing that we play the most important part in the history of the world, for it is we who 'mother the men' who have to uphold the honour and traditions not only of our Empire but of the whole civilized world.

To the man who pathetically calls himself a 'common soldier', may I say that we women, who demand to be heard, will tolerate no such cry as 'Peace! Peace!' where there is no peace. The corn that will wave over land watered by the blood of our brave lads shall testify to the future that their blood was not spilt in vain. We need no marble monuments to remind us. We only need that force of character behind all motives to see this monstrous world tragedy brought to a victorious ending. The blood of the dead and the dying, the blood of the 'common soldier' from his 'slight wounds' will not cry to us in vain. They have all done their share, and we, as women, will do ours without murmuring and without complaint. Send the Pacifists to us and we shall very soon show them, and show the world, that in our homes at least there shall be no 'sitting at home warm and cosy in the winter, cool and "comfy" in the summer'. There is only one temperature for the women of the British race, and that is white heat. With those who disgrace their sacred trust of motherhood we have nothing in common. Our ears are not deaf to the cry that is ever ascending from the battlefield from men of flesh and blood whose indomitable courage is borne to us, so to speak, on every blast of the wind. We women pass on the human ammunition of 'only sons' to fill up the gaps, so that when the 'common soldier' looks back before going 'over the top' he may see the women of the British race at his heels, reliable, dependent, uncomplaining.

The reinforcements of women are, therefore, behind the 'common soldier'. We gentle-nurtured, timid sex did not want the war. It is no pleasure to us to have our homes made desolate and the apple of our eye taken away. We would sooner our lovable, promising, rollicking boy stayed at school. We would have much preferred to have gone on in a light-hearted way with our amusements and our hobbies. But the bugle call came, and we have hung up the tennis racquet, we've fetched our laddie from school, we've put his cap away, and we have glanced lovingly over his last report which said 'Excellent' – we've wrapped them all in a Union Jack and locked them up, to be taken out only after the war to be looked at. A 'common soldier', perhaps, did not count on the women, but they have their part to play, and *we* have risen to our responsibility. We are proud of our men, and they in turn have to be proud of us. If the men fail, Tommy Atkins, the women won't.

> *Tommy Atkins to the front,*
> *He has gone to bear the brunt.*
> *Shall 'stay-at-homes' do naught but snivel and but sigh?*
> *No, while your eyes are filling*
> *We are up and doing, willing*
> *To face the music with you – or to die!*

Women are created for the purpose of giving life, and men to take it. Now we are giving it in a double sense. It's not likely we are going to fail Tommy. We shall not flinch one iota, but when the war is over he must not grudge us, when we hear the bugle call of 'Lights out', a brief, very brief, space of time to withdraw into our secret chambers and share, with Rachel the Silent, the lonely anguish of a bereft heart, and to look once more on the college cap, before we emerge stronger women to carry on the glorious work our men's memories have handed down to us for now and all eternity.

Yours, etc.,
A Little Mother.

EXTRACTS AND PRESS CRITICISMS

'The widest possible circulation is of the utmost importance.' – *The Morning Post.*

'Deservedly attracting a great deal of attention, as expressing with rare eloquence and force the feelings with which the British wives and mothers have faced and are facing the supreme sacrifice.' – *The Morning Post.*

'Excites widespread interest.' – *The Gentlewoman.*

'A letter which has become celebrated.' – *The Star.*

'We would like to see it hung up in our wards.' – *Hospital Blue*.

'One of the grandest things ever written, for it combines a height of courage with a depth of tenderness which should be, and is, the stamp of all that is noblest and best in human nature.' – *A Soldier in France*.

'Florence Nightingale did great and grand things for the soldiers of her day, but no woman has done more than the "Little Mother", whose now famous letter in *The Morning Post* has spread like wild-fire from trench to trench. I hope to God it will be handed down in history, for nothing like it has ever made such an impression on our fighting men. I defy any man to feel weak-hearted after reading it . . . My God! she makes us die happy.' – *One who has Fought and Bled*.

'Worthy of far more than a passing notice; it ought to be reprinted and sent out to every man at the front. It is a masterpiece and fills one with pride, noble, level-headed, and pathetic to a degree.' – *Severely Wounded*.

'I have lost my two dear boys, but since I was shown the "Little Mother's" beautiful letter a resignation too perfect to describe has calmed all my aching sorrow, and I would now gladly give my sons twice over.' – *A Bereaved Mother*.

'The "Little Mother's" letter should reach every corner of the earth – a letter of the loftiest ideal, tempered with courage and the most sublime sacrifice.' – *Percival H. Monkton*.

'The exquisite letter by a "Little Mother" is making us feel prouder every day. We women desire to fan the flame which she has so superbly kindled in our hearts.' – *A British Mother of an Only Son*.

At Harlech, Siegfried and I spent the time getting our poems in order; Siegfried was at work on his *Old Huntsman*. We made a number of changes in each other's verses; I proposed amendments, which he accepted, in an obituary poem 'To His Dead Body' – written for me when he thought me dead.

We defined the war in our poems by making contrasted definitions of peace. With Siegfried it was hunting, nature, music, and pastoral scenes; with me, chiefly children. In France, I used to spend much of my spare time playing with the French children of the villages in which we were billeted. When Siegfried had gone, I began the novel on which the earlier chapters of this book are based, but soon abandoned it.

Towards the end of September, I stayed in Kent with a recently wounded First Battalion friend. An elder brother had been killed in the Dardanelles, and their mother kept the bedroom exactly as he had left it, with the sheets aired, the linen always freshly laundered, flowers and cigarettes by the bedside. She went around with a vague, bright religious look on her face. The first night I spent there, my friend and I sat up talking about the war until past twelve o'clock. His mother had gone to bed early, after urging us not to get too tired. The talk had excited me, and though I managed to fall asleep an hour later, I was continually awakened by sudden rapping noises, which I tried to disregard but which grew louder and louder. They seemed to come from everywhere. Soon sleep left me and I lay in a cold sweat. At nearly three o'clock, I heard a diabolic yell and a succession of laughing, sobbing shrieks that sent me flying to the door. In the passage I collided with the mother who, to my surprise, was fully dressed. 'It's nothing,' she said. 'One of the maids had hysterics. I'm so sorry you have been disturbed.' So I went back to bed, but could not sleep again, though the noises had stopped. In the morning I told my friend: 'I'm leaving this place. It's worse than France.' There were thousands of mothers like her, getting in touch with their dead sons by various spiritualistic means.

In November, Siegfried and I rejoined the battalion at Litherland, and shared a hut. We decided not to make any public protest against war. Siegfried said that we must 'keep up the good reputation of the poets' – as men of courage, he meant. Our best place would be back in France, away from the more shameless madness of home-service. There, our function would not be to kill Germans, though that might happen, but to make things easier for the men under our command. For them, the difference between being commanded by someone whom they could count as a friend – someone who protected them as much as he could from the grosser indignities of the military system – and having to study the whims of any petty tyrant in an officer's tunic, made all the difference in the world. By this time, the ranks of both line battalions were filled with men who had enlisted for patriotic reasons and resented the professional-soldier tradition . . . Siegfried had already shown what he meant. The Fricourt attack was rehearsed over dummy trenches in the back areas until the whole performance, having reached perfection, began to grow stale. Siegfried, ordered to rehearse once more on the day before the attack, led his platoon into a wood and instead read to them – nothing military or literary, just the *London Mail*. Though the *London Mail*, a daring new popular weekly, was hardly in his line, Siegfried thought that the men would enjoy the '*Things We Want To Know*' column.

Officers of the Royal Welch were honorary members of the Formby Golf Club. Siegfried and I went there often. He played golf seriously, while I hit a ball alongside him. I had once played at Harlech as a junior member of the Royal St David's, but resigned when I found it bad for my temper. Afraid of taking the game up again seriously, I now limited myself to a single iron. My mis-hits did not matter. I played the fool and purposely put Siegfried off his game. This was a time of great food shortage; German submarines sank about every fourth food ship, and strict meat, butter, and sugar ration had been imposed. But the war had not reached the links. The leading Liverpool businessmen were members of the club, and did not mean to go short while there was any food at all coming in at the docks. Siegfried and I went to the club-house for lunch on the day before Christmas, and found a cold-buffet in the club dining-room, offering hams, barons of beef, jellied tongues, cold roast turkey, and chicken. A large, meaty-faced waiter presided. Siegfried asked him sarcastically: 'Is this all? There doesn't seem to be quite such a good spread as in previous years.' The waiter blushed. 'No, sir, this isn't quite up to the usual mark, sir, but we are expecting a more satisfactory consignment of meat on Boxing Day.' The dining-room at the club-house was always full, the links practically deserted.

We officers of the Mersey garrison made the Adelphi Hotel our favourite rendezvous. It had a swimming bath, and a cocktail bar generally crowded with very drunk Russian naval officers. One day, I met a major of the King's Own Scottish Borderers there. I saluted him. Taking me aside, he muttered confidentially: 'It's nice of you to salute me, my boy, but I must confess that I am not what I seem. I wear a crown on my sleeve, and so does a C.S.M.; but then he's not entitled to wear these three cuff-bands and the wavy border. Aren't they pretty? No, I'm not what I seem to be. I'm a sham. I've got a sergeant-major's stomach.' Accustomed by now to drunken senior officers, I answered respectfully: 'Really, sir, and how did you come to acquire that?' He said: 'You think I'm drunk. Well, perhaps I am, but it's true about my stomach. You see, I got shot in the guts at the Beaumont-Hamel show. It hurt like hell, let me tell you. They took me down to the field-hospital. I was busy dying; but a company sergeant-major had got it through the head, and *he* was busy dying, too; and he did die. Well, as soon as ever the sergeant-major died, they took out that long gut, whatever you call the thing, the thing that unwinds – they say it's as long as a cricket pitch – and they put it into me, grafted it on somehow. Wonderful chaps these medicos! They supply spare parts as though one were a motor-car . . . Well, this sergeant-major seems to have been an abstemious man. The lining of the new gut is much better than my old one; so I'm celebrating it. I only wish I'd borrowed his kidneys, too.'

An R.A.M.C. captain, sitting close by, broke into the conversation. 'Yes, major, a stomach wound's the worst of the lot. You were lucky to reach the field-ambulance alive. The best chance is to lie absolutely still. I got mine out between the lines, while I was bandaging a fellow. I flopped into a shell-hole. My stretcher-bearers wanted to carry me back, but I wouldn't have any of that. I kept everyone off with a revolver for forty-eight hours, and saved my own life. I couldn't count on a spare gut waiting for me at the dressing-station. My only chance was to lie still and let it heal.'

In December, I attended a medical board; they sounded my chest and asked how I was feeling. The president wanted to know whether I wanted a few months more home-service. I said: 'No, sir, I should be much obliged if you would pass me fit for service overseas.' In January I got my sailing orders.

I went back an old soldier, as my kit and baggage proved. I had reduced the original Christmas-tree to a pocket-torch with a fourteen-day battery, and a pair of insulated wire-cutters strong enough to cut German wire (the ordinary Army issue would cut only British wire). Instead of a haversack, I bought a pack like the ones carried by the men, but lighter and waterproof. I had lost my revolver when wounded and not bought another; a rifle and bayonet could always be got from the battalion. (Not carrying rifle and bayonet made officers conspicuous during an attack; in most divisions now they carried them; and also wore trousers rolled down over their puttees, like the men, instead of riding-breeches – because the Germans had learned to recognize officers by their thin knees.) The heavy blankets I had brought out before were now replaced by an eiderdown sleeping-bag in an oiled-silk cover. I also took a Shakespeare and a Bible, both printed on India paper, a Catullus and a Lucretius in Latin; and two light-weight folding canvas arm-chairs – one as a present for Yates, the quartermaster, the other for myself. I wore a very thick whip-cord tunic, with a neat patch above the second button and another between the shoulders – my only salvage from the last time out, except for the reasonably waterproof pair of ski-ing boots, in which also I had been killed – my breeches had been cut off me in hospital.

I commanded a draft of ten young officers. Young officers, at this period, were expected, as someone has noted in his war-memoirs, to be roistering blades over wine and women. These ten did their best. Three of them got venereal disease at the Rouen Blue Lamp. They were strictly brought-up Welsh boys of the professional classes, had never hitherto visited a brothel, and knew nothing about prophylactics. One of them shared a hut with me. He came in very late and very drunk one night, from the *Drapeau Blanc*, woke me up and began telling me about his experiences. 'I never knew before,' he said, 'what a wonderful thing sex is!'

I said irritably, and in some disgust: 'The *Drapeau Blanc*? Then I hope to God you washed yourself.'

He was very Welsh, and on his dignity. 'What do you mean, captain? I did wass my fa-ace and ha-ands.'

There were no restraints in France; these boys had money to spend and knew that they stood a good chance of being killed within a few weeks anyhow. They did not want to die virgins. The *Drapeau Blanc* saved the life of scores by incapacitating them for future trench service. Base venereal hospitals were always crowded. The troops took a lewd delight in exaggerating the proportion of army chaplains to combatant officers treated there.

At the Bull Ring, the instructors were full of bullet-and-bayonet enthusiasm, with which they tried to infect the drafts. The drafts consisted, for the most part, either of forcibly enlisted men, or wounded men returning; and at this dead season of the year could hardly be expected to feel enthusiastic on their arrival. The training principles had recently been revised. *Infantry Training, 1914*, laid it down politely that the soldier's ultimate aim was to put out of action or render ineffective the armed forces of the enemy. The War Office no longer considered this statement direct enough for a war of attrition. Troops learned instead that they must HATE the Germans, and KILL as many of them as possible. In bayonet-practice, the men had to make horrible grimaces and utter blood-curdling yells as they charged. The instructors' faces were set in a permanent ghastly grin. 'Hurt him, now! In at the belly! Tear his guts out!' they would scream, as the men charged the dummies. 'Now that upper swing at his privates with the butt. Ruin his chances for life! No more little Fritzes!... Naaoh! Anyone would think that you *loved* the bloody swine, patting and stroking 'em like that! BITE HIM, I SAY! STICK YOUR TEETH IN HIM AND WORRY HIM! EAT HIS HEART OUT!'

Once more I felt glad to be sent up to the trenches.

22

I FOUND the Second Battalion near Bouchavesnes on the Somme, but a very different Second Battalion. No riding-school, no battalion mess, no Quetta manners, no regular officers, except for a couple of newly arrived Sandhurst boys. I was more warmly welcomed this time; my supposed spying activities had been forgotten. But the day before I reported, Colonel Crawshay had been wounded while out in No Man's Land inspecting the battalion wire: shot in the thigh by one of the 'rotten crowd' of his letter, who mistook him for a German and fired without challenging. He has been in and out of nursing homes ever since.

Doctor Dunn asked me with kindly disapproval what I meant by returning so soon. I said: 'I couldn't stand England any longer.' He told the acting C.O. that I was, in his opinion, unfit for trench service, so I took command of the headquarter company and went to live with transport, back at Frises, where the Somme made a bend. My company consisted of regimental clerks, cooks, tailors, shoemakers, pioneers, transport men, and so on, who in a break-through could turn riflemen and be used as a combatant force, as at the First Battle of Ypres. We lived in dug-outs, close to the river, which was frozen over completely but for a narrow stretch of fast-running water in the middle. I have never been so cold in all my life. I used to go up to the trenches every night with the rations, Yates being sick; it was about a twelve-mile walk there and back.

General Pinney, now commanding the Thirty-third Division, felt teetotal convictions on behalf of his men and stopped their issue of rum, unless in emergencies; the immediate result being the heaviest sick-list that the battalion had ever known. Our men looked forward to their tot of rum at the dawn stand-to as the brightest moment of the twenty-four hours; when this was denied them, their resistance weakened. I took the rations up through Cléry, not long before a wattle-and-daub village with some hundreds of inhabitants. The highest part of it now standing was a short course of brick wall about three feet high; the remainder consisted of enormous overlapping shell-craters. A broken-down steamroller by the roadside had 'CLÉRY' chalked on it as a guide to travellers. We often lost a horse or two at Cléry, which the Germans went on shelling from habit.

Our reserve billets for these Bouchavesnes trenches were at Suzanne: not really billets, but dug-outs and shelters. Suzanne also lay in ruins. This winter was the hardest since 1894–5. The men played inter-company football matches on the river, now frozen two feet thick. I remember a meal here, in a shelter-billet: stew and tinned tomatoes on aluminium plates. Though the food arrived hot from the kitchen next-door, ice had formed on the edge of our plates before we finished eating. In all this area one saw no French civilians, no unshelled houses, no signs of cultivation. The only living creatures besides soldiers, horses, and mules, were a few moorhen and duck paddling in the unfrozen central stream of the river. The fodder ration for the horses, many of them sick, was down to three pounds a day, and they had open standings only. I have kept no records of this time, but the memory of its misery survives.

Then I got toothache, which forced me to take a horse and ride twenty miles to the nearest army dental station at corps headquarters. I found the dentist under the weather, like everyone else. He would do nothing at first but grumble what a fool he had been to offer his services to the King at such a low salary. 'When I think,' he complained, 'of the terrible destruction to the nation's teeth now being done by unqualified men at home, and the huge fees that they exact for their wicked work, it makes me boil with rage.' There followed further complaints against his treatment at headquarters, and the unwillingness of the R.A.M.C. to give dentists any promotion beyond lieutenant's rank. Later he examined my tooth. 'An abscess,' he said. 'No good tinkering about with this; must pull it out.' So he yanked at the tooth irritably, and the crown broke off. He tried again, damning the ineffective type of forceps which the Government supplied, found very little purchase, and broke off another piece. After half an hour he had dug the tooth out in sections. The local anaesthetic supplied by the Government seemed as ineffective as the forceps. I rode home with lacerated gums.

Brigade appointed me a member of a field general court-martial that was to sit on an Irish sergeant charged with 'shamefully casting away his arms in the presence of the enemy'. I had heard about the case unofficially; the man, maddened by an intense bombardment, had thrown away his rifle and run with the rest of his platoon. An army order, secret and confidential, addressed to officers of captain's rank and above, laid down that, in the case of men tried for their life on other charges, sentence might be mitigated if conduct in the field had been exemplary; but cowardice was punishable only with death, and no medical excuses could be accepted. Therefore I saw no choice between sentencing the man to death and refusing to take part in the proceedings. If I refused, I should be court-martialled myself, and a reconstituted court would sentence the sergeant to death anyhow. Yet I could not sign a death-verdict for an offence which I might have committed myself in similar circumstances. I evaded the dilemma. One other officer in the battalion, besides the acting C.O., had the necessary year's service as a captain entitling him to sit on a field general court-martial. I found him willing enough to take my place. He was hard-boiled and glad of a trip to Amiens, and I took over his duties.

Executions were frequent in France. I had my first direct experience of official lying when I arrived at Le Havre in May 1915, and read the back-files of army orders at the rest camp. They contained something like twenty reports of men shot for cowardice or desertion; yet a few days later the responsible minister in the House of Commons, answering a question from a pacifist, denied that sentence of death for a military offence had been carried out in France on any member of His Majesty's Forces.

James Cuthbert, the acting C.O., a Special Reserve major, felt the strain badly and took a lot of whisky. Dr Dunn pronounced him too sick to be in the trenches; so he came to Frises, where he shared a dug-out with Yates and myself. Sitting in my arm-chair, reading the Bible, I stumbled on the text: 'The bed is too narrow to lie therein and the coverlet too small to wrap myself therewith.' 'Listen, James,' I said, 'here's something pretty appropriate for this dug-out.' I read it out.

He raised himself on an elbow, genuinely furious. 'Look here, von Runicke,' he shouted, 'I am not a religious man. I've cracked a good many of the commandments since I've been in France; but while I'm in command here I refuse to hear you, or anyone bloody else blaspheme the Bible!'

I liked James, whom I had first met on the day I arrived at Wrexham to join the Regiment. He was then just back from Canada, and how hilariously he threw the chairs about in the junior anteroom of the mess! He had been driving a plough through virgin soil, he told us, and reciting Kipling to the prairie-dogs. His favourite piece was (I may be misquoting):

> Are ye there, are ye there, are ye there?
> Four points on a ninety-mile square –
> With a helio winking like fun in the sun,
> Are ye there, are ye there, are ye there?

James, who had served with the Special Reserve a year or two before he emigrated, cared for nobody, was most courageous, inclined to sentimentality, and probably saw longer service with the Second Battalion in the war than any officer except Yates.

A day or two later, because James was still sick, I found myself in temporary command of the battalion, and attended a commanding officers' conference at brigade headquarters – 'that it should ever have come to this!' I thought. Opposite our trenches a German salient protruded, and the brigadier wanted to 'bite it off' in proof of the division's offensive spirit. Trench soldiers could never understand the Staff's desire to bite off an enemy salient. It was hardly desirable to be fired at from both flanks; if the Germans had got caught in a salient, our obvious duty must be to keep them there as long as they could be persuaded to stay. We concluded that a passion for straight lines, for which headquarters were well known, had dictated this plan, which had no strategic or tactical excuse. The attack had been twice postponed, and twice cancelled. I still have a field-message referring to it, dated February 21st (see next page).

Even this promise of special rum could not, however, hearten the battalion. Everyone agreed that the attack was unnecessary, foolish, and impossible. A thaw had now set in, and the four company commanders assured me that to cross three hundred yards of No Man's Land, which constant shelling and the thaw had turned into a morass of mud more than knee-deep, would take even lightly armed troops four or five minutes. Not a man would be able to reach the enemy lines so long as a single section of Germans with rifles remained to defend them.

Please	cancel	Form 4	of	my
AA 202	units	will	draw	from
19th	brigade	B. Echelon	the	following
issue	of	rum	which	will
be	issued	to	troops	taking
part	in	the	forth	coming
operations	at	the	discretion	of
O.C.	units	2nd R.W.F.	7 1/2	gallons.

The general, when I arrived, inquired in a fatherly way whether I were not proud to be attending a commanding officers' conference at the age of twenty-one. I answered irritably that I had not examined my feelings, but that I was an old enough soldier to realize the impossibility of the attack. The colonel of the Cameronians, who were also to be engaged, took the same line. So the brigadier finally called off the show. That night, I went up with rations as usual; the officers were much relieved to hear of my stand at the conference.

We had been heavily shelled on the way, and while I took a drink at battalion headquarters, someone sent me a message about a direct hit on 'D' Company limber. Going off to inspect the damage, I passed our chaplain, who had come up with me from Frises Bend, and a group of three or four men. The chaplain was gabbling the burial service over a corpse lying on the ground covered with a waterproof sheet – the miserable weather and fear of the impending attack were responsible for his death. This, as it turned out, was the last dead man I saw in France and, like the first, he had shot himself.

I found the shattered limber, and remains of the petrol tins, full of water, which it was carrying, but no sign of the team. They were highly valued horses, having won a prize offered at a divisional horse show some months previously for the best-matched pair. So Meredith the transport sergeant and I sent the transport back, and went looking for the horses in the dark. We stumbled through miles of morass that night, but could not find hoof or hide of them. We used to boast that our transport animals were the best in France, and our transport men the best horse-thieves. No less than eighteen of our stable had been stolen from other units at one time or another, for their good looks. We even had 'borrowed' two from the Scots Greys. The horse I rode to the dentist came from the French police; its only fault being that, as the left-hand horse of a police squadron, it always pulled to the wrong side of the road. We had never lost a horse to any other battalion; so, naturally, Sergeant Meredith and I, who had started out with the rations at four o'clock in the afternoon, continued our search until long after midnight. When we reached Frises at 3 a.m. I collapsed on my bunk, completely exhausted.

The next day, Dr Dunn diagnosed bronchitis, and I went back in an ambulance to Rouen, once more to No. 8 Red Cross Hospital. The R.A.M.C. major recognized me and said: 'What on earth are *you* doing out in France, young man? If I find you and those lungs of yours in my hospital again, I'll have you court-martialled.'

Yates wrote to reassure me that the horses had been found shortly after I left – unhurt except for grazes on their bellies, and in possession of the Fourth Division machine-gun company. The machine-gunners were caught disguising them with stain, and trying to remove the regimental marks.

At Rouen they asked me where in England I should like to be hospitalized. I said, at random: 'Oxford.'

23

So I was sent to Oxford: to Somerville College which, like the Examination Schools, had been converted into a hospital. It occurred to me here that I had perhaps finished with the war, which would surely not last long now. I both liked and disliked the idea. I disliked being away from the regiment in France, but I liked to believe that I might still be alive when the war ended. Meanwhile, Siegfried had got boarded too and tried to follow me to the Second Battalion; but arrived only to find me gone. I felt that I had somehow let him down. But he wrote that he was unspeakably relieved to think of me safely back home.

We were now wondering whether the war ought to continue. It was said that, in the autumn of 1915, Asquith had been offered peace terms on the basis of *status quo ante*, which he was willing to consider; but that his colleagues' opposition had brought about the fall of the Liberal Government and its supersession by the 'Win-the-War' Coalition Government of Lloyd George. Siegfried vehemently asserted that the terms should have been accepted; I agreed. We no longer saw the war as one between trade-rivals: its continuance seemed merely a sacrifice of the idealistic younger generation to the stupidity and self-protective alarm of the elder. I made a facetious note about this time:

War should be a sport for men above forty-five only, the Jesses, not the Davids. 'Well, dear father, how proud I am of you serving your country as a very gallant gentleman prepared to make even the supreme sacrifice! I only wish I were your age: how willingly would I buckle on my armour and fight those unspeakable Philistines! As it is, of course, I can't be spared; I have to stay behind at the War Office and administrate for you lucky old men. What sacrifices I have made!' David would sigh, when the old boys had gone off with a draft to the front, singing *Tipperary*: 'There's father and my Uncle Salmon, and both my grandfathers all on active service. I must put a card in the window about it.'

Deciding to stay in Oxford, I applied, on the strength of a chit from Currie the Bull Ring commandant at Harfleur, for an instructional job in one of the Officer-Cadet Battalions quartered in the men's colleges. They posted me to the Wadham Company of No. 4 Battalion. These battalions had grown out of instructional schools for young officers. The cadet course was three months – later increased to four – but a severe one, and particularly intended for the training of platoon commanders in the handling of the platoon as an independent unit. About two-thirds of the cadets had been recommended for commissions in France by battalion commanders, the remainder being public school boys from the O.T.C.

We taught drill and musketry, and 'conduct befitting officers and gentlemen', but chiefly tactical exercises with limited objectives. The Army Text-book S.S. 143, or *Instructions for the training of platoons for offensive action*, *1917*, perhaps the most important War Office publication issued during the war, was our stand-by. The author is said to have been General Solly-Flood, who wrote it after a visit to a French Army School. Since 1916, the largest body of infantrymen possible to control in sustained action had been the platoon – which now superseded the company as the chief tactical unit.

Though the quality of the officers had deteriorated from the regimental point of view, their greater efficiency in action amply compensated for their deficiency in manners. The cadet-battalion system saved the army in France from becoming a mere rabble. We failed about a sixth of the candidates for commissions; the failures were sometimes public-school boys without the necessary toughness, but usually men from France, recommended on compassionate grounds – rather stupid platoon-sergeants and machine-gun corporals who had been out too long and needed a rest. Our final selection was made by watching the candidates play games, principally rugger and soccer. Those who played rough but not dirty, and had quick reactions, were the sort needed, and we spent most of our spare time playing games with them.

My platoon consisted of New Zealanders, Canadians, South Africans, two men from the Fiji Island contingent, an English farm labourer, a Welsh miner, and two or three public-school boys. Most of them were killed during the next year and a half of war. The New Zealanders went in for rowing; the record time for the river at Oxford was made by a New Zealand eight that summer. Hard work in the damp Oxford climate, however, proved too much for my lungs. I kept myself going for two months on a strychnine tonic, then fainted and fell down a staircase one evening in the dark, cutting my head; I was taken back to Somerville.

The Wadham dons had elected me a member of the senior common-room, which gave me access to the famous brown sherry which is especially mentioned in a Latin grace among the blessings vouchsafed to the Collegians by their Creator. My commanding officer, Colonel Stenning, in better times University Professor of Hebrew, was a fellow of the college. The social system at Oxford had been dislocated. Mr J. V. Powell, the St John's don destined to be my moral tutor when I came up, now wore the grey uniform of a corporal in the General Reserve, drilled in the parks, and saluted me whenever we met. A college scout held a commission, and was instructing in the other cadet-battalion. There cannot have been more than a hundred and fifty undergraduates in residence at this time: American Rhodes Scholars, Indians, and the unfit. I saw a good deal of Aldous Huxley, Wilfred Childe, and Thomas Earp who, together, ran an undergraduates' literary paper of necessarily limited circulation, called *The Palatine Review*, to which I contributed. Earp had set himself the task of keeping the Oxford tradition alive through the dead years – as president and sole member, he said, of some seventeen undergraduate social and literary societies. In 1919, still in residence, he handed over the minute-books to the returning university. Most of the societies were then re-formed.

I enjoyed my stay at Somerville. The sun shone, and the discipline was easy. We used to lounge around the hospital grounds in our pyjamas and dressing-gowns, and sometimes walked out into St Giles's and down the Cornmarket (still in pyjamas and dressing-gowns) for a morning cup of coffee at the Cadena. And I fell in love with Marjorie, a probationer nurse, though I did not tell her so at the time. My heart had remained whole, if numbed, since Dick's disappearance from it, yet I felt difficulty in adjusting myself to the experience of woman love. I used to meet Marjorie, who was a professional pianist, when I visited a friend in another ward; but we had little talk together, except once when she confided in me how beastly a time the other nurses gave her – for having a naturalized German father. I wrote to her after I had left hospital, but finding that she was engaged to a subaltern in France, I stopped writing. I had seen what it must feel like to be in France and have a rival at home. Yet her reproofs of my silence suggested that she was at least as fond of me as of him. I did not press the point, but let the affair end almost before it started.

While with the cadet-battalion, I went out nearly every Sunday to the village of Garsington. Siegfried's friends, Philip and Lady Ottoline Morrell, lived at the manor house there. The Morrells were pacifists, and I first heard from them that there was another side to the question of war guilt. Clive Bell, England's leading art critic and a conscientious objector, looked after the cows on the manor farm; he had been allowed to do this 'work of national importance' instead of going into the army. Aldous Huxley, Lytton Strachey, and the Hon. Bertrand Russell were frequent visitors. Aldous was unfit, otherwise he would certainly have been in the army like Osbert and Sacheverell Sitwell, Herbert Read, Siegfried, Wilfred Owen, myself, and most other young writers of the time, none of whom now believed in the war.

Bertrand Russell, too old for military service, but an ardent pacifist (a rare combination), turned sharply on me one afternoon and asked: 'Tell me, if a company of your men were brought along to break a strike of munition makers, and the munition makers refused to go back to work, would you order the men to fire?'

'Yes, if everything else failed. It would be no worse than shooting Germans, really.'

He asked in surprise: 'Would your men obey you?'

'They loathe munition-workers, and would be only too glad of a chance to shoot a few. They think that they're all skrim-shankers.'

'But they realize that the war's all wicked nonsense?'

'Yes, as well as I do.'

He could not understand my attitude.

Lytton Strachey was unfit, but instead of allowing himself to be rejected by the doctors preferred to appear before a military tribunal as a conscientious objector. He told us of the extraordinary impression caused by an air-cushion which he inflated in court as a protest against the hardness of the benches. Asked by the chairman the usual question: 'I understand, Mr Strachey, that you have a conscientious objection to war?', he replied (in his curious falsetto voice): 'Oh, no, not at all, only to *this* war.' And to the chairman's other stock question, which had previously never failed to embarrass the claimant: 'Tell me, Mr Strachey, what would you do if you saw a German soldier trying to violate your sister?' he replied with an air of noble virtue: 'I would try to get between them.'

In 1916, I met more well-known writers than ever before or since. There were two unsuccessful meetings. George Moore had recently written *The Brook Kerith*, and my neurasthenic twitchings interrupted the calm, easy flow of his conversational periods. He told me irritably not to fidget; in return I taunted him with having introduced cactus into the Holy Land some fifteen centuries before the discovery of America, its land of origin.

At the Reform Club, H. G. Wells, who was 'Mr Britling' in those days, and full of military optimism, talked without listening. He had just been taken for a 'Cook's Tour' to France, and staff-conductors had shown him the usual sights that royalty, prominent men of letters, and influential neutrals were allowed to see. He described his experience at length, and seemed unaware that I and Siegfried, who was with me, had also seen the sights.

But I liked Arnold Bennett for his kindly unpretentiousness; and I liked Augustine Birrell, who had been Asquith's Lord Lieutenant of Ireland. I dared correct him when he remarked that the Apocrypha was never read in church services; and again, when he described Elihu the Jebusite as one of Job's comforters. Birrell tried to override me on both points, but I called for a Bible and proved them.

He glowered very kindly at me: 'I will say to you what Thomas Carlyle once said to a young man who caught him out in a misquotation: "Young man, you are heading straight for the pit of Hell!"'

And who else? John Galsworthy; or did I first meet him a year or two later? He was editing a literary magazine called *Reveille*, published under Government auspices, the proceeds of which were to go to a disabled-soldier fund. I contributed to it. When we met, he asked me technical questions about soldier-slang – he was writing a war-play and wanted it to be accurate. He seemed a humble man and, except for these questions, listened without talking; which is, apparently, his usual practice.

I met Ivor Novello, in 1918, two years older than myself, and already world-famous as the author and composer of the patriotic song:

> *Keep the home fires burning*
> *While the hearts are yearning . . .*

There was some talk of his setting a song of mine. I found him wearing a silk dressing-gown, in an atmosphere of incense and cocktails. He and his young stage-friends were all sitting or lying on cushions scattered about the floor. Feeling uncomfortably military, I removed my spurs (I was a temporary field-officer at the time) in case anyone got pricked. Novello had joined the Royal Navy Air Service but, his genius being officially recognized, was allowed to keep the home fires burning until the boys came home . . .

The War Office now stopped the privilege that officers enjoyed, after leaving hospital, of going to their own homes for convalescence. It had been noticed that many of them took no trouble to get well and return to duty; they kept late nights, drank, and overtaxed their strength. Therefore, when somewhat recovered, I was sent to a convalescent home in the Isle of Wight – none other than Osborne Palace; my bedroom had once been the royal night-nursery of King Edward VII and his brothers and sisters. This was the strawberry season and fine weather; we patients could take all Queen Victoria's favourite walks through the woods and along the quiet seashore, play billiards in the royal billiard-room, sing bawdy songs in the royal music-room, drink the Prince Consort's favourite Rhine wines among his Winterhalters, play golf-croquet, and visit Cowes when in need of adventure. We were made honorary members of the

Royal Yacht Squadron. Another of the caricature scenes of my life: myself as pseudo-yachtsman, sitting in a leather chair in the smoking-room of what had been, and is now again, the most exclusive club in the world, drinking gin and ginger, and sweeping the Solent with a powerful telescope.

I made friends with the French Benedictine Fathers, who lived near by. Driven from Solesmes in France by the anti-clerical laws of 1906, they had built themselves a new abbey at Quarr. The abbey had a special commission from the Vatican to collect and edit ancient church music. Hearing the fathers at their plain-song made me for the moment forget the war completely. Many of them were ex-Army officers who, I was told, had turned to religion after the ardours of campaign or disappointments in love. They saw the war as a dispensation of God for restoring France to Catholicism, and told me that the Freemason element in the French Army, represented by General 'Papa' Joffre, had now been discredited, and that the present Supreme Command, Foch's, was predominantly Catholic – an augury, they claimed of Allied victory.

The Guest-master showed me a library of twenty thousand volumes, hundreds of them black-letter. The librarian, an old monk from Béthune, begged me for an accurate account of the damage done to his quarter of the town. The Guest-master asked whether I should like to read any of the books. There were all kinds: history, botany, music, architecture, engineering, almost every other lay subject. I asked him whether they had a poetry section. He smiled kindly and said, no, poetry could not be regarded as improving.

The Father Superior inquired whether I were a *bon catholique*.

I replied politely, that, no, I did not belong to the 'true religion'. To spare him a confession of agnosticism, I explained that my parents were Protestants.

'But if ours is the true religion, why do you not turn Catholic?' He asked the question so simply that I felt ashamed.

Having to put him off somehow, I said: 'Reverend Father, we have a proverb in England, never to swap horses while crossing a stream. I am still caught up in the war, you know.'

When he looked disappointed, I offered him: '*Peut-être après la guerre*' – the stock-answer that the Pas de Calais girls were ordered by their priests to give Allied soldiers who asked for a '*Promenade, mademoiselle?*' It was seldom given, I heard, except for the purpose of bargaining.

All the same, I half-envied the Fathers (finished with wars and love-affairs) their abbey on the hill, and admired their kindness, gentleness, and seriousness. Those clean, whitewashed cells and meals eaten in silence at the long oaken tables, while a novice read *The Lives of the Saints*! The food, mostly cereals, vegetables, and fruit, was the best I had tasted for years – I had eaten enough ration beef, ration jam, ration bread, and cheese to last me a lifetime. At Quarr, Catholicism ceased to repel me.

Many of the patients at Osborne were neurasthenic and should have been in a special neurasthenic hospital. A. A. Milne was there, as a subaltern in the Royal Warwickshire Regiment, and in his least humorous vein. One Vernon Bartlett, of the Hampshire Regiment, decided with me that something new must be started. So we founded the 'Royal Albert Society', its pretended aim being to revive interest in the life and times of the Prince Consort. My regalia as president consisted of a Scottish dirk, Hessian boots, and a pair of side-whiskers. Official business might not proceed until the announcement had been duly made that 'The whiskers are on the table'. Membership was open only to officers who professed themselves students of the life and works of the Prince Consort; those who had been born in the province of Alberta in Canada; those who had resided for six months or longer by the banks of the Albert Nyanza; those who held the Albert Medal for saving life; or those who were linked with the Prince Consort's memory in any other signal way. This must have been the first of the now popular burlesques of Victorianism. The members were instructed to report at each meeting reminiscences collected from old palace-servants and Osborne cottagers, throwing light on the human side of the Consort's life. We had fifteen members and ate quantities of strawberries.

On one occasion, a dozen officers came in to join the society, professing to have the necessary qualifications. One claimed to be the grandson of the man who had built the Albert Memorial; one had worked at the Albert Docks; and one actually did possess the Albert Medal for saving life; the others were all interested students. They submitted quietly at first to the ceremonies and business, but it was soon apparent that they had come to break up the society; they were, in fact, most of them drunk. They began giving indecent accounts of the Prince Consort's private life, alleging that they could substantiate them with photographic evidence. Bartlett and I got worried; it was not that sort of society. Therefore, as president, I

208

rose and told in an improved version the story which had won the 1914 All-England Inter-regimental Competition at Aldershot for the filthiest story of the year. I linked it up with the Prince Consort by saying that he had heard it from the lips of John Brown, the Balmoral ghillie, in whose pawky humour Queen Victoria used to find such delight; and that, having prevented him from sleeping for three days and nights, it had been a contributory cause of his premature death. The interrupters threw up their hands, in shocked surrender, and walked out. It struck me how far I had come since my first years at Charterhouse. If only I had used the same technique there!

On the beach one day, Bartlett and I found an old ship's fender. Because the knotted ropes at the top had frayed into something resembling hair, Bartlett said, sighing: 'Poor fellow, I knew him well. He was in my platoon in the Hampshires, but went mad and jumped overboard from the hospital ship.' A little farther along the beach, we found an old pair of trousers half in the water, and a coat, and then some socks and a boot. So we dressed up Bartlett's old comrade, draped sea-weed over him where necessary, and walked on. Soon after, we met a coastguard and turned back with him. We said: 'There's a dead man on the beach.' He stopped a few yards off, and exclaimed, holding his nose: 'Pooh, don't he 'alf stink!' We turned again, leaving the coastguard with the dead, and the next day read in the Isle of Wight paper of a hoax that certain 'convalescent officers at Osborne' had played on the coroner. Among our laboriously nonsensical games was one of changing the labels on all the pictures in the galleries. Anything to make people laugh. But we found the going hard.

24

SIEGFRIED had written in March 1917 from the Second Battalion, asking me to pull myself together and send him a letter because he felt horribly low in spirits. He complained of his welcome there. The battalion was now restocked with senior officers, and my enemy, the Special Reserve second-lieutenant with the regular commission, now an acting-captain, had gone so far as to call him a bloody wart, and allude to the bloody First Battalion. Siegfried swallowed the insult, but tried to get transferred to the First Battalion.

The Second was resting until the end of the month about two miles from our beloved Morlancourt, surrounded by billows of mud slopes and muddy woods and aerodromes, and fine new railroads where he used to lollop about on the black mare of an afternoon. (David Thomas and I once watched Siegfried breaking in that black mare, a beautiful combative creature with a homicidal kink, and wondered at his patience. He would put the mare at a jump and, when she sulked, not force her but simply turn her around and then lead her back to it. Time after time she refused, yet could neither provoke his ill-temper nor make him give up his intention. Finally she took the jump in mere boredom – a six-footer, and she could manage higher than that.)

He was posted to 'C' Company now, he wrote, with a half-witted platoon awaiting his orders to do or die, and a beast of a stiff arm where Dr Dunn had inoculated him, sticking his needle in and saying: 'Toughest skin of the lot, but you're a tough character, I know.' Siegfried hoped that the battalion would get into some sort of a show soon; it would be a relief after all these weeks of irritation and discomfort and disappointment. (One usually felt like that in the Second Battalion.) He supposed that his *Old Huntsman* would not be published until the autumn. He had seen the last issue of *The Nation*, and commented what fun it was for us two to appear as a military duet in a pacifist organ. 'You and me, the poets who mean to work together some day and scandalize the jolly old Gosses and Stracheys.' (Re-reading this letter, I am reminded that the occasion of my final breach with Siegfried, ten years later, was my failure to observe the proper literary punctilios in a correspondence with the late Sir Edmund Gosse, C.B. And that, when the *Old Huntsman* appeared, Sir Edmund had severely criticized some lines of an allegorical poem in it:

> . . . *Rapture and pale Enchantment and Romance*
> *And many a slender sickly lord who'd filled*
> *My soul long since with lutanies of sin*
> *Went home because he could not stand the din.*

This, he considered, might be read as a libel on the British House of Lords. The peerage, he said, was proving itself splendidly heroic in the war.)

Heavy fighting in the Hindenburg Line broke out soon afterwards. Siegfried's platoon went to support the Cameronians, and when these were driven out of some trenches they had won, he regained the position with a bombing-party of six men. Though shot through the throat, he continued bombing until he collapsed. The Cameronians rallied and returned, and the brigadier sent Siegfried's name in for a Victoria Cross – a recommendation refused, however, on the ground that the operations had been unsuccessful; for the Cameronians were later driven out again by a bombing-party under some German Siegfried.

Back in London now, and very ill, he wrote that often when he went for a walk he saw corpses lying about on the pavements. In April, Yates had sent him a note saying that four officers were killed and seven wounded in a show at Fontaine-les-Croiselles – a 'perfectly bloody battle'. But the battalion advanced nearly half a mile which, to Siegfried, seemed some consolation. Yet in the very next sentence he wrote how mad it made him to think of the countless good men being slaughtered that summer, and all for nothing. The bloody politicians and ditto generals with their cursed incompetent blundering and callous ideas would go on until they tired of it or had got as much kudos as they wanted. He wished he could do something in protest, but even if he were to shoot the Premier or Sir Douglas Haig, they would only shut him up in a mad-house like Richard Dadd of glorious memory. (I recognized the allusion. Dadd, a brilliant nineteenth-century painter, and incidentally a great-uncle of Edmund and Julian, had made out a list of people who deserved to be killed. The first on the list was his father. Dadd picked him up one day in Hyde Park and carried him on his shoulders for nearly half a mile before publicly drowning him in the Serpentine.) Siegfried went on to say that if, as a protest, he refused to go out again, they would only accuse him of being afraid of shells. He asked me whether I thought we should be any better off by the end of that summer of carnage. We would never break the German line by hammering at it. So far our losses were heavier than the Germans'. The Canadians at Vimy had suffered appallingly, yet the official *communiqués* told unblushing lies about the casualties. Julian Dadd had visited him in hospital and, like everyone else, urged him to take a safe job at home – but he knew that this could only be a beautiful dream: he would be morally compelled to go on until he got killed. The thought of going back now was agony, just when he had come out into the light again – 'Oh, life, oh, sun!' (A quotation from a poem of mine about my return from the grave.) His wound was nearly healed, and he expected to be sent for three weeks to a convalescent home. He didn't like the idea, but *anywhere* would be good enough if he could only be quiet and see no one, simply watch the trees dressing up in green and feel the same himself. He was beastly weak and in a rotten state of nerves. A gramophone in the ward plagued him beyond endurance. The *Old Huntsman* had come out that spring after all, and for a joke he would send a copy to Sir Douglas Haig. He couldn't be prevented from doing *that* anyhow.

In June, he had visited the Morrells at Oxford, not knowing that I was still there, but wrote that perhaps it was as well we didn't meet, neither of us being at our best; at least one of us should be in a normal frame of mind when we were together. Five poems of his had appeared in *The Cambridge Magazine* (one of the few aggressively pacifist journals published in England at the time, the offices of which were later sacked by Flying Corps cadets). None of them, he admitted, was much good except as a dig at the complacent and perfectly unspeakable people who thought the war ought to go on indefinitely until everyone got killed but themselves. The pacifists were now urging him to produce something red hot in the style of Barbusse's *Under Fire*, but he couldn't do it. He had other things in his head, *not poems*. (I didn't know what he meant by this, but hoped that it was not a Richard Dadd assassination programme.) The thought of France nearly drove him dotty sometimes. Down in Kent he could hear the guns thudding ceaselessly across the Channel, on and on, until he didn't know whether he wanted to rush back and die with the First Battalion, or stay in England and do what he could to prevent the war going on. But both courses were hopeless. To go back and get killed would be only playing to the gallery – the wrong gallery – and he could think of no means of doing any effective preventive work at home. His name had gone in for an officer-cadet battalion appointment in England, which would keep him safe if he pleased; but it seemed a dishonourable way out.

At the end of July, another letter from Siegfried reached me at Osborne. It felt rather thin. I sat down to read it on the bench dedicated by Queen Victoria to John Brown ('A truer and more faithful heart never burned within human breast.'). As I opened the envelope, a newspaper cutting fluttered out, marked in ink: '*Bradford Pioneer*, Friday, July 27th, 1917'. I read the wrong side first:

THE C.O.s MUST BE SET FREE
by
Philip Frankford

The conscientious objector is a brave man. He will be remembered as one of the few noble actors in this world drama when the impartial historian of the future sums up the history of this awful war.

The C.O. is putting down militarism. He is fighting for freedom and liberty. He is making a mighty onslaught upon despotism. And, above all, he is preparing the way for the final abolition of war.

But thanks to the lying, corrupt, and dastardly capitalist Press these facts are not known to the general public, who have been taught to look upon the conscientious objectors as skunks, cowards, and shirkers.

Lately a renewed persecution of C.O.s has taken place. In spite of the promises of 'truthful' Cabinet Ministers, some C.O.s have been sent to France, and there sentenced to death – a sentence afterwards transferred to one of 'crucifixion' or five or ten years' hard labour. But even when allowed to remain in this country we have to chronicle the most scandalous treatment of these men – the salt of the earth. Saintly individuals like Clifford Allen, Scott Duckers, and thousands of others, no less splendid enthusiasts in the cause of anti-militarism, are in prison for no other reason than because they refuse to take life; and because they will not throw away their manhood by becoming slaves to the military machine. These men MUST BE FREED.

The political 'offenders' of Ireland . . .

Then I turned over and read:

FINISHED WITH THE WAR
A Soldier's Declaration

(This statement was made to his commanding officer by Second-Lieutenant S. L. Sassoon, Military Cross, recommended for D.S.O., Third Battalion Royal Welch Fusiliers, as explaining his grounds for refusing to serve further in the army. He enlisted on 3rd August 1914, showed distinguished valour in France, was badly wounded and would have been kept on home service if he had stayed in the army.)

I am making this statement as an act of wilful defiance of military authority, because I believe that the war is being deliberately prolonged by those who have the power to end it.

I am a soldier, convinced that I am acting on behalf of soldiers. I believe that this war, upon which I entered as a war of defence and liberation, has now become a war of aggression and conquest. I believe that the purposes for which I and my fellow-soldiers entered upon this war should have been so clearly stated as to have made it impossible to change them, and that, had this been done, the objects which actuated us would now be attainable by negotiation.

I have seen and endured the sufferings of the troops, and I can no longer be a party to prolong these sufferings for ends which I believe to be evil and unjust.

I am not protesting against the conduct of the war, but against the political errors and insincerities for which the fighting men are being sacrificed.

On behalf of those who are suffering now I make this protest against the deception which is being practised on them; also I believe that I may help to destroy the callous complacence with which the majority of those at home regard the continuance of agonies which they do not share, and which they have not sufficient imagination to realize.

July, 1917.   S. Sassoon.

This filled me with anxiety and unhappiness. I entirely agreed with Siegfried about the 'political errors and insincerities' and thought his action magnificently courageous. But more things had to be considered than the strength of our case against the politicians. In the first place, he was in no proper physical condition to suffer the penalty which the letter invited: namely to be court-martialled, cashiered, and imprisoned. I found myself most bitter with the pacifists who had encouraged him to make this gesture. I felt that, not being soldiers, they could not understand what it cost Siegfried emotionally. It was wicked that he should have to face the consequences of his letter on top of those Quadrangle and Fontaine-les-Croiselles experiences. I also realized the inadequacy of such a gesture. Nobody would follow his example, either in England or in Germany. The war would inevitably go on and on until one side or the other cracked.

I at once applied to appear before a medical board that sat next day; and asked the doctors to pass me fit for home service. I was not fit, and they knew it, but I asked it as a favour. I had to get out of Osborne and attend to this Siegfried business. Next, I wrote to the Hon. Evan Morgan, with whom I had canoed at Oxford a month or two previously, the private secretary to one of the Coalition Ministers. I asked him to do everything possible to prevent republication of, or comment on, the letter; and arrange that a suitable answer should be given to Mr Lees-Smith, the leading pacifist Member of Parliament, when he asked a question about it in the House. I explained to Evan that I was on Siegfried's side really, but that he should not be allowed to become a martyr to a hopeless cause in his present physical condition. Finally, I wrote to the Third Battalion. I knew that Colonel Jones-Williams was narrowly patriotic, had never been to France, and could not be expected to take a sympathetic view. But the second-in-command, Major Macartney-Filgate, was humane; so I pleaded with him to make the colonel see the affair in a reasonable light. I told him of Siegfried's recent experiences in France and suggested that he should be medically boarded and given indefinite leave.

Presently, Siegfried wrote from the Exchange Hotel, Liverpool, that no doubt I was worrying about him. He had come up to Liverpool a day or two before and walked into the Third Battalion orderly room at Litherland, feeling like nothing on earth, but probably looking fairly self-possessed. Major Macartney-Filgate, whom he found in command, the colonel being away on holiday, had been unimaginably decent, making him feel an utter brute, and had consulted the general commanding the Mersey Defences. Now the general was 'consulting God, or someone like that'. Meanwhile, I could write to him at the hotel, because he had promised not to run away to the Caucasus. He hoped, in time, to persuade them to be nasty – they probably didn't realize that his performance would soon be given great publicity. Though he hated the whole business more than ever, he knew more than ever that he was right and would never repent of what he had done. He added that things were looking better in Germany, but that Lloyd George would probably call it a 'plot'. The politicians seemed to him incapable of behaving like human beings.

The general consulted not God but the War Office; and Evan's Minister persuaded the War Office not to press the matter as a disciplinary case, but to give Siegfried a medical board. Evan had done his part well. I next set myself somehow to get Siegfried in front of the medical board. I rejoined the battalion and met him at Liverpool. He looked very ill; he told me that he had just been down to the Formby links and thrown his Military Cross into the sea. We discussed the political situation; I took the line that everyone was mad except ourselves and one or two others, and that no good could come of offering common sense to the insane. Our only possible course would be to keep on going out until we got killed. I expected myself to go back soon, for the fourth time. Besides, what would the First and Second Battalions think of him? How could they be expected to understand his point of view? They would accuse him of ratting, having cold feet, and letting the regiment down. How would Old Joe, even, the most understanding man in the regiment, understand it? To whom was his letter addressed? The army could, I repeated, only read it as cowardice, or at the best as a lapse from good form. The civilians would take an even unkinder view, especially when they found out that 'S.' stood for 'Siegfried'.

He refused to agree with me, but I made it plain that his letter had not been given, and would not be given, the publicity he intended. At last, unable to deny how ill he was, Siegfried consented to appear before the medical board.

So far, so good. Next, I had to rig the medical board. I applied for permission to give evidence as a friend of the patient. There were three doctors on the board – a regular R.A.M.C. colonel and major, and a 'duration of the war' captain. I very soon realized that the colonel was patriotic and unsympathetic; the major reasonable but ignorant; and the captain a competent nerve-specialist, right-minded, and my only hope. I had to go through the whole story again, treating the colonel and major with the utmost deference, but using the captain as an ally to break down their scruples. Much against my will, I had to appear in the rôle of a patriot distressed by the mental collapse of a brother-in-arms – a collapse directly due to his magnificent exploits in the trenches. I mentioned Siegfried's 'hallucinations' of corpses strewn along on Piccadilly. The irony of having to argue to these mad old men that Siegfried was not sane! Though conscious of a betrayal of truth, I acted jesuitically. Being in nearly as bad a state of nerves as Siegfried myself, I burst into tears three times during my statement. Captain McDowell, who proved to be a well-known Harley Street psychologist, played up well. As I went out, he said to me: 'Young man, you ought to be before this board yourself.' I prayed that when Siegfried came into the board-room after me he would not undo my work by appearing too sane. But McDowell argued his seniors over to my view.

Macartney-Filgate detailed me as Siegfried's escort to a convalescent home for neurasthenics at Craiglockhart, near Edinburgh. Siegfried and I both thought this a great joke, especially when I missed the train and he reported to 'Dottyville', as he called it, without me. At Craiglockhart, Siegfried came under the care of Professor W. H. R. Rivers, whom we now met for the first time, though we already knew him as a leading Cambridge neurologist, ethnologist, and psychologist. He had made a point of taking up a new department of research every few years, and incorporating it in his comprehensive anthropological scheme.

Rivers died shortly after the war, when on the point of contesting the London University parliamentary seat as an independent Labour candidate; intending to round off his scheme with a study of politics. He was now busily engaged with morbid psychology. He had over a hundred neurasthenic cases in his care, and diagnosed their condition largely through a study of their dream-life, based on Freud's work, though he energetically repudiated Freud's more idiosyncratic theses. His posthumous work *Conflict and Dream* is a record of his labours at Craiglockhart. Dick, by the way, had come under Rivers' observation as a result of the police-court episode and, after treatment, been pronounced sufficiently cured to enlist in the army.

Siegfried and Rivers soon became close friends; Siegfried was interested in Rivers' diagnostic methods, and Rivers in Siegfried's poems. On my return from Edinburgh I felt much happier. Siegfried began to write the terrifying sequence of poems, some of them published in the Craiglockhart hospital magazine, *The Hydra*, which appeared next year as *Counter-Attack*. Another patient was Wilfred Owen of the Manchester Regiment. It preyed on his mind that he had been unjustly accused of cowardice by his commanding officer. Meeting Siegfried here set Owen, a quiet, round-faced little man, writing war-poems.

25

THE president of the Osborne medical board had been right: I should not have been back on duty. The training at the Third Battalion camp was intensive, and being given command of a trained-men company I did not get enough rest. I realized how bad my nerves were when one day, marching through the streets of Litherland on a battalion route-march, I saw three workmen in gas-masks beside an open man-hole, bending over a corpse which they had just hauled up from a sewer. His clothes were sodden and stinking; face and hands, yellow. Waste chemicals from the munitions factory had got into the sewage system and gassed him when he went down to inspect. My company did not pause in its march, and I had only a glimpse of the group; but it reminded me so strongly of France that, but for the band-music, I should have fainted.

The colonel detailed me as member of a court-martial on a civilian alleged to have enlisted under the Derby Scheme, but not to have presented himself when his class was called to the colours. I tried to feel sympathetic with the nasty-looking little man, who closely resembled a rabbit, but found it difficult, even when he proved never to have enlisted. His solicitor handed us a letter from a corporal in France, explaining that he had enlisted in the rabbit's name while on leave, because the rabbit had recently been rabbiting with his wife. This the rabbit denied; but he showed that the colour of his eyes recorded on the enlistment-form was blue, while his own were rabbit-brown, so he seemed to have a case. But a further question arose: why had he not enlisted under the Military Service Act, if he was a fit rabbit? He claimed to be starred, having done responsible work in a munitions factory for the necessary length of time before the Military Service Act became law. However, police evidence on the table showed that his 'protection certificates' were forged, that he had not been working on munitions before the Military Service Act, and thus, coming into the class of those 'deemed to have enlisted', was a deserter in any case. Having no legal alternative, we sentenced him to the prescribed two years' imprisonment. He broke down, squealed rabbit-fashion, and declared conscientious objections against war. Getting involved in the trial made me feel contemptible.

Large drafts now frequently went off to the First, Second, Ninth, and Tenth Battalions in France, and to the Eighth Battalion in Mesopotamia. Very few of the men warned for draft absented themselves. But they were always more cheerful about going in the spring and summer, when there was heavy fighting, than in the quieter winter months. (The regiment kept up its spirits even in the last year of the war. Attwater told me that big drafts sent off during the critical weeks of the 1918 spring, when the Germans had broken through the Fifth Army, went down to the station singing and cheering enthusiastically. They might have been the reservists whom he and I had seen assembling at Wrexham on August 12th, 1914, to rejoin the Second Battalion just before it sailed for France.)

Colonel Jones-Williams always made the same speech to the drafts. The day I joined the battalion from Osborne, I went via Liverpool Exchange Station and the electric railway to Litherland. Litherland station was crowded with troops. I heard a familiar voice making a familiar speech: the colonel bidding Godspeed to a small draft of men on their way back to the First Battalion. '. . . going cheerfully like British soldiers to fight the common foe . . . some of you perhaps may fall . . . upholding the magnificent traditions of the Royal Welch Fusiliers . . .' The draft cheered vigorously; rather too vigorously, I felt – perhaps even ironically? When he had finished, I went over and greeted a few old friends: 79 Davies, 33 Williams, and the Davies who was nicknamed 'Dym Bacon', which was Welsh for 'there isn't any bacon'. (He had won the nickname in his recruit days. The son of a Welsh farmer and accustomed to good food, he had complained about his first morning's breakfast, shouting to the orderly-sergeant: 'Do you call this a bloody breakfast, man? Dym bacon, dym sausages, dym herrings, dym bloody anything! Nothing but bloody bread and jaaam!')

I saw another well-remembered First Battalion face – D.C.M. and rosette, Médaille Militaire, Military Medal, no stripe. 'Lost them again, Sergeant Dickens?' I asked.

He grinned. 'Easy come, easy go, sir.'

Then the train came in, and I stretched out my hand with 'Good Luck!'

'You'll excuse us, sir,' said Dickens.

The draft shouted with laughter, and I saw why my hand had not been wrung, and also why the cheers had been so loud. Everyone of them was in hand-cuffs. They had been detailed a fortnight before for a draft to Mesopotamia, but wanted to get back to the First Battalion, so they overstayed their leave. The colonel, not understanding the situation, put them into the guardroom to make sure of them for the next draft. They were now going back in hand-cuffs, under an escort of military police, to the battalion of their choice. The men bore Colonel Jones-Williams no ill-will for the hand-cuffs. A good-hearted man, he took a personal interest in the camp kitchens, had built a cinema-hut within the camp, been reasonably mild in orderly room, and done his best not to drive returned soldiers too hard.

I decided to leave Litherland somehow, forewarned what the winter would be like, with the mist steaming up from the Mersey and hanging about the camp, full of T.N.T. fumes. During the previous winter I used to sit in my hut, and cough and cough until I was sick. The fumes tarnished buttons and cap-badges, and made our eyes smart. I thought of going back to France, but realized the absurdity of the notion. Since 1916, the fear of gas obsessed me: any unusual smell, even a sudden strong scent of flowers in a garden, was enough to send me trembling. And I couldn't face the sound of heavy shelling now; the noise of a car back-firing would send me flat on my face, or running for cover. But what about Palestine, where gas was unknown and shell-fire inconsiderable by comparison with France?

Siegfried wrote from Craiglockhart in August: 'What do you think of the latest push? How splendid this attrition is! As Lord Crewe says: "We are not the least depressed."' I matched this with a remark of Lord Carson's: 'The necessary supply of heroes must be maintained at all costs.'

At my next medical board I asked to be passed in the category of B2, which meant: 'Fit for garrison service at home.' I reckoned on being sent to the Third Garrison Battalion of the regiment, now under canvas at Oswestry in Wales. From there, when I felt a bit better, I would get myself passed B1, or: 'Fit for garrison service abroad', and would, in due course, be sent to a Royal Welch garrison battalion in Egypt. Once there, it should be easy to get passed A1 and join the Twenty-fourth or Twenty-fifth (New Army) Battalion in Palestine.

So presently I was sent to Oswestry. We had a good colonel, but the men were mostly compulsory enlistments; and the officers, with few exceptions, useless. My first task on arrival was to superintend the entraining of battalion stores and transport; we were moving to Kinmel Park Camp, near Rhyl. The adjutant gave me one hundred and fifty men, and allowed me six hours for the job. I chose fifty of the stronger men and three or four N.C.O.s who looked capable, then sent the remainder away to play football. By organizing the mob in First Battalion style, I got my fifty men to load the train in two hours less than the scheduled time. The colonel congratulated me. At Rhyl, he gave me the job of giving 'further instruction' to the sixty or so young officers sent to him from the cadet-battalions. Few officers in the battalion had seen any active service.

It was at this point that I remembered Nancy Nicholson. I had first met her in April, 1916, at the Nicholsons' Harlech house, while on leave after the operation on my nose. She was sixteen at the time, on holiday from school, and I knew her brother Ben, the painter, whose asthma kept him out of the army. When I returned to France in 1917, I had called on Ben and the rest of the family in Chelsea, and the last person to say goodbye to me on my way to Victoria

Station was Nancy. I remembered her standing in the doorway, in a black velvet dress with coral necklace. She was ignorant, of independent mind, good-natured, and as sensible about the war as anybody at home could be. In the summer of 1917, shortly after the episode with Marjorie, I had taken her to a musical review, the first review of my life. It was *Cheep*; with Lee White, singing of Black-eyed Susans, and how 'Girls must all be Farmers' Boys, off with skirts, wear corduroys'. Nancy told me that she was now on the land herself. She showed me her paintings, illustrations to Stevenson's *Child's Garden of Verses*; my child-sentiment and hers answered each other. I liked all the family, particularly her mother, Mabel Nicholson, the painter, a beautiful, wayward Scotch-melancholy person. William Nicholson, again 'the painter', is still among my friends. Tony, a brother, just older than Nancy, was a gunner-officer, waiting to go to France.

I began a correspondence with Nancy, about some children's rhymes of mine which she wanted to illustrate. Soon I fell in love with her. On my next leave, in October 1917, I visited her at the farm where she worked in Huntingdonshire – alone, except for her black poodle, among farmers, farm-labourers, and wounded soldiers who had been put on land-service – and helped her to run mangolds through a slicer. Our letters became more intimate after this. She warned me that she was a feminist and that I had to be careful what I said about women; the attitude of the Huntingdon farmers to their wives and daughters kept her in a continual state of anger. But Nancy's crude summary of the Christian religion: 'God is a man, so it must be all rot,' took a load off my shoulders.

I had been passed B1 now, but the orders that came for me to proceed to Gibraltar upset my plans. Gibraltar being a dead-end, it would be as difficult to get from there to Palestine as it would from England. A friend in the War Office undertook to cancel the order until a vacancy could be found for me in the battalion stationed at Cairo. At Rhyl, I was enjoying my first independent command. I got it because of a rumoured invasion of the north-east coast, to follow a sortie of the German fleet. A number of battalions were sent across England for its defence. All fit men of the Third Garrison Battalion were ordered to move at twenty-four hours' notice to York. A slight error occurred, however, in the Morse message from War office to Western Command. Instead of dash-dot-dash-dash, they sent dash-dot-dash-dot, so the battalion was sent to Cork instead;

where, on second thoughts, it seemed just as much needed as in York – so there it stayed for the remainder of the war.

Ireland had been seething since the Easter Rebellion in 1916, and Irish troops at the depôts were now giving away their rifles to the Sinn Feiners. On getting these orders, the colonel told me that I was the only officer he could trust to look after the rest of the battalion – thirty young officers, four or five hundred crocks engaged in camp duties, and a draft of two hundred trained men under orders for Gibraltar. He left me a competent adjutant, and three officers' chargers to ride, also asking me to keep an eye on his children, whom he had to leave behind until a house could be found for them at Cork; I had been playing with them a good deal. I got the draft off all right, and their soldier-like appearance so impressed the inspecting general that he sent them all to the camp cinema at his own expense. This gave me another good mark with the colonel in Ireland. The climax of my faithful services was when I checked an attempt on the part of the camp quartermaster to make our battalion responsible for the loss of five hundred blankets.

It happened like this. Suddenly, one night, I had three thousand three hundred leave-men from France thrown under my command – Irishmen, from every regiment in the army, held up at Holyhead on the way home by the presence of submarines in the Irish Sea. They were rowdy and insubordinate, and during the four days of their stay gave me little rest. The five hundred missing blankets, part of the six thousand six hundred issued to them, had probably been sold in Rhyl to pay for cigarettes and beer. I was able to prove at the Court of Inquiry that the men, though attached to the battalion for purposes of discipline, had been issued with blankets direct from the quartermaster's stores, before reporting to me. The loss of the blankets might be presumed to have taken place between the time of issue and the time that the men arrived in the battalion lines; for I had given the camp quartermaster no receipt for the blankets. The Court of Inquiry was convened in the camp quartermaster's private office; and I insisted that he should leave the room during the taking of evidence, because it was now no longer his private office but a Court of Inquiry. The president agreed, and his consequent ignorance of my line of defence saved the case. This success, and the evidence that I turned up of presents accepted by the battalion mess-president, when at Rhyl, from wholesale caterers (the mess-president had tried to make me pay my mess-bill twice over, and I retaliated by investigating his private life) so pleased the colonel that he recommended me for the Russian Order of St Anne, with Crossed Swords, of the Third Class. After all, then, I should not have left the army undecorated but for the October Bolshevik revolution, which cancelled the award-list.

I saw Nancy again when I visited London in December, and we decided to get married at once. Though attaching no importance to the ceremony, Nancy did not want to disappoint her father, who liked weddings and parties. I was still expecting orders for Egypt, and intended to go on from there to Palestine. However, Nancy's mother made it a condition of marriage – Nancy being still a minor – that I should visit a London lung-specialist to find out whether I would be fit for active service in the course of the next year or two. I went to Sir James Fowler, who had visited me at Rouen when I was wounded. He told me that my lungs were healthy enough, though I had bronchial adhesions and my wounded lung had only a third of its proper expansion; but that my general nervous condition made it folly for me to think of active service in any theatre of war.

Nancy and I were married in January 1918 at St James's Church, Piccadilly. She being just eighteen, and I twenty-two. George Mallory acted as the best man. Nancy had read the marriage-service for the first time that morning, and been so horrified that she all but refused to go through with the wedding, though I had arranged for the ceremony to be modified and reduced to the shortest possible form. Another caricature scene to look back on: myself striding up the red carpet, wearing field-boots, spurs, and sword; Nancy meeting me in a blue-check silk wedding-dress, utterly furious; packed benches on either side of the church, full of relatives; aunts using handkerchiefs; the choir boys out of tune; Nancy savagely muttering the responses, myself shouting them in a parade-ground voice.

Then the reception. At this stage of the war, sugar could not be got except in the form of rations. There was a three-tiered wedding-cake and the Nicholsons had been saving up their sugar and butter cards for a month to make it taste like a real one; but when George Mallory lifted off the plaster-case of imitation icing, a sigh of disappointment rose from the guests. However, champagne was another scarce commodity, and the guests made a rush for the dozen bottles on the table. Nancy said: 'Well, I'm going to get something out of this wedding, at any rate,' and grabbed a bottle. After three or four glasses, she went off and changed back into her land-girl's costume of breeches and smock. My mother, who had been thoroughly enjoying the proceedings, caught hold of her neighbour, E. V. Lucas, the essayist, and exclaimed: 'Oh, dear, I wish she had not done that!' The embarrassments of our wedding-night (Nancy and I being both virgins) were somewhat eased by an air-raid: Zeppelin bombs dropping not far off set the hotel in an uproar.

A week later, Nancy returned to her farm, and I to my command at Kinmel Park. It was an idle life now. No men attended parade; all were employed on camp duties. And I found a lieutenant with enough experience to attend to the 'further instruction' of the young officers. My orderly room took about ten minutes each day; crime was rare, and the adjutant always kept ready and in order the few documents to be signed; which left me free to ride all my three chargers over the countryside, in turn, for the rest of the day. I frequently used to visit the present Archbishop of Wales in his palace at St Asaph; his son had been killed in the First Battalion. We discovered a common taste for the curious; I have kept a postcard from him, which runs as follows:

The Palace, St Asaph.
Hippophagist banquet held at Langham's Hotel, February 1868
A. G. Asaph.

(I met several bishops during the war, but none afterwards; except the Bishop of Oxford, in a railway carriage, two years ago, discussing the beauties of Samuel Richardson. And the Bishop of Liverpool, at Harlech, in 1932 – I was making tea on the sandhills, when he came out from the sea with cries of pain, having been stung in the thigh by a jellyfish. He gladly accepted a cup of tea, tut-tutting miserably to himself that he had been under the impression that jellyfish stung only in foreign parts.)

Wearying of this idleness, I arranged to be transferred to the Sixteenth Officer Cadet Battalion in another part of the same camp. There I did the same sort of work as with the Fourth at Oxford, and stayed from February 1918 until the Armistice on November 11th. Rhyl being much healthier than Oxford, I could play games without danger of another break-down. Nancy got a job at a market-gardener's near the camp, and came up to live with me. A month or two later she found that she was having a baby, stopped land work, and went back to her drawing.

None of my friends had approved of my engagement, particularly to a girl as young as Nancy. One of them, Robbie Ross, Oscar Wilde's literary executor, whom I first met through Siegfried, tried to dissuade me from marriage, hinting, very unkindly that there was Negro blood in the Nicholson family – that perhaps one of our children might revert to coal-black. Siegfried could not easily accustom himself to the idea of Nancy, whom he had not met, but he still wrote from Craiglockhart. A few months later, though in no way renouncing his pacifist views, he decided that his only possible course was, after all, to return to France. He had written to me in the previous October that seeing me again made him more restless than ever. He found the isolation of hospital life nearly unbearable. Old Joe had written him a long letter to say that the First Battalion were just back at rest-billets from the Polygon Wood fighting; the conditions and general situation were more appalling than anything yet known – three miles of morass, shell-holes, corpses, and dead horses through which to bring up the rations. Siegfried felt he would rather be anywhere than in hospital; he couldn't bear to think of poor Old Joe lying out all night in shell-holes and being shelled. Several of the transport-men had been killed, but at least, according to Joe, 'the Battalion got its rations'. If only the people who wrote leading articles in the *Morning Post* about victory could read Joe's letter! (When this feat won Joe a D.S.O., he was sent a slip to complete with biographical details for a new edition of *The Companionage and Knightage*, but looked contemptuously at the various headings. Disregarding 'date and place of birth', and even 'military campaigns', he filled in two items only:

> *Issue: Rum, rifles, etc.*
> *Family seat: My khaki pants.*)

Siegfried now wrote the poem 'When I'm asleep, dreaming and lulled and warm' about the ghosts of soldiers, reproaching him in dream for his absence – they had looked for him in the line from Ypres to Frise and not found him. He told Rivers that he would go back to France if they agreed to send him, but made it quite clear that his views were what they had been in July when he wrote the letter of protest – if possible, more violently so. He demanded a written guarantee that he would be sent overseas at once, and not kept hanging around a training battalion. In a letter to me he reprehended the attitude I had taken in July, when I reminded him that the regiment would either think him a coward, or regard his protest as a lapse from good form. It was suicidal stupidity and credulity, he wrote, to identify oneself in any way with good form; a man of real courage would not acquiesce as I did. I admitted, he pointed out, that the people who sacrificed the troops were callous bastards, and that the same thing was happening everywhere, except in Russia. What my answer was, I forget; perhaps that, while in France, I had never seen such a fire-eater as he – the number of Germans whom I killed or caused to be killed could hardly be compared with his wholesale slaughter. In fact, Siegfried's unconquerable idealism changed direction with his environment: he varied between happy warrior and bitter pacifist. His poem:

> To these I turn, in these I trust,
> Brother Lead and Sister Steel;
> To his blind power I make appeal,
> I guard her beauty clean from rust . . .

had originally been inspired by Colonel Campbell, V.C.'s bloodthirsty 'Spirit of the Bayonet' address at an army school. Later, Siegfried offered it as a satire; and it certainly comes off, whichever way you read it. I was both more consistent and less heroic than Siegfried.

Whether I pulled any strings escapes my memory; at any rate this time he got posted to the Twenty-fifth Royal Welch – dismounted Yeomanry – in Palestine. He seemed to enjoy the life there, but in April a letter from 'somewhere in Ephraim', gave me the distressing news that the division had orders for France. He wrote that he would be sorry to get back to trenches, and perhaps go over the top at Morlancourt or Méaulte. The mention of Morlancourt in the *communiqués* had brought things home to him. He expected that the First and Second Battalions had about ceased to exist by now, for the *n*th time.

I heard again, at the end of May, from France. Siegfried quoted Duhamel: 'It was ordained that you should suffer without purpose and without hope, but I will not let all your sufferings be lost in the abyss.' Yet he wrote the next paragraph in his happy-warrior vein, saying that his men were the best he'd ever served with. He wished I could see them. Though I mightn't believe it, he was training them bloody well and couldn't imagine whence his flame-like ardour had come; but come it had. His military efficiency derived from the admirable pamphlets now being issued: so different from the stuff we used to get two years before. He said that when he read my letter he began to think: 'Damn Robert, damn everyone except my company, the smartest turn-out, ever seen, and damn Wales, and damn leave, and damn being wounded, and damn everything except staying with my company until it has melted away! Limping and crawling among the shell-holes, lying very still in the afternoon sunshine in dignified desecrated attitudes.' He asked me to remember this mood when I saw him (*if* I saw him) worn out and smashed up again, querulous and nerve-ridden. Or when I read something in the Casualty List and got a polite letter from Mr Lousada, his solicitor. There had never been such a battalion, he said, since 1916, but in six months it would have ceased to exist.

Nancy's brother, Tony, had also gone to France now, and her mother made herself ill by worrying about him. Early in July he should be due for leave. I was on leave myself at the end of one of the four-months' cadet courses, staying with the rest of Nancy's family at Maesyneuardd, a big Tudor house near Harlech. This was the most haunted house that I have ever been in, though the ghosts, with one exception, were not visible, except occasionally in the mirrors. They would open and shut doors, rap on the oak panels, knock the shades off lamps, and drink the wine from the glasses at our elbows when we were not looking. The house belonged to an officer in the Second Battalion, whose ancestors had most of them died of drink. The visible ghost was a little yellow dog that would appear on the lawn in the early morning to announce deaths. Nancy saw it through the window that time.

The first Spanish influenza epidemic began, and Nancy's mother caught it, but did not want to miss Tony's leave and going to the London theatres with him. So when the doctor came, she took quantities of aspirin, reduced her temperature, and pretended to be all right. But she knew that the ghosts in the mirrors knew the truth. She died in London on July 13th, a few days later. Her chief solace, as she lay dying, was that Tony had got his leave prolonged on her account. I was alarmed at the effect that the shock of her death might have on Nancy's baby. Then I heard that Siegfried had been shot through the head that same day while making a daylight patrol through long grass in No Man's Land; but not killed. And he wrote me a verse-letter from a London hospital (which I cannot quote, though I should like to do so) beginning:

It is the most terrible of his war-poems.

Tony was killed in September. I went on mechanically at my cadet-battalion work. The new candidates for commissions were mostly Manchester cotton clerks and Liverpool shipping clerks – men with a good fighting record, quiet and well behaved. To forget about the war, I was writing *Country Sentiment*, a book of romantic poems and ballads.

In November came the Armistice. I heard at the same time of the deaths of Frank Jones-Bateman, who had gone back again just before the end, and Wilfred Owen, who often used to send me poems from France. Armistice-night hysteria did not touch our camp much, though some of the Canadians stationed there went down to Rhyl to celebrate in true overseas style. The news sent me out walking alone along the dyke above the marshes of Rhuddlan (an ancient battlefield, the Flodden of Wales), cursing and sobbing and thinking of the dead.

Siegfried's famous poem celebrating the Armistice began:

> *Everybody suddenly burst out singing,*
> *And I was filled with such delight*
> *As prisoned birds must find in freedom . . .*

But 'everybody' did not include me.

26

IN the middle of December the cadet battalions were wound up, and the officers, after a few days' leave, sent back to their units. I had orders to rejoin the Royal Welch Third Battalion, now at the Castle Barracks, Limerick, but decided to overstay my leave until the baby was born. Nancy expected it early in January 1919, and her father took a house at Hove for the occasion. Jenny, born on Twelfth Night, was neither coal-black nor affected by the shocks of the previous months. Nancy had no foreknowledge of the experience – I assumed that she must have been given some sort of warning – and it took her years to recover from it. I went over to Limerick, and there lied my way out of the overstaying of leave.

Limerick being a Sinn Fein stronghold, constant clashes occurred between the troops and the young men of the town, yet little ill-feeling; Welsh and Irish always got on well together, just as Welsh and Scottish were sure to disagree. The Royal Welch had the situation comfortably in hand; they made a joke of politics and turned their entrenching-tool handles into shillelaghs. Limerick looked like a war-ravaged town. The main streets were pitted with holes like shell-craters and many of the bigger houses seemed on the point of collapse. Old Reilly at the antique shop, who remembered my grandfather well, told me nobody built new houses at Limerick now; the birth-rate was declining and when one fell down the survivors moved into another. He also said that everyone died of drink in Limerick except the Plymouth Brethren, who died of religious melancholia.

Life did not start in the town before nine in the morning. Once, at about that time, I walked down O'Connell Street, formerly King George Street, and found it deserted. When the hour chimed, the door of a magnificent Georgian house flew open and out came, first a shower of slops, which just missed me, then a dog, which lifted up its leg against a lamp-post, then a nearly naked girl-child, who sat down in the gutter and rummaged in a heap of refuse for filthy pieces of bread; finally a donkey, which began to bray. I had pictured Ireland exactly so, and felt its charm as dangerous. When detailed to search for concealed rifles at the head of a task force, in a neighbouring village, I asked Attwater, then still adjutant, to find a substitute; explaining that as an Irishman I did not care to be mixed up in Irish politics. That January I played my last game of rugger: as full-back for the battalion against Limerick City. We were all crocks and our opponents seemed bent on showing what fine fighting material England had lost by withholding Home Rule. How jovially they jumped on me, and rubbed my face in the mud!

My new loyalty to Nancy and Jenny tended to overshadow regimental loyalty, now that the war seemed to be over. Once I began writing a rhymed nonsense letter to them in my quarters overlooking the barrack square:

> *Is there any song sweet enough*
> *For Nancy or for Jenny?*
> *Said Simple Simon to the Pieman:*
> *'Indeed, I know not any.'*

> *I have counted the miles tò Dubylon,*
> *I have flown the earth like a bird,*
> *I have ridden cock-horse to Banbury Cross,*
> *But no such song have I heard.*

At that moment some companies of the battalion returned to barracks from a route-march; the drums and fifes drew up under my window, making the panes rattle with *The British Grenadiers*. The insistent repetition of the tune and the hoarse words of command as the parade formed up in the square, company by company, challenged Banbury Cross and Babylon. *The British Grenadiers* succeeded for a moment in forcing their way into the poem:

> *Some speak of Alexander,*
> *And some of Hercules,*

and then were repulsed:

> *But where are there any like Nancy and Jenny,*
> *Where are there any like these?*

Had I ceased to be a British Grenadier?

I decided to resign my commission at once. Consulting the priority list of trades for demobilization, I found that agricultural workers and students were among the first classes to go. I did not particularly want to be a student again and would rather have been an agricultural worker – Nancy and I had spoken of farming when the war ended – but where was my agricultural background? And I could take a two years' course at Oxford with a Government grant of two hundred pounds a year, and be excused the intermediate examination (Mods.) on account of war-service. The preliminary examination I had already been excused because of a 'higher certificate examination' passed at Charterhouse; so there remained only the finals. The grant would be increased by a children's allowance. It seemed absurd at the time to suppose that university degrees would count for anything in a regenerated post-war England; but Oxford offered itself as a convenient place to mark time until I felt more like earning a livelihood. We were all accustomed to the war-time view, that the sole qualification for peace-time employment would be a good record of service in the field, that we expected our scars and our commanding officers' testimonials to get us whatever we wanted. A few of my fellow-officers did manage, as a matter of fact, to take advantage of the employers' patriotic spirit before it cooled again; sliding into jobs for which they were not properly qualified.

I wrote to a friend in the War Office Demobilization Department, asking him to hurry through my release. He wrote back that he would do his best, but that I must not have had charge of Government moneys for the past six months. As it happened, I had not at the time; but Attwater suddenly decided to put me in command of a company. He complained of being disastrously short of officers who could be trusted with company accounts. The latest arrivals from the New Army battalions were a constant shame to the senior officers. Paternity-orders, stumer cheques, and drunkenness on parade grew frequent; not to mention table manners at which Sergeant Malley stood aghast. We now had two mess ante-rooms, the junior and the senior; yet if a junior officer happened to be regimentally a gentleman (belonged, that is, to the North Wales landed gentry, or came from Sandhurst) the colonel invited him to use the senior ante-room and mix with his own class. The situation must have seemed very strange to the three line-battalion second-lieutenants captured at Mons in 1914, now promoted captains by the death of most of their contemporaries and set free by the terms of the Armistice.

Attwater cancelled the intended appointment only when I promised to help him with the battalion theatricals now being arranged for St David's Day; I undertook to play Cinna in *Julius Caesar*. His change of mind saved me over two hundred pounds, because next day the senior lieutenant of the company which I was to have taken over went off with the cash-box, and I should have been legally responsible for its loss. Before the war he used to give displays on Blackpool Pier as 'The Handcuff King'. He got away safely to the United States.

I rode out a few miles from Limerick to visit my uncle, Robert Cooper, at Cooper's Hill. He was a farmer, a retired naval commander, and the Sinn Feiners had begun burning his ricks and driving his cattle. Through the window he showed me distant herds grazing beside the Shannon. 'They have been there all winter,' he said despondently, 'but I haven't had the heart to take a look at them these three months.' I spent the night at Cooper's Hill, and woke up with a sudden chill, which I recognized as the first symptoms of Spanish influenza.

Back at the barracks, I found that a War Office telegram had come through for my demobilization, but that all demobilization among troops in Ireland was to be stopped on the following day for an indefinite period because of the Troubles. Attwater, showing me the telegram, said: 'We're not going to let you go. You promised to help me with those theatricals.' I protested; he stood firm; but I did not intend to have influenza at an Irish military hospital with my lungs in their present condition.

I decided to make a run for it. The orderly-room sergeant had made out my papers on receipt of the telegram; all my kit lay ready packed. There remained only two things to get: the commanding officer's signature to the statement that I had handled no company moneys, and the secret code-marks which the battalion demobilization officer alone could supply – but he was hand-in-glove with Attwater, so I dared not ask him for them. The last train before demobilization ended would be the six-fifteen from Limerick that same evening, February 13th. My one hope was to wait until Attwater left the orderly-room and then casually ask the commanding officer to sign the statement, without mentioning Attwater's objection to my going. Attwater remained in the orderly-room until five minutes past six. As soon as he was out of sight I hurried in, saluted, got the necessary signature – fortunately my old friend Macartney-Filgate was now in command, saluted again, and hurried away to collect my baggage. I had counted on a jaunting-car at the barrack gates but found none. About five minutes left, and the station a good distance away! A First Battalion corporal passed. I shouted to him: 'Corporal Summers, quick! Get a squad of men! I've *got my ticket* and must catch the last train home.' Summers promptly called four men; they picked up my stuff and doubled off with it, left, right, left, to the station. I tumbled into the train as it moved slowly out and threw a pound-note to Corporal Summers. 'Goodbye, corporal, drink my health!'

Yet still I had not got my code-marks, and knew that when I reached the demobilization centre at Wimbledon the officers there would refuse to let me go. Not that I cared very much. I should at least have my influenza in an English, and not an Irish, hospital. My temperature was running high, and my mind working clearly, as it always does in fever, with its visual imagery, which is cloudy and partial at ordinary times, defined and complete. We reached Fishguard after a rough crossing. I bought a copy of the *South Wales*

Echo and read that a strike of London Electric Railwaymen would take place the next day, February 14th, unless the railway directors met the union's demands. So as the train steamed into Paddington, I jumped out, fell down, picked myself up, and ran across to the station entrance where, in spite of competition from porters – a feeble crew at this period – I seized the only taxi in sight as its occupant paid the fare. I had foreseen the taxi-shortage and could afford to waste no time. I brought my taxi back to the train, where scores of stranded officers eyed me with envy. One, a fellow-traveller in my compartment, had been met by his wife. 'Excuse me,' I said, 'but would you like to share my taxi anywhere? (I have influenza, I warn you.) I'm going down to Wimbledon, so I shall be getting out at Waterloo; the steam-trains are still running.' That delighted them, because they lived at Ealing and had no idea how to get home except by taxi.

On the way to Waterloo he said: 'I wish there were some way of showing our gratitude – something we could do for you.'

'Well, there's only one thing in the world that I want at the moment. But you can't give it to me, I'm afraid. And that's the set of secret code-marks to complete my demobilization papers. I've bolted from Ireland without them, and there'll be hell to pay if the Wimbledon people send me back.'

He rapped on the glass of the taxi, told the driver to stop, got down his bag, opened it, and produced a satchel of army forms. 'Well,' he said, 'I happen to be the Cork District Demobilization officer, and here's the whole bag of tricks.'

Then he filled in my papers.

At Wimbledon, instead of having to wait in a queue for the expected nine or ten hours, I got released at once; Ireland was officially a 'theatre of war', and demobilization from theatres of war had priority over home-service demobilization. After a hurried visit to my parents, now back in our own house half a mile across the Common, I went on to Hove. Arriving at supper-time, I warned Nicholson about my influenza, and hurried away to bed. Within a day or two, the whole family caught it, except Nicholson, Jenny, and the housemaid, a Welsh gipsy, who kept it off by a charm – the leg of a lizard tied in a bag round her neck. A new epidemic, as bad as the summer one, had started; not a nurse could be found in all Brighton. Nicholson at last rounded up two ex-nurses: one competent, but frequently drunk, and with the habit, when drunk, of ransacking all the wardrobes in the house and piling the contents into her own bag. The other sober, but incompetent, would stand a dozen times a day in front of the open window, arms outspread, and cry in a stage-voice: 'Sea, sea, give my husband back to me!' The husband, by the way, was not drowned, merely unfaithful.

A doctor, found with equal difficulty, gave me no hope of recovery; it was septic pneumonia now, and had affected both my lungs. But, having come through the war, I refused to die of influenza. This made the third time in my life that I had been given up, and each time because of my lungs. I should have mentioned in my first chapter the double-pneumonia following measles, which nearly did for me at the age of seven. Maggie, the gipsy-servant, wept whenever she dusted my room – I thought because of a tiff with her young man, but these were tears for me, my widow, and my orphan girl. I focused attention on a poem, 'The Troll's Nosegay', which was giving me trouble; I had taken it through thirty drafts and still it would not come right. The thirty-fifth draft passed scrutiny, I felt better, and Maggie smiled again. Nancy's attack was a light one, fortunately.

A few weeks later, I watched a mutiny of the Guards, when about a thousand men of all regiments marched out from Shoreham Camp and paraded through the Brighton streets, in protest against unnecessary restrictions. The troops' impatience of military disipline between the Armistice and the signing of peace delighted Siegfried; he had taken a prominent part in the General Election which Lloyd George forced immediately after the Armistice, asking for a warrant to hang the Kaiser and make a stern peace. Siegfried, supporting Philip Snowden's candidature on a Pacifist platform, had faced a threatening civilian crowd; he trusted that his three wound-stripes and the mauve and white Military Cross ribbon (which he had not thrown away with the Cross itself) would give him a privileged hearing. Snowden and Ramsay MacDonald were now perhaps the two most unpopular men in England, and whatever hopes we had nursed of a general anti-Governmental rising by ex-service men soon faded. Once back in England, they were content with a roof over their heads, civilian food, beer that was at least better than French beer, and enough blankets at night. Any overcrowding in their home was as nothing compared to what they had grown accustomed to; a derelict French four-roomed cottage would provide billets for sixty men. Having won the war, they were satisfied and left the rest to

Lloyd George. The only serious outbreak took place at Rhyl. There a two days' mutiny of young Canadians caused much destruction and several deaths. The signal for the rising was a cry: 'Come on, the Bolsheviks!'

Nancy, Jenny, and I went up to Harlech, where Nicholson lent us his house to live in. We were there for a year. I discarded my uniform, having worn nothing else for four and a half years, and looked into my trunk to see what civilian clothes I still had. The one suit, other than school uniform which I found, no longer fitted. The Harlech villagers treated me with the greatest respect. At the Peace Day celebrations in the castle, I was asked, as the senior Man of Harlech who had served overseas, to make a speech about the glorious dead. I spoke in commendation of the Welshman as a fighting man and earned loud cheers. But not only did I have no experience of independent civilian life, having gone straight from school into the army: I was still mentally and nervously organized for war. Shells used to come bursting on my bed at midnight, even though Nancy shared it with me; strangers in daytime would assume the faces of friends who had been killed. When strong enough to climb the hill behind Harlech and revisit my favourite country, I could not help seeing it as a prospective battlefield. I would find myself working out tactical problems, planning how best to hold the Upper Artro valley against an attack from the sea, or where to place a Lewis-gun if I were trying to rush Dolwreiddiog Farm from the brow of the hill, and what would be the best cover for my rifle-grenade section. I still had the army habit of commandeering anything of uncertain ownership that I found lying about; also a difficulty in telling the truth – it was always easier for me now, when charged with any fault, to lie my way out in army style. I applied the technique of taking over billets or trenches to a review of my present situation. Food, water supply, possible dangers, communication, sanitation, protection against the weather, fuel and light – I ticked off each item as satisfactory.

Other loose habits of war-time survived, such as stopping cars for a lift, talking without embarrassment to my fellow-travellers in railway carriages, and unbuttoning by the roadside without shame, whoever might be about. Also, I retained the technique of endurance: a brutal persistence in seeing things through, somehow, anyhow, without finesse, satisfied with the main points of any situation. But at least I modified my unrestrainedly foul language. The greatest difficulty lay in facing the problem of money, which had not worried me since those first days at Wrexham; but at the moment my savings of some £150, my war-bonus of £250, the disability pension of £60 a year that I now drew, and occasional sums that came in from poems, seemed plenty. Nancy and I engaged a nurse and a general servant, and lived as though we had an income of a thousand a year. Nancy spent much of her time illustrating some poems of mine; I got my *Country Sentiment* in order, and wrote reviews.

Very thin, very nervous, and with about four years' loss of sleep to make up, I was waiting until I got well enough to go to Oxford on the Government educational grant. I knew that it would be years before I could face anything but a quiet country life. My disabilities were many: I could not use a telephone, I felt sick every time I travelled by train, and to see more than two new people in a single day prevented me from sleeping. I felt ashamed of myself as a drag on Nancy, but had sworn on the very day of my demobilization never to be under anyone's orders for the rest of my life. Somehow I must live by writing.

Siegfried had gone to live at Oxford as soon as demobilized, expecting me to join him. However, after a couple of terms there, he accepted the literary editorship of the newly-published *Daily Herald*. He sent me books to review for it. In those days, the *Daily Herald* was not respectable, but violently anti-militarist and the only daily newspaper that dared protest against the Versailles Treaty and the blockade of Russia by the British fleet. The Treaty of Versailles shocked me; it seemed destined to cause another war some day, yet nobody cared. While the most critical decisions were being taken in Paris, public interest concentrated entirely on three home-news items: Hawker's Atlantic flight and rescue; the marriage of England's reigning beauty, Lady Diana Manners; and a marvellous horse called The Panther – the Derby favourite, which came in nowhere.

The *Herald* spoiled our breakfast every morning. We read in it of unemployment all over the country due to the closing of munition factories; of ex-service men refused reinstatement in the jobs they had left when war broke out, of market-rigging, lockouts, and abortive strikes. I began to hear news, too, of the penury to which my mother's relatives in Germany had been reduced, particularly the retired officials whose pensions, by the collapse of the mark, now amounted to only a few shillings a week. Nancy and I took all this to heart and called ourselves socialists.

My family, who were living permanently in Harlech, having sold the house at Wimbledon, did not know quite how to treat me. I had fought gallantly for my country – indeed, of six brothers, I alone had seen active service, and my shell-shocked state entitled me to every consideration; but my sympathy for the Russian rebellion against the corrupt Czarist Government outraged them. I once more forfeited the good will of my Uncle Charles. My father tried to talk me over, reminding me that my brother Philip, once a pro-Boer and a Fenian, had recovered from his youthful revolutionary idealism and come out all right in the end. Most of my elder brothers and sisters were in the Near East, either British officials, or married to British officials. My father hoped that when I recovered I would go to Egypt, perhaps in the consular service, where the family influence would help me, and there get over my 'revolutionary enthusiasm'.

Socialism with Nancy was a means to a single end: namely judicial equality between the sexes. She ascribed all the wrong in the world to male domination and narrowness, and would not see my experiences in the war as anything comparable with the sufferings that millions of working-class married women went through without complaint. This, at least, had the effect of putting the war into the background for me; my love for Nancy made me respect her views. But male stupidity and callousness became such an obsession with her that she began to include me in her universal condemnation of men. Soon she could not bear a newspaper in the house, for fear of reading some paragraph that would horrify her – about the necessity of keeping up the population; or about women's limited intelligence; or about the shameless, flat-chested modern girl; or anything at all about women written by clergymen. We joined the newly formed Constructive Birth Control Society, and distributed its literature among the village women, to the scandal of my family.

What made things worse was that neither of us went to Harlech church, and we refused to baptize Jenny. My father even wrote to Nancy's godfather, who happened to be my publisher, asking him to persuade Nancy, for whose religion he had promised at the font to be responsible, into giving her child Christian baptism. It scandalized them, too, that Nancy kept her own name for all purposes, refusing to be called 'Mrs Graves' in any circumstances. She explained that, as 'Mrs Graves', she had no personal validity. Children, at that time, were the sole property of the father; the mother not being legally a parent.

27

In October 1919, I went to Oxford at last, and Nicholson gave us the Harlech furniture to take along. Oxford was overcrowded; the lodging-house keepers, some of whom nearly starved during the war, now had their rooms booked up terms ahead, and charged accordingly. Keble College built a row of huts for its surplus students. Not an unfurnished house could be rented anywhere within the three-mile radius. I solved the difficulty by pleading ill-health and getting permission from St John's College to live five miles out, on Boar's Hill – where John Masefield, who thought well of my poetry, had offered to rent us a cottage at the bottom of his garden.

We found the University remarkably quiet. The returned soldiers did not feel tempted to rag about, break windows, get drunk, or have tussles with the police and races with the Proctors' 'bulldogs', as in the old days. The boys straight from the public schools kept quiet too, having had war preached at them continually for four years, with orders to carry on loyally at home while their brothers served in the trenches, and make themselves worthy of such sacrifices. Since the boys went off to cadet-battalions at the age of seventeen, the masters kept firm control of the schools; trouble there nearly always came from the eighteen-year-olds. G. N. Clark, a history don at Oriel, who had got his degree at Oxford just before the war and meanwhile been an infantryman in France and a prisoner in Germany, told me: 'I can't make out my pupils at all. They are all "Yes, sir" and "No, sir". They seem positively to thirst for knowledge and scribble away in their note-books like lunatics. I can't remember a single instance of such stern endeavour in pre-war days.'

The ex-service men, who included scores of captains, majors, colonels, and even a one-armed twenty-five year old brigadier, insisted on their rights. At St John's, they formed a 'College Soviet', successfully demanded an entire revision of the scandalous catering system, and chose an undergraduate representative to sit on the kitchen-committee. The elder dons, whom I had often seen during the war trembling in fear of an invasion, with the sacking and firing of the Oxford colleges and the rape of their families in the Woodstock and Banbury Roads, and who then regarded all soldiers, myself included, as their noble saviours, now recovered their pre-war self-possession and haughtiness. The change in their manner amused me. My moral tutor, however, though he no longer saluted me when we met, remained a friend; he persuaded the College to let me change my course from Classics to English Language and Literature, and take up my £60 Classical Exhibition notwithstanding. I felt glad now that it was only an exhibition, not a scholarship, though in 1913 this had disappointed me: College regulations permitted exhibitioners to be married, scholars must remain single.

I found the English Literature course tedious, especially the insistence on eighteenth-century poets. My tutor, Percy Simpson, the editor of Ben Jonson's plays, sympathized, telling me that he had suffered once, as a boy, for preferring the Romantic Revivalists. When his schoolmaster beat him for reading Shelley, he had protested between the blows: 'Shelley is beautiful! Shelley is beautiful!' Yet he warned me not on any account to disparage the eighteenth century when I sat for my finals. I also found it difficult to concentrate on cases, genders, and irregular verbs in Anglo-Saxon grammar. The Anglo-Saxon lecturer was candid about his subject: it was, he said, a language of purely linguistic interest, and hardly a line of Anglo-Saxon poetry extant possessed the slightest literary merit. I disagreed. I thought of Beowulf lying wrapped in a blanket among his platoon of drunken thanes in the Gothland billet; Judith going for a *promenade* to Holofernes's staff-tent; and *Brunanburgh* with its bayonet-and-cosh fighting – all this came far closer to most of us than the drawing-room and deer-park atmosphere of the eighteenth century. Edmund Blunden, who also had leave to live on Boar's Hill because of gassed lungs, was taking the same course. The war still continued for both of us, and we translated everything into trench-warfare terms. In the middle of a lecture I would have a sudden very clear experience of men on the march up the Béthune–La Bassée road; the men would be singing, while French children ran along beside us, calling out: 'Tommee, Tommee, give me bullee beef!' and I would smell the stench of the knacker's yard just outside the town. Or it would be in Laventie High Street, passing a company billet; an N.C.O. would roar: 'Party, 'shun!' and the Second Battalion men in shorts, with brown knees, and brown, expressionless faces, would spring to their feet from the broken steps where they were sitting. Or I would be in a barn with my first platoon of the Welsh Regiment, watching them play nap by the light of dirty candle stumps. Or in a deep dug-out at Cambrin, talking to a signaller; I would look up the shaft and see somebody's muddy legs coming down the steps; then there would be a sudden crash and the tobacco smoke in the dug-out would shake with the concussion and twist about in patterns like the marbling on books. These day-dreams persisted like an alternate life and did not leave me until well in 1928. The scenes were nearly always recollections of my first four months in France; the emotion-recording apparatus seemed to have failed after Loos.

The eighteenth century owed its unpopularity largely to its Frenchness. Anti-French feeling among most ex-soldiers amounted almost to an obsession. Edmund, shaking with nerves, used to say at this time: 'No more wars for me at any price! Except against the French. If there's ever a war with them, I'll go like a shot.' Pro-German feeling had been increasing. With the war over and the German armies beaten, we could give the German soldier credit for being the most efficient fighting-man in Europe. I often heard it said that only the blockade had beaten the Fritzes; that in Haig's last push they never really broke, and that their machine-gun sections held us up long enough to cover the withdrawal of the main forces. Some undergraduates even insisted that we had been fighting on the wrong side: our natural enemies were the French.

At the end of my first term's work, I attended the usual college board to give an account of myself. The spokesman coughed, and said a little stiffly: 'I understand, Mr Graves, that the essays which you write for your English tutor are, shall I say, a trifle temperamental. It appears, indeed, that you prefer some authors to others.'

A number of poets were living on Boar's Hill; too many, Edmund and I agreed. It was now almost a tourist centre, dominated by Robert Bridges, the Poet Laureate, with his bright eye, abrupt challenging manner, and a flower in his buttonhole – one of the first men of letters to sign the Oxford recantation of war-time hatred against the Germans. Dr Gilbert Murray lived there, too, gentle-voiced and with the spiritual look of the strict vegetarian, doing preliminary propaganda work for the League of Nations. Once, as I sat talking to him in his study about Aristotle's *Poetics*, while he walked up and down, I suddenly asked: 'Exactly what is the principle of that walk of yours? Are you trying to avoid the flowers on the rug, or are you trying to keep to the squares?' My own compulsion-neuroses made it easy for me to notice them in others. He wheeled around sharply: 'You're the first person who has caught me out,' he said. 'No, it's not the flowers or the squares; it's a habit that I have got into of doing things in sevens. I take seven steps, you see, then I change direction and go another seven steps, then I turn around. I consulted Browne, the Professor of Psychology, about it the other day, but he assured me it isn't a dangerous habit. He said: "When you find yourself getting into multiples of seven, come to me again."'

I saw most of John Masefield, a nervous, generous, correct man, very sensitive to criticism, who seemed to have suffered greatly in the war, as an orderly in a Red Cross unit; he was now working on *Reynard the Fox*. He wrote in a hut in his garden, surrounded by tall gorse-bushes, and only appeared at meal-times. In the evening he used to read his day's work over to Mrs Masefield, and they corrected it together. Masefield being at the height of his reputation at the time, a constant stream of American visitors washed against his door. Mrs Masefield protected 'Jan'. She came from the North of Ireland, and put a necessary brake on Jan's generosity and sociability. We admired her careful housekeeping, and the way she stood up for her rights where less resolute people would have shrunk. As an example: some neighbours of ours had a particularly stupid Airedale; they were taking it for a walk when a wild rabbit ran across the road from the Masefield's gorse plantation. The Airedale dashed at the rabbit, and missed as usual. The rabbit, not giving it sufficient credit for stupidity and slowness, doubled back; but found the dog not yet recovered from its mistake and ran right into its open jaws. The dog's owners, delighted at the brilliant performance of their pet, retrieved the rabbit, which was a small and inexperienced one, and took it home for the pot. Mrs Masefield had been watching through the plantation fence. This not being, strictly, a public road, the rabbit was legally hers. That evening they heard a knock at the door. 'Come in, oh, do come in, Mrs Masefield!' She had called to demand the skin of her rabbit. Mrs Masefield's one extravagance was bridge; she used to play at a halfpenny a hundred, to steady her play. But she was a considerate landlord to us, and advised Nancy to keep up with me intellectually, if she wished to hold my affections.

Another poet on Boar's Hill was Robert Nichols, one more neuras-thenic ex-soldier, with his flame-opal ring, his wide-brimmed hat, his flapping arms, and a 'mournful grandeur in repose' (the phrase comes from a review by Sir Edmund Gosse). Nichols served only three weeks in France, with the gunners, and got involved in no show; but, being highly strung, he got invalided out of the army and went to lecture on British war-poets in America for the Ministry of Information. He read Siegfried's poetry and mine, and started a legend of Siegfried, himself, and me as the new Three Musketeers, though the three of us had never once been together in the same room.

That winter, George and Ruth Mallory invited Nancy and myself to go climbing with them. But Nancy could not stand heights and was having another baby; and I realized that my climbing days were over. I could never again now deliberately take chances with my life. In March, the baby arrived and we called him David. My mother was overjoyed to have secured the first Graves grandson. My elder brothers had only girls; here, at last, was an heir for the family silver and documents. At Jenny's birth she had condoled with Nancy: 'Perhaps it is as well to have a girl first, to practise on.' Nancy was determined to have four children; they were to resemble the children in her drawings, and be girl, boy, girl, boy, in that order. She intended to get it all over with quickly; she believed in young parents with families of three or four children fairly close together in age. She had her way exactly, but began to regret her marriage, as a breach of faith with herself – a concession to patriarchy. She wanted somehow to be dis-married – not by divorce, which was as bad as marriage – so that she and I could live together without any legal or religious obligation to do so.

I now met Dick again, for the last time, and found him disagreeably pleasant. He was up at Oxford, about to enter the diplomatic service, and so greatly changed that it seemed absurd to have ever suffered on his account. Yet the caricature likeness to the boy I had loved persisted.

28

THE first time I met Colonel T. E. Lawrence, he happened to be wearing full evening dress. That must have been in February or March 1920, and the occasion was a guest-night at All Souls', where he had been awarded a seven-years' Fellowship. The formality of evening dress concentrates attention on eyes, and Lawrence's eyes immediately held me. They were startlingly blue, even by artificial light, and never met the eyes of the person he addressed, but flickered up and down as though making an inventory of clothes and limbs. I was only an accidental guest and knew few people there. Lawrence, talking to the Regius Professor of Divinity about the influence of the Syrian Greek philosophers on early Christianity, and especially of the importance of the University of Gadara close to the Lake of Galilee, mentioned that St James had quoted one of the Gadarene philosophers (I think, Mnasalcus) in his *Epistle*. He went on to speak of Meleager, and the other Syrian-Greek contributors to the Greek Anthology, whose poems he intended to publish in English translation. I joined in the conversation and mentioned a morning-star image which Meleager once used in rather an un-Greek way. Lawrence turned to me. 'You must be Graves the poet? I read a book of yours in Egypt in 1917, and thought it pretty good.'

This was embarrassing, but kind. He soon began asking me about the younger poets: he was out of touch with contemporary work, he said. I told him what I knew.

Lawrence had not long finished with the Peace Conference, where he acted as adviser to the Emir Feisal, and was now tinkering at the second draft of *The Seven Pillars of Wisdom*, his Fellowship having been granted him on condition that he wrote the book as a formal history of the Arab Revolt.

I used to visit his rooms in the mornings between lectures, but not before eleven o'clock or half past, because he worked by night, going to bed at dawn. Though he never drank himself, he would always send his scout to fetch me a silver goblet of audit ale. Audit ale, brewed in the College, was as soft as barley-water but of great strength. Prince Albert of Schleswig-Holstein had once come down to Oxford to open a new museum; he lunched at All Souls' before the ceremony, the mildness of the audit ale deceived him, and later that afternoon they took him back to the station in a cab with the blinds drawn.

I knew nothing definite of Lawrence's wartime activities, though my brother Philip had been with him in the Intelligence Department at Cairo in 1915, making out the Turkish Order of Battle. I did not question him about the Revolt, partly because he seemed to dislike the subject – Lowell Thomas was now lecturing in the United States on 'Lawrence of Arabia' – and partly because of a convention between him and me that the war should not be mentioned: we were both suffering from its effects and enjoying Oxford as a too-good-to-be-true relaxation. Thus, though the long, closely-written fool-scap sheets of *The Seven Pillars* were always stacked in a neat pile on his living-room table, I restrained my curiosity. He occasionally spoke of his archaeological work in Mesopotamia before the war; but poetry, especially modern poetry, was what we discussed most.

He wanted to meet what poets there were, and through me came to know, among others, Siegfried Sassoon, Edmund Blunden, Masefield, and, later, Thomas Hardy. He frankly envied poets. He felt that they had some sort of secret which he might be able to grasp and profit from. He made Charles Doughty his chief hero and got an introduction to him through Hogarth, Curator of the Ashmolean Museum, whom he regarded as a second father. Lawrence envisaged the poet's secret as a technical mastery of words rather than as a particular mode of living and thinking. I had not yet learned enough to be able to dispute this, and when I did begin to learn, some years later, found Lawrence difficult to convince. To him, painting, sculpture, music, and poetry were parallel activities, differing only in the medium used. Lawrence told me: 'When I asked Doughty why he had made that Arabian journey, his answer was that he had gone there "to redeem the English language from the slough into which it has fallen since the time of Spenser".' These words of Doughty's seem to have made a great impression on Lawrence, and largely account, I think, for his furious keying-up of style in *The Seven Pillars*.

Vachel Lindsay, the American poet, an extremely simple man – Middle-Western clay with a golden streak – came to Oxford, and I persuaded Sir Walter Raleigh, the Professor of English Literature, to let him have a lecture hall for a poetry-reading. Everyone enjoyed the performance, which was an exercise in elocution and mime, not a reading. Afterwards, Lawrence invited Lindsay and his old mother and myself to lunch in his rooms. Lawrence's scout, scandalized to hear that Lindsay belonged to the Illinois Anti-Saloon League, asked permission to lay on his place a copy of verses composed in 1661 by a fellow of the College. One stanza ran:

> *The poet divine that cannot reach wine,*
> *Because that his money doth many times faile,*
> *Will hit on the vein to make a good strain,*
> *If he be but inspired with a pot of good ale.*

Mrs Lindsay had been warned by friends to comment on nothing unusual that she met at Oxford, and when Lawrence brought out the College gold service in her honour, she took this to be the ordinary thing at a University luncheon party – apologized for it as being of no great antiquity: but the College had been patriotic during the Civil War and melted down all its plate to help pay King Charles's expenses while he made Oxford his headquarters.

Lawrence's rooms were dark and oak-panelled, with a large table and a desk as the principal furniture. There were also two heavy leather chairs, simply acquired. An American oil-financier had come in suddenly one day when I was there and said: 'I am here from the States, Colonel Lawrence, to ask a single question. You are the only man who will answer it honestly. Do Middle-Eastern conditions justify my putting any money in South Arabian oil?'

Lawrence, without rising, quietly answered: 'No.'

'That's all I wanted to know; it was worth coming for. Thank you, and good day!' In his brief glance about the room he missed something and, on his way home through London, chose the chairs and had them sent to Lawrence with his card.

Other things in the room were pictures, including Augustus John's portrait of the Emir Feisal, which Lawrence, I believe, bought from John with the diamond he had worn as a mark of honour in his Arab headdress; his books, including a Kelmscott *Chaucer*; three prayer-rugs, the gift of Arab leaders, one of them with a lapis-lazuli sheen on the nap; the Tell Shawm station bell from the Hedjaz Railway; and on the mantelpiece a four-thousand-year-old toy – a clay soldier on horseback from a child's grave at Carchemish, where Lawrence had dug before the war.

I was working on a new book of poems, which reflected my haunted condition; it appeared later under the title of *The Pierglass*. Lawrence made a number of suggestions for improving these poems, most of which I adopted. He behaved very much like an undergraduate at times. One day I happened to visit the top of the Radcliffe Camera and look down on the roofs of neighbouring colleges. From a pinnacle of All Souls' fluttered a small crimson Hedjaz flag: Lawrence had been a famous roof-climber when up at Jesus College twelve years before this. He told me of two or three schemes for brightening All Souls' and Oxford generally. One was for improving the rotten turf in the Quadrangle; he had suggested at a College meeting that it should be manured or replaced; no action was taken.

He now proposed to plant mushrooms on it, so that they would be forced to returf the whole extent; and consulted a mushroom expert in town. But the technical difficulties of mushroom culture proved to be great, and Lawrence went away to help Winston Churchill with the Middle-Eastern settlement of 1922 before they could be overcome.

Another scheme, for which he enlisted my help, was to steal the Magdalen College deer. We would drive them one early morning into the small inner quadrangle of All Souls', having persuaded the College to answer the Magdalen protests with a declaration that it was the All Souls' herd, pastured there from time immemorial. Great things were expected of this raid, but we needed Lawrence as the stage-manager; so it fell through when he left us. However, he engineered a successful strike by the College servants for better pay and hours, and such a thing had never happened before since the foundation of the University. Lawrence also proposed to present the College with a peacock which, once accepted, would be found to bear the name 'Nathaniel' – after Lord Curzon, an enemy of Lawrence's, and Vice-Chancellor of the University. One morning I went to his rooms, and he introduced me to a visitor there: 'Ezra Pound: Robert Graves – you will dislike each other,' he said.

'What's wrong with him?' I asked afterwards, having felt very uncomfortable in Pound's presence.

'They tell me that he's Longfellow's grand-nephew, and when a man's a modernist that takes some living down.'

At the same time Lawrence was getting to know the leading painters and sculptors, and trying to grasp their secret, too. He used to sit as a model, to see what they made of him, and compare the results.

Recently, I saw Sir William Orpen's version – a curious almost libellous magnification of a seldom-seen element in Lawrence's character – a sort of street-urchin furtiveness. It counter-balances Augustus John's too sentimentally heroic portrait.

Professor Edgeworth, of All Souls', avoided conversational English, persistently using words and phrases that one expects to meet only in books. One evening, Lawrence returned from a visit to London, and Edgeworth met him at the gate. 'Was it very caliginous in the Metropolis?'

'Somewhat caliginous, but not altogether inspissated,' Lawrence replied gravely.

I remember having tea with him at Fuller's Tea Shop, and the scandal he caused by clapping his hands for the waitress in oriental fashion. And one afternoon he rang the station bell from his window into the Quadrangle. 'Good God,' I said, 'you'll wake the whole College!'

'It needs waking up.'

We planned to collaborate in a burlesque on contemporary writers, in the style of a Government Blue-book. I said: 'First we must get a Blue-book and study it.' He agreed to buy one next time he went to London. When he asked at the Stationery Office for a Blue-book, the clerk asked: 'Which Blue-book? We have hundreds.'

'Whichever you like.'

Mistaking his indifference for guilty embarrassment, the clerk handed him the report of a Royal Commission on Venereal Disease.

I teased him once for standing on the fender over the fire; I pretended that he did it to make himself look taller. He denied this hotly, insisting that the onus of proving oneself of any use in the world lay with tall people like myself. This encouraged me to a ragging pretence of physical violence; but I immediately stopped when I caught the look in his face. I had surprised his morbid horror of being touched.

I took no part in undergraduate life, seldom visiting St John's except to draw my Government grant and Exhibition money; and refused to pay the College games' subscription, as being unfit for games myself and having no leisure to watch them. Most of my friends were at Balliol and Queen's, and Wadham had a prior claim on my loyalty.

At this time I had little to do with the children; they were in the hands of Nancy and the nurse. Nancy felt that she needed some activity besides drawing, but could not decide what. One evening, in the middle of the long vacation, she suddenly said: 'I must get away out of all this at once. Boar's Hill stifles me. Let's go off on bicycles somewhere.'

We packed a few things and rode off in the general direction of Devon. The nights were coldish and, not having brought any blankets, we bicycled by night and slept by day. We rode across Salisbury Plain in the moonlight, passing Stonehenge, and several deserted army camps which had an even more ghostly look. They could provide accommodation for a million men: the number of men killed in the British and Overseas Forces during the war. Finding ourselves near Dorchester, we turned aside to visit Thomas Hardy, whom we had met not long before when he came to get his honorary doctor's degree at Oxford. Hardy was active and gay, with none of the aphasia and wandering of attention that we had noticed in him there.

I have kept a record of our talk with him. He welcomed us as representatives of the post-war generation, claiming to live such a quiet life at Dorchester that he feared he was altogether behind the times. He wanted, for instance, to know whether we had any sympathy with the Bolshevik regime, and whether he could trust the *Morning Post*'s account of the Red Terror. Then he asked about Nancy's hair, which she wore short, in advance of the fashion, and why she kept her own name. His comment on the name question was: 'Why, you *are* old-fashioned! I knew an old couple here sixty years ago who did the same. The woman was called Nanny Priddle (descendant of an ancient family, the Paradelles, long decayed into peasantry), and she would never change her name either.' Then he wanted to know why I no longer used my army rank. I explained that I had resigned my commission. 'But you have a right to it; I should certainly keep my rank if I had one, and feel very proud to be called Captain Hardy.'

He told us that he was now engaged in restoring a Norman font in a church near by – only the bowl, but he enjoyed doing a bit of his old work again. Nancy mentioned that our children were not baptized. Interested, but not scandalized, he remarked that his mother had always said that, at any rate, there could be no harm in baptism, and that she would not like her children to blame her in after-life for leaving any duty to them undone. 'I have usually found that what my mother said was right.' He told us that, to his mind, the new generation of clergymen were very much better than the last . . . Though he now went to church only three times a year – one visit to each of the three neighbouring churches – he could not forget that in his boyhood the church had been the centre of all musical, literary, and artistic education in a village. He talked about the string-orchestras at Wessex churches, in one of which his father, grandfather, and he himself had taken part; and regretted their disappearance. He mentioned that the clergyman who appears as Mr St Clair in *Tess of the D'Urbervilles* had protested to the War Office about the Sunday brass-band performances at the Dorchester Barracks, and been the cause of headquarters' no longer being sent to this very popular station.

We took tea in the drawing-room which, like the rest of the house, was cluttered with furniture and ornaments. Hardy had an affection for accumulated possessions, and Mrs Hardy loved him too well to suggest that anything at all should be removed. With a cup of tea in his hand, he made jokes about bishops at the Athenaeum Club and imitated their episcopal tones when they ordered: 'China tea and a little bread and butter.' 'Yes, my lord!' Apparently, he considered bishops fair game, but soon began censuring Sir Edmund Gosse, who had recently stayed with them, for a breach of good taste in imitating his old friend Henry James's way of drinking soup. Loyalty to his friends was always a passion with Hardy.

After tea we went into the garden, where he asked to see some of my new poems. I fetched him one, and he wondered whether he might offer a suggestion: the phrase 'the scent of thyme', which occurred in it was, he said, one of the *clichés* which poets of his generation had studied to avoid. Could I perhaps alter it? When I replied that his contemporaries had avoided it so well that I could now use it without offence, he withdrew the objection.

'Do you write easily?' he inquired.

'This poem is in its sixth draft and will probably be finished in two more.'

'Why!' he said, 'I have never in my life taken more than three, or perhaps four, drafts for a poem. I am afraid of it losing its freshness.'

He said that he could once sit down and write novels by a time-table, but that poetry always came to him by accident, which perhaps was why he prized it more highly.

He spoke disparagingly of his novels, though admitting that he had enjoyed writing certain chapters. As we walked around the garden, Hardy paused at a spot near the greenhouse. He had once been pruning a tree when an idea for a story suddenly entered his head. The best story he had ever conceived, and it came complete with characters, setting, and even some of the dialogue. But not having pencil or paper with him, and wanting to finish his pruning before the weather broke, he took no notes. By the time he sat down at his table to recall the story, all was utterly gone. 'Always carry a pencil and paper,' he said, adding: 'Of course, even if I remembered that story now, I couldn't write it. I'm past novel-writing. But I often wonder what it can have been.'

That night at dinner he grew enthusiastic in praise of cyder, which he had drunk since a boy, as the finest medicine he knew. I suggested

249

that in his *Message to the American People*, which he had just been asked to write, he might take the opportunity to recommend cyder.

Hardy complained of autograph-hunters and their persistence. He did not like leaving letters unanswered, and if he did so, these people pestered him the more. He was upset that morning by a letter from an autograph-fiend, which began:

Dear Mr Hardy,

I am interested to know why the devil you don't reply to my request...

He asked me for advice, and jumped at the suggestion that a mythical secretary should reply offering his autograph at one or two guineas, the amount to be sent to a hospital – 'Swanage Children's Hospital', he put in – which would forward a receipt.

He regarded professional critics as parasites, no less noxious than autograph-hunters, wished the world rid of them, and also regretted having listened to them as a young man; on their advice he had cut out from his early poems dialect-words which possessed no ordinary English equivalents. And still the critics were plaguing him. One of them complained of a line: 'his shape smalled in the distance.' Now, what in the world else could he have written? Hardy then laughed a little. Once or twice recently he had looked up a word in the dictionary for fear of being again accused of coining, and found it there right enough – only to read on and discover that the sole authority quoted was himself in a half-forgotten novel! He talked of early literary influences, saying that these were negligible because he did not come of literary stock. But he admitted that a fellow-apprentice in the architect's office where he worked as a young man used to lend him books. (His taste in literature was certainly most unexpected. Once, a few years later, when Lawrence ventured to say something disparaging about Homer's *Iliad*, he protested: 'Oh, but I admire it greatly. Why, it's in the *Marmion* class!' Lawrence at first thought that Hardy was having a little joke.)

We left the next day, after another of Hardy's attacks on the critics at breakfast. He complained that they accused him of pessimism. One critic singled out as an example of gloom his poem on the woman whose house burned down on her wedding night. 'Of course it's a humorous piece,' said Hardy, 'and the man must have been thick-witted not to see that. On reading his criticism, I went through

250

my last collection of poems with a pencil, marking them S, N, and C according as they were sad, neutral, or cheerful. I found them in pretty equal proportions; which nobody could call pessimism.'

In his opinion, *vers libre* could come to nothing in England. 'All we can do is to write on the old themes in the old styles, but try to do a little better than those who went before us.' Of his own poems he told me that, once written, he cared very little what happened to them.

He described his war-work, rejoicing to have been chairman of the Anti-Profiteering Committee, and to have succeeded in bringing a number of rascally Dorchester tradesmen to book. 'It made me unpopular, of course,' he admitted, 'but it was a hundred times better than sitting on a Military Tribunal and sending young men to the war who did not want to go.'

We never saw Hardy again, though he gave us a standing invitation to stay with him.

From Dorchester we bicycled to Tiverton in Devonshire, where Nancy's old nurse kept a fancy-goods shop. Nancy helped her dress the shop-window, and advised her about framing the prints which she was selling. She also gave the shop a good turn-out, dusted the stock, and took her turn behind the counter. As a result of Nancy's work, the week's receipts went up several shillings and continued at the improved figure for a week or two after we were gone. This gave Nancy the idea of starting a shop herself on Boar's Hill, a large residential district with no shop nearer than three miles away. We could buy a second-hand army hut, stock it with confectionery, groceries, tobacco, hardware, medicines, and all the other things that one finds in a village shop, run it tidily and economically, and make our fortune. I promised to help her while the vacation lasted.

But army huts could not be bought at any reasonable price (the timber-merchants were in a ring); so a local carpenter built a shop to Nancy's design. A neighbour rented us a corner of his field close to the road. The work got finished in good time, and we bought the stock. The *Daily Mirror* advertised the opening on its front page with the heading 'SHOP-KEEPING ON PARNASSUS' and crowds came up from Oxford to look at us. We soon began to realize that it must either be a large general shop which made Boar's Hill more or less independent of Oxford (and of the unsatisfactory system of vans calling at the door and bringing inferior foods with 'take it or leave it'), or a small sweet and tobacco shop that offered no challenge to the Oxford tradesmen. We decided on the challenge. The building had to be enlarged, and two or three hundred pounds' worth of stock purchased. I used to serve in the shop several hours of the day, while Nancy went round to the big houses for the daily orders. Term had now begun, and I should have been attending lectures in Oxford. Another caricature scene: myself, wearing a green-baize apron this time, with flushed face and disordered hair, selling a packet of Bird's Eye tobacco to the Poet Laureate with one hand, and with the other weighing out half a pound of brown sugar for Sir Arthur Evans's gardener's wife.

Finally, the shop business ousted everything, not only Nancy's painting but my University work, and Nancy's proper supervision of the house and children. We engaged a boy to call for orders, and soon had the custom of every resident on Boar's Hill, except two or three. Even Mrs Masefield used to visit us once a week. She always bought the same tin of sink-powder and packet of soap-flakes, paying money down from a cash-box which she carried with her. The moral problems of trade interested me. Nancy and I both found it very difficult at this time of fluctuating prices to be really honest; we could not resist the temptation of under-charging the poor villagers of Wootton, who were frequent customers, and recovering our money from the richer residents. Playing at Robin Hood came easily to me. Nobody ever detected the fraud; it was as easy as shelling peas, the boy said, who also took his turn behind the counter. We found that most people bought tea by price and not by quality. If we happened to be out of the tea, selling at ninepence a quarter, which Mrs So-and-so always bought, refusing the eightpenny tea, and if Mrs So-and-so asked for it in a hurry, we used to make up a pound of the sevenpenny, which was the same colour as the ninepenny, and charge it at ninepence. The difference would not be noticed.

We felt sorry for commercial travellers who sweated up the hill with their heavy bags of samples, usually on foot, and had to be sent away without any orders. They would pitch a hard-luck tale, and often we relented and got in more stock than we needed. In gratitude they would tell us some of the tricks of the trade, advising us, for instance, never to cut cheese or bacon exactly to weight, but to make it an ounce or two more and overcharge for this extra piece. 'There's few can do the sum before you take the stuff off the scales, and there's fewer still who take the trouble to weigh up again when they get back home.'

The shop lasted six months. Prices began falling at the rate of about five per cent every week, the stock on our shelves had depreciated greatly in value, we had let several of the Wootton villagers run up bad debts. Then I went down with influenza, at the same time as Nancy quarrelled with the nurse and had to take the house and children herself. When we came to reckon things up, we decided to cut our losses; hoping to recoup the original expenditure, and even to be in pocket on the whole transaction, by selling the shop and goodwill to a large firm of Oxford grocers who wished to buy it as a branch establishment. Unfortunately, however, the site was not ours, and Mrs Masefield prevailed on the landlord not to let any ordinary business firm take over the shop from us, and thus spoil local amenities. No other site being available, we had to sell off what stock remained at bankruptcy prices to the wholesalers, and find a buyer for the building. Unfortunately again, the building was not made in bolted sections to be re-erected elsewhere; it could be sold only as timber, and during these six months the corner in timber had also been broken and prices fallen steeply. We recovered twenty pounds of the two hundred that had been spent on it, but were some five hundred pounds in debt to the wholesalers and others. A lawyer took everything in hand for us, and disposed of our assets; finally reducing the debt to some three hundred pounds. Nicholson sent Nancy a hundred-pound note (in a match-box) as his contribution, and Lawrence unexpectedly contributed the remainder. He gave me four chapters of *The Seven Pillars of Wisdom*, to sell for serial publication in the United States. As a point of honour, Lawrence refused to make any money out of the Revolt, even in the most indirect way; but if it could help a poet in difficulties, he saw no harm in that.

We gave the Masefields notice that the cottage would be free by the end of the June quarter 1921; but did not have any idea where to go, or what to do next. It seemed clear that we must get another cottage somewhere, live quietly, look after the children ourselves, and try to make what money we needed by writing and drawing. Nancy, who had taken charge of everything while I was ill, now set me the task of getting the cottage. It must be found in three weeks' time.

I protested: 'But you know there isn't a single cottage for rent anywhere.'

'Yes, but we simply *have* to get one.'

'All right, then, describe it in detail. Since there are no cottages, we might as well get a no-cottage that we really like.'

'Well, it must have six rooms, water indoors, a beamed attic, a walled-in garden, and it must be near the river. It must be in a village with shops, and yet a little removed from the village. The village must lie five or six miles from Oxford in the opposite direction from Boar's Hill. The church must have a tower and not a spire – I've always hated spires. And we can afford only ten shillings a week unfurnished.'

I took down other details about soil, sanitation, windows, stairs, and kitchen sinks; laid a ruler across the Oxford ordnance map, and found five riverside villages which corresponded in general direction and distance with Nancy's stipulation. Of these five villages, two proved on inquiry to possess shops; and, of these two, one had a towered church and the other a spired church.

I went to a firm of house-agents in Oxford and asked: 'Have you any cottages to let unfurnished?'

The clerk laughed politely. 'What I want is a cottage just outside the village of Islip, with a walled garden, six rooms, water in the house, a beamed attic, and at a rent of ten shillings a week.'

'Oh, you mean the World's End cottage? But that's for sale, not for rent. However, it's failed to find a buyer for two years, so perhaps the owner will let it go now at five hundred pounds, which is only half of what he originally asked.'

The next day Nancy came to Islip with me. She looked around and said: 'Yes, this is the cottage all right, but I shall have to cut down the cypress trees, and change those window-panes. We'll move in on quarter-day.'

'But the money! We haven't the money.'

Nancy answered: 'If we could find the exact house, surely we can find a mere lump sum of money?'

She was right. My mother very kindly bought the cottage for five hundred pounds and let it to us at ten shillings a week.

29

My mother, in letting us the Islip house, put a clause in the agreement that it must be used as a residence only, and not for the carrying on of any trade or business. She wanted to guard herself against any further commercial enterprise on our part; but need not have worried – we had learned our lesson. Islip, an agricultural village, lay far enough from Oxford not to be contaminated with the roguery for which the outskirts of most university towns are notorious. The policeman led an easy life. During the four years we lived there nothing of ours was ever stolen, and no Islip cottager cheated or offended us. Once, by mistake, I left my bicycle at the station for two days and, when I recovered it, not only were both lamps, the pump, and the repair outfit still in place, but an anonymous friend had even cleaned it.

Every Saturday during the winter months I played football for the village team. We ex-soldiers reintroduced the game at Islip after a lapse of some eighty years. The village nonagenarian complained that football was not so manly now as in his boyhood. He pointed across the fields to a couple of aged willow trees: 'Them used to be our home goals,' he said. 'T'other pair stood half a mile upstream. Constable stopped our play in the end. Three men were killed in the last game – one kicked to death; t'other two drowned each other in a scrimmage. Her was a grand game.' I found Islip football, though not unmanly, ladylike by comparison with the Charterhouse game. When playing centre-forward, I often got booed for charging the goalkeeper as he fumbled with the shot he had saved. The cheers were reserved for my inside-left, who spent most of his time stylishly dribbling the ball in circles round and round the field until robbed of it; he seldom went anywhere near the goal. But the football club was democratic, unlike the cricket club. I played cricket the first season, but resigned because the team seldom consisted of the best eleven men available; regular players would be dropped to make room for visiting gentry.

Nancy and I did all the work ourselves, including the washing. I undertook the cooking; she made and mended the children's clothes; we shared the other chores. Catherine was born in 1922, and Sam in 1924. By the end of 1925, we had lived for eight successive years in an atmosphere of teething, minor accidents, epidemics, and perpetual washing of babies' napkins. I did not dislike this sort of life, except for the money difficulties and almost never getting away to London. 'Love in a cottage, I'm afraid' had been the prophetic phrase current at our wedding. The strain told on Nancy, who was constantly ill, and I often had to take charge of everything. She tried to draw; but by the time she got her materials together some alarm from the nursery would always disturb her. At last she decided not to start again until all the children were house-trained and old enough for school. I kept on with my work because the responsibility for making money rested with me, and because nothing has ever stopped me writing. Nancy and I kept the cottage clean in a routine that left us little leisure for anything else: we had accumulated a number of brass ornaments and utensils that needed polishing and our children wore five times as many clean dresses as the neighbours' children did.

I worked through constant interruptions. I could recognize the principal varieties of babies' screams: hunger, indigestion, wetness, pins, boredom, wanting to be played with; and learned to disregard all but the more important ones. Most of my prose books published in those four years betray the conditions under which I wrote: they are scrappy, not properly considered, and obviously written out of reach of a reference library. Poetry alone did not suffer. When working at a poem in my head, I went on doing my mechanical tasks in a trance until I had time to sit down and record it. At one period I could allow myself only half an hour's writing a day, and then had to scribble hard in an effort to disburden my mind – I never sat chewing a pen. My poetry-writing has always been a painful process of continual corrections, corrections on top of corrections, and persistent dissatisfaction.

The children were all healthy and gave us little trouble. Nancy had strong views about giving them no meat or tea but as much fruit as they wanted, putting them to bed early, making them rest in the afternoon. We did our best to avoid the mistakes of our own childhood; but when they went to the village school we could not protect them from formal religion, class snobbery, political prejudice, and mystifying fairy stories of the facts of sex. Islip seemed as good a place as any for the happy childhood that we wanted them to have. They had fields to play in, and animals all around, and play-fellows of their own age. The river was close and we could borrow a canoe. They even liked school.

The villagers called me 'The Captain'; otherwise I had few reminders of the war, except my yearly visit to the standing Medical Board. The Board continued for some years to recommend me for a disability pension. My particular disability was neurasthenia; the train journey and the first-class army railway-warrant filled out with my rank and regiment usually produced reminiscential neurasthenia by the time I reached the Board.

Ex-service men were continually coming to the door selling boot-laces and asking for cast-off shirts and socks. We always gave them a cup of tea and money. Islip was a convenient halt between the Chipping Norton and the Oxford workhouses. One day an out-of-work ex-serviceman, a steamroller driver by trade, called with his three children, including a baby. Their mother had recently died in childbirth. We felt very sorry for them, and Nancy offered to adopt the eldest child, Daisy, who was about thirteen years old and her father's greatest anxiety. She undertook to train Daisy in house-work, so that she would be able later to go into service. The steam-roller-man shed tears of gratitude; and Daisy, a big, ugly girl, strong as a horse and toughened by her three years on the roads, seemed happy enough to be a member of the family. Nancy made her new clothes, we cleaned her, bought her shoes, and gave her a bedroom. The steamroller-man wanted Daisy to continue her education, which had been interrupted by their wanderings. But the schoolmistress put Daisy into the baby class, and the bigger girls used to tease her. In return, she pulled their hair and thumped them, and learned to hate school. After a while she grew homesick for the road.

'That was a good life,' she used to say. 'Dad and me and my brother and the baby. The baby was a blessing. When I fetched him along to the back doors I nearly always won something. 'Course, I was artful. If they tried to slam the door in my face, I used to put my foot in it and say: "This is my little orphan brother." Then I used to look around and anything I seen I used to ast for. I used to ast for a pram for the baby, if I seen an old one in a shed; and I'd get it, too. 'Course, we had a pram really, a good one, and then we'd sell the pram I'd won in the next town we come to. Good beggars always ast for something particular, something they seen lying about. It's no good asting for food or money. I used to pick up a lot for my dad. I was a better beggar nor he was, he said. We used to go along singing "On the Road to Anywhere". And there was always the Spikes to go to when the weather got bad. They was very good to us there. The Spike at Chippy Norton was our winter home. We used to go to the movies once a week there. We had fine grub at Chippy. We been all over the country: Wales, and Devonshire, right up to Scotland, but we always come back to Chippy.'

Nancy and I were shocked one day when a tramp came to the door and Daisy slammed it in his face and told him to 'clear out of it, Nosey, and don't poke your ugly mug into respectable people's houses.' She went on: 'I know you, Nosey Williams, you and your ex-service papers what you pinched from a bloke down in Salisbury, and them bigamy charges against you a-waiting down at Plymouth. Hop it now, quick, or I'll run for the cop!'

Daisy told us the true stories of many of the beggars we had befriended. 'There's not one decent man in ten among them bums,' she said. 'My dad's the only decent one of the lot. The reason most of them is on the road is the cops have something against them, so they has to keep moving. 'Course, my dad don't like the life; he took to it too late. And my mum was very respectable, too. She kept us clean. Most of them bums is lousy, with nasty diseases, and they keeps out of the Spike as much as they can, 'cause they don't like the carbolic baths.'

Daisy stayed with us for a whole winter. When spring came, and the roads dried, her father called for her again. He couldn't manage the little ones without her, he said. That was the last we saw of Daisy, though she wrote once from Chipping Norton asking us for money.

My Government grant and College Exhibition had ended at the time we moved to Islip. Peace brought a slump in the sale of poetry, and our total income, counting birthday and Christmas cheques from relatives, now amounted to one hundred and thirty pounds a year, of which perhaps half came from my writing. As Nancy reminded me, this meant fifty shillings a week, and some farm-labourers at Islip, with more children than ourselves, earned only thirty shillings. They lived a much harder life than we did, and had no one to fall back on, in case of sudden illness or other emergency. We used to get holidays, too, at Harlech, when my mother would insist on paying the train-fare as well as giving us our board free. Thinking how difficult conditions were for the labourers' wives kept Nancy permanently depressed.

We still called ourselves socialists, and when a branch of the Parliamentary Labour Party was formed in the village, lent the cottage for its weekly meetings throughout the winter months. Islip, though a rich agricultural area, had a reputation for slut-farming. Mr Wise, a farm-labourer, one of our members, once heckled a speaker in the Conservative interest about a protective duty imposed by the Conservative Goverment on dried currants. The speaker answered patronizingly: 'Well, surely a duty on Greek currants won't hurt you working men at Islip? You don't grow currants in these parts, do you?'

'No, sir,' replied Mr Wise, 'the farmers' main crop hereabouts is squitch.'

They persuaded me to stand for the parish council, of which I became a member for a year. I wish now I had taken records of the smothered antagonism at the council meetings. There were seven members, with three representatives of Labour and three Conservative representatives of the farmers and gentry; the chairman was a Liberal, whom we supported as a generous employer, and the only farmer for miles around with training at an agricultural college. He held the balance very fairly. The Council nearly came to blows over a proposed application to the District Council for the building of new cottages; many returned ex-soldiers who wanted to marry had nowhere to live with their wives. The Conservative members opposed this application, because it would mean a penny on the rates.

Then there was the question of getting a recreation ground for the village. The football team did not wish to be dependent on the generosity of a big farmer who rented it to us at a nominal fee. The Conservatives opposed this plan, again in the interest of the rates, and pointed out that shortly after the Armistice the village had turned down a recreation ground scheme, preferring to spend the memorial subscription money on a cenotaph. The Labour members replied that the vote was taken, as at the 1918 General Election, before the soldiers could return to express their views. Nasty innuendoes were then aimed at farmers who had stayed at home and made their pile, while their labourers fought and bled. The chairman calmed the antagonists. Another caricature scene: myself in corduroys and a rough frieze coat, sitting in the village schoolroom (this time with no 'Evils of Alcoholism' around the walls, but nature drawings and mounted natural history specimens instead), debating, as an Oxfordshire village elder, whether or not Farmer Tomkins could use a footpath across the allotments as a bridle-path – having first over-turned the decayed stile which, I urged, disproved his right.

This association with the Labour Party severed our friendly relations with the village gentry, who had hitherto regarded us as in their camp. My mother had taken the trouble to call on the Rector when she viewed the property, and he later asked me to speak from the chancel steps of the village church at a War Memorial service. He suggested that I should read war-poems. But instead of Rupert Brooke on the glorious dead, I read some of the more painful poems by Sassoon and Wilfred Owen about men dying from gas-poisoning, and about buttocks of corpses bulging from the mud. I also suggested that the men who had died, destroyed as it were by the fall of the Tower of Siloam, were not particularly virtuous or particularly wicked, but just average soldiers, and that the survivors should thank God they were alive, and do their best to avoid wars in the future. Though the Church party, apart from the liberal-minded Rector, professed to be scandalized, the ex-service men had not been too well treated on their return, and liked to be told that they stood on equal terms with the glorious dead. They were modest men: I noticed that though respecting the King's desire to wear their campaign medals on this occasion, they kept them buttoned up inside their coats.

The leading Labourite at Islip was William Beckley, senior. He bore an inherited title dating from the time of Oliver Cromwell: being always known as 'Fisher' Beckley. A direct ancestor, fishing one day on the Cherwell during the siege of Oxford, had ferried Cromwell himself and a body of Parliamentary troops over the river. In return, Cromwell granted him perpetual fishing-rights from Islip to the stretch of river where the Cherwell Hotel now stands. The cavalry skirmish at Islip bridge still remained fresh in local tradition, and a cottager at the top of the hill showed me a small stone cannon-ball, fired on this occasion and found stuck in his chimney-stack. But even Cromwell came late in the history of the Beckley family; the Beckleys had been watermen on the river long before the seventeenth century. Indeed, Fisher Beckley knew, by family tradition, the exact spot in the river bed where a barge lay – sunk while conveying stone for the building of Westminster Abbey before the Norman Conquest. Islip was the birthplace of Edward the Confessor, who had awarded the Islip lands to the Abbey; they remained Abbey property after a thousand years. The Abbey stone came from a quarry on the hillside close to the river; our cottage stood on the old slipway down which the stone-barges were launched. Some time in the 1870s, American weed was introduced into the river and net-fishing at last became impossible. Fisher Beckley turned agricultural labourer. His socialist views prevented him from getting employment in the village, so he daily trudged to a farm some miles away. But he was still 'Fisher' Beckley, and for us cottagers the most respected man in Islip.

30

My parents were most disappointed when, because of the shop crisis and my illness, I failed to take the B.A. degree at Oxford. But Sir Walter Raleigh, as head of the English School, allowed me to sit for the later degree of Bachelor of Letters, and present a written thesis on any subject I chose. He also agreed to be my tutor on condition that he should not be expected to tutor me. He thought well of my poetry, and suggested that we should only meet as friends. Sir Walter was engaged at the time on the official history of the war in the air, and wanted practical flying experience for the task. The R.A.F. took him up as often as he needed, but he caught typhoid fever on a flight out East and died. His death so saddened me that I did not apply for another tutor.

I found it difficult to write my thesis, *The Illogical Element in English Poetry*, in the required academic style, and decided to make it an ordinary book. I rewrote it some nine times; and did not like the final result. I was trying to show the nature of the supra-logical element in poetry, which could only be fully understood, I wrote, by studying the latent associations of the words used – the obvious prose sense being often in direct opposition to the latent content. The book's weakness lay in its not clearly distinguishing between a poet's supra-logical thought processes and the sub-logical process of the common psychopath.

I published a volume of poems every year from 1920 to 1925; after *The Pierglass*, which appeared in 1921, I made no attempt to please the ordinary reading public, and did not even flatter myself that I was conferring benefits on posterity; I had no reason to suppose that posterity would be more appreciative than my contemporaries. I never wrote unless a poem pressed to be written. Though assuming a reader of intelligence and sensibility, and envisaging his possible reactions to my words, I no longer identified him with any particular group of readers or (taking courage from Hardy) with critics of poetry. He was no more real a person than the conventional figure put in the foreground of an architectural design to indicate the size of a building. This greater strictness in writing, which showed in *Whipperginny*, laid me open to accusations of trying to get publicity and increase my sales by a wilful clowning modernism.

I made several attempts during these years to rid myself of the poison of war memories by finishing my novel, but had to abandon it – ashamed at having distorted my material with a plot, and yet not sure enough of myself to turn it back into undisguised history, as here.

I knew most of the poets then writing; they included Walter de la Mare, W. H. Davies, T. S. Eliot, the Sitwells, and many more. I liked Davies because he came from South Wales and was afraid of the dark, and because once, I heard, he made out a list of poets and crossed them off one by one as he decided that they were not true poets – until only two names were left – his own, and mine! He was very jealous of de la Mare and had bought a pistol, with which he used to take pot-shots at a photograph of de la Mare's on the upper landing of his house. But I liked de la Mare, too, for his gentleness, and the hard work he obviously put into his poems – I was always interested in the writing-technique of my fellow-poets. I once asked whether he had not worried for hours over the lines:

> *Ah, no man knows*
> *Through what wild centuries*
> *Roves back the rose . . .*

and, in the end, been dissatisfied. De la Mare ruefully admitted that he was forced to leave the assonance 'Roves and rose', because no synonym for 'roves' seemed strong enough. In 1925, I agreed to collaborate with T. S. Eliot, then a harassed bank clerk, in a book about modern poetry to which we would each contribute essays, but the plan fell through.

I seldom saw Osbert and Sacheverell Sitwell now. When I did, I always felt uncomfortably rustic in their society. One autumn, Osbert sent me a present of a brace of grouse. They came from

Renishaw, the Derbyshire family seat, in a bag labelled: 'With Captain Sitwell's compliment to Captain Graves.' Nancy and I could neither of us face the task of plucking and gutting and roasting the birds, so we gave them to a neighbour. I wrote to Osbert: 'Captain Graves acknowledges with thanks Captain Sitwell's gift of Captain Grouse.' But we made friends with his sister Edith. It was a surprise, after reading her wild *avant garde* poems, to find her gentle, domesticated, and even devout. When she came to stay with us she spent her time sitting on the sofa and hemming handkerchiefs. She used to write to Nancy and me frequently, but our friendship ended in 1926.

I met none of my surviving army friends, with the very occasional exception of Siegfried. Edmund Blunden had gone as Professor of English Literature to Tokyo. Lawrence enlisted in the R.A.F. as soon as the Middle Eastern settlement went through, but a Labour member gave notice of a question in the House about his presence there under an assumed name, and the Air Ministry dismissed him. He was now a private in the Royal Tank Corps and hating it. When Sir Walter Raleigh died, I felt my connexion with Oxford University broken; and when Rivers died, and George Mallory on Everest, the death of my friends seemed to be following me in peacetime as relentlessly as in war.

A feeling of ill luck clouded these years. Islip had ceased to be a country refuge. I found myself resorting to the wartime technique of getting through things somehow, anyhow, in the hope that they would mend. Nancy's poor health led her to do less and less work. Our finances were improved by an allowance from her father that covered the extra expense of the new children – we now had two hundred pounds a year – but cottage life with four of them under six years old, and Nancy ill, showed signs of palling. I might have, after all, had to violate my oath and take a teaching job. But for that I needed a degree; so I completed my thesis, which I published as *Poetic Unreason*, and handed it in, already printed, to the examining board. To my surprise, they accepted it, and now I had my B.Litt.'s degree. However, I did not want a preparatory or secondary school job, which would keep me away from home all day; Nancy could not bear having anyone else but myself and her taking care of the children. There seemed no solution to my problem.

Then the doctor told us that if Nancy wished to regain her health she must spend the winter in Egypt. Thus, the only appointment that could possibly meet the case would be an independent teaching job in Egypt, at a very high salary, and with little work to do. A week or two later (this is how things have always happened in emergencies) I was invited to offer myself as a candidate for the post of Professor of English Literature at the newly-founded Royal Egyptian University, Cairo. I had been recommended, I found out afterwards, by two or three influential men, among them Arnold Bennett, always a good friend to me, and the first critic who spoke out strongly for my poems in the daily Press; and Lawrence, who had known Lord Lloyd, then High Commissioner of Egypt, during the Arab Revolt. The salary, including the passage money, amounted to fourteen hundred pounds a year. I fortified these recommendations with others: from my neighbour, Colonel John Buchan, and from Mr Asquith, now the Earl of Oxford, who had taken a fatherly interest in me and often visited our cottage at Islip.

I got the appointment. The indirect proceeds from poem-writing can be enormously higher than the direct ones.

31

So, second-class, by P. & O. to Egypt, with a nurse for the children, new clothes in the new cabin-trunks, and a Morris-Oxford in the hold. Lawrence had written to me:

Egypt, being so near Europe, is not a savage country. The Egyptians ... you need not dwell among. Indeed, it will be a miracle if an Englishman can get to know them. The bureaucrat society is exclusive, and lives smilingly unaware of the people. Partly because so many foreigners come there for pleasure, in the winter; and the other women, who live there, must be butterflies too, if they would consort with the visitors.

I thought the salary attractive. It has just been raised. The work may be interesting, or may be terrible, according to whether you get keen on it, like [Lafcadio] Hearn, or hate it, like [Robert] Nichols. Even if you hate it, there will be no harm done. The climate is good, the country beautiful, the things admirable, the beings curious and disgusting; and you are stable enough not to be caught broadside by a mere dislike for your job. Execute it decently, as long as you draw the pay, and enjoy your free hours (plentiful in Egypt) more freely. Lloyd will be a good friend.

Roam about – Palestine. The Sahara oases. The Red Sea province. Sinai (a jolly desert). The Delta Swamps. Wilfred Jennings Bramly's buildings in the Western Desert. The divine mosque architecture of Cairo town.

Yet, possibly, you will not dislike the job. I think the coin spins evenly. The harm to you is little, for the family will benefit by a stay in the warm (Cairo isn't warm, in winter) and the job won't drive you into frantic excesses of rage. And the money will be useful. You should save a good bit of your pay after the expense of the first six months. I recommend the iced coffee at Groppi's.

And so, my blessing.

My elder brother Dick, and my elder sister Mollie, had both been living in Egypt since I was a little boy. Dick, a leading Government official (at a salary less than my own), and his wife viewed my arrival with justifiable alarm. They knew of my political opinions. But Mollie, to whom I was devoted, had no suspicions and wrote a letter of most affectionate welcome.

Siegfried came to see me off. 'Do you know who's on board?' he asked. '"The Twisted Image"! He's still in the regiment, going out to join the First Battalion in India. Last time I saw him, he was sitting in the bottom of a dug-out, gnawing a chunk of bully-beef like a rat.' The Twisted Image – his nickname referred to the Biblical proposition that we are all created in the image of our Maker – went to Copthorne school with me and won a scholarship at the same time as I did; we served at Wrexham and Liverpool together; he also was wounded with the Second Battalion at High Wood; and now we were travelling East together. We had absolutely nothing in common, even mutual dislike; so I saw no natural reason why we should have been thrown so often in each other's company.

The ship touched at Gibraltar, where we disembarked, bought figs, and rode round the town; I remembered the cancelled War Office telegram and thought what a fool I had been to prefer Rhyl. Luckily, a P. & O. director, who happened to be aboard, persuaded the captain to take the ship within half a mile of Stromboli, then in eruption; by dusk in a hailstorm, with the lava hissing into the sea. At Port Said, a friend of my sister's helped us through the Customs; I still felt sea-sick, but knew that I was in the East because he began talking about Kipling and Kipling's 'wattles of Lichtenburg', and whether they were really wattles or some allied plant. Then on to Cairo, looking out of the windows all the way, delighted at summer fields in January.

My sister-in-law advised us against the more exclusive residential suburb of Gizereh, where she lived, so with her assistance we rented a flat at Heliopolis, a few miles east of Cairo. We found the cost of living very high, this being the tourist season, but reduced the grocery bill by taking advantage of the more reasonable prices at the British Army Canteen, where I presented myself as an officer on the Pension List. Our two Sudanese servants, contrary to all warnings about the natives, were temperate, punctual, respectful, and never, to my knowledge, stole a thing beyond the remains of a single joint of mutton. It seemed queer, no longer looking after the children, or doing housework; and wonderful to have as much time as I needed for my work.

The University was founded by King Fuad, who wished to be known as a patron of the arts and sciences. The Cairo University before this one had been nationalistic in its policy and, because not staffed with European experts, or supported by the Government, soon came to an end. King Fuad's University began ambitiously: Faculties of Science, Medicine, and Letters, and a full complement of highly-paid professors, few of them Egyptians. The Medicine and Science faculties were predominantly English, but the appointments to the Faculty of Letters had been made in the previous summer, when the British High Commissioner went on holiday; else he would no doubt have discountenanced them, as being predominantly French and Belgian. Only one of my colleagues could speak English, and none had any knowledge of Arabic; yet of the two hundred Egyptian students, mostly sons of rich merchants and landowners, fewer than twenty knew more than a smattering of French – just enough for shopping purposes in the elegant stores – though every one of them had learned English in the secondary schools. All official University correspondence was conducted in classical Arabic, which admits no word of later date than Mohammed's time – not that I should have noticed any neologisms myself. The 'very learned Sheikh' Graves, as I was there described, used to take his hand-outs to the post office for interpretation. My twelve or thirteen French colleagues were men of the highest academic distinction, but two or three English village-schoolmasters would have gladly undertaken their work at one-third of their salaries, and done it far better. The University building, a former harem-palace of the Khedive, was built in luscious French style with mirrors and gilding.

British officials at the Ministry of Education begged me to keep the British flag flying in the Faculty of Letters. I assented. Though I had not come to Egypt as an ambassador of Empire, it irked me to let the French indulge in semi-political activities at my expense. The Dean, M. Grégoire, was an authority on Slav poetry: tough, witty, and capable. He had acquired a certain slyness and adaptability during the war when, as a Belgian civilian in the German occupation, he edited an underground publication. The one-legged Professor of French Literature, a war hero, patronized me at first. I was his young friend, rather than his dear colleague. But when he learned that I also had bled in the cause of civilization and France, I became his most esteemed chum.

The Frenchmen lectured with the help of Arabic interpreters, which made neither for speed nor for accuracy. I should have delivered two lectures a week. The Dean, however, soon decided that if the students were ever to dispense with the interpreters, they must be given special instruction in French – and this reduced the time for lectures, so that he could allow me only one a week. That one was pandemonium. The students were not hostile, merely excitable and anxious to show their regard for me and liberty and Zaghlul Pasha and the well-being of Egypt – all at the same time. They obliged me to shout at the top of my loudest barrack-square voice, which I had learned to pitch high for greater carrying-power, in order to restore silence.

No text-books of any sort were available, the University Library having no English department; and it took months to get books through the French librarian. This was January, and the students faced an examination in May. They professed themselves anxious to master Shakespeare, Wordsworth, and Byron in that time. I had no desire to teach Wordsworth and Byron to anyone, and wished to protect Shakespeare from them. Deciding to lecture on the most rudimentary forms of literature possible, I chose the primitive ballad and its development into epic and the drama. I might at least, perhaps, teach them the meaning of the simpler literary terms. But though they had taken English for eight years or so in the schools, I could not count on their understanding half what I told them. Nobody, for instance, when I spoke of a ballad-maker singing to his harp, knew what a harp looked like. I told them that it was what King David played upon, and drew a picture on the blackboard; at which they shouted: 'Oh, *anur*!' I had myself seen a communal ballad-group in action at the hind legs of the Sphinx, while a gang of fellaheen cleared away the sand; one of the gang acted as chantey-man to keep the others moving. But my students thought it beneath their dignity to admit the existence of ballads in Egypt. The fellaheen did not exist, in their eyes, except as lazy and rather disgusting ani-mals. Printed notes of my lectures, with which to prepare for the examinations, were much in demand. I asked the clerical staff of the faculty to duplicate some of them, but they were kept too busy by the French professors and in spite of promises never got the job done. My lectures soon degenerated into lecture-notes for lectures that could not be given – but, at any rate, I kept the students busy scrib-bling in their note-books.

My wide trousers, the first 'Oxford bags' to reach Egypt, interested them profoundly; their own being still the peg-top sort, narrow at the ankles. Soon everyone who was anyone wore Oxford bags. One evening the Rector of the University asked me to dinner; two of my students, sons of Ministers, happened also to be invited. For fun, I was wearing white silk socks with my evening dress. Afterwards I heard from the Vice Rector, Ali Bey Omar, whom I liked best of the University officials, that a day or two later he had seen the same students wearing white silk socks at a Government banquet. When they looked round on the distinguished assembly, they found they they were so far in advance of fashion as to be the only white socks present. Ali Bey Omar gave a pantomime account of how, in embarrassment, they tried to loosen their braces surreptitiously and stroke down their trousers.

For some weeks I missed even my single weekly lecture, because the students went on strike. This was Ramadan, when they had to fast for a month between sunrise and sunset. Between sunset and sunrise they ate rather more than usual, to make up: a tax on the digestive processes which affected their nerves. The pretext for strik-ing was the intensive French instruction; but really they wanted leisure to cram for the examination at home. Then the blind Pro-fessor of Arabic, one of the few Egyptians with fame as an orientalist, published a book calling attention to pre-Islamic sources of the Koran. His lectures demanded greater mental effort than any of the rest, so when the examinations were held, most students absented them-selves from the Arabic paper on religious grounds. To an orthodox Moslem the Koran, since dictated by God to Mohammed, could have no pre-Islamic sources.

I came to know only two of my students fairly well: a Greek and a Turk. The Turk was rich, intelligent, good-natured, perhaps twenty years old, and twice took me for a drive to the pyramids in his motor-car. He spoke both French and English fluently, being almost the only student (except for twelve who had attended a French Jesuit college) with this facility. He apologized one day for having to miss my lecture: he was about to be married. I asked whether this would be the first or second part of the ceremony. He said: 'The first. I will not be allowed to see my wife's face, because her family is orthodox; that must wait until the second ceremony.' But his sister, he explained, had been at school with the girl and told him that she was pretty and a good sort; also, his father respected her father. When the second ceremony took place, he confessed to perfect satisfaction. I learned that the bridegroom seldom refused the bride when she lifted her veil, though he had the right to do so; and she had a similar right. Usually, the couple contrived to meet before even the first ceremony. The girl would slip the man a note saying: 'I shall be at Maison Cicurel by the hat-counter about three-thirty tomorrow afternoon, if you want to know what I look like. It will be quite in order for me to lift my veil as I try on a hat. You can recognize me by my purple parasol.'

I inquired about the rights of Moslem women in Egypt. Apparently divorce was simple. The man had only to declare in the presence of a witness: 'I divorce you, I divorce you, I divorce you,' and that did it. On the other hand, she could recover her original dowry, plus the interest accrued on it during her married life. Dowries were always heavy and divorces comparatively rare. The gentry considered it very low-class to keep more than one wife, unless she behaved so badly that the husband decided to shame her by taking another. I heard of an Egyptian who got angry with his wife one morning because the breakfast-coffee came in cold. He shouted: 'I divorce you, I divorce you, I divorce you!'

'Oh, my dear,' she exclaimed, 'now you've done it! The servants heard what you said. I must go back to my father with my ten thousand pounds and my sixty camels.'

He apologized for his hasty temper. 'Light of my eyes, we must get re-married as soon as possible.'

She reminded him that the Law prevented them from marrying again unless another marriage had intervened.

So he called in the aged man who watered the lawn and ordered him to marry her; but it must be a marriage of form only. The obedient gardener did as he was told and, immediately after the ceremony, returned to his watering-pot.

Two days later the woman got run over by a taxi, so the gardener inherited the money and the camels.

The Greek invited me to tea once. He had three beautiful sisters named Pallas, Aphrodite, and Artemis, who gave me tea in their garden, with European cakes that they had learned to make at the American College. Next door, a pale-faced man stood on a third-floor balcony addressing the world. I asked Pallas what his speech was about. 'Oh,' she laughed, 'don't mind him. He's a mad millionaire, so the police leave him alone. He lived ten years in England. He's saying now that they're burning him up with electricity, and telling the birds all his troubles. Also that his secretary accuses him of stealing five piastres, but it isn't true ... And that there can't be a God because God wouldn't allow the English to steal the fellaheen's camels for the war and not return them ... Now he's saying that all religions are very much the same, and that Buddha is as good as Mohammed. Really, he's quite mad. He keeps a little dog in his house, actually in his very room, plays with it and talks to it as though it were a human being!'

Pallas told me that in another twenty years the women of Egypt would control everything. The feminist movement had just started, and since the woman were by far the most active and intelligent part of the population, great changes might be expected. Neither she nor her sisters would stand her father's attempt to keep them in their places. Her brother, who was doing the literature course as a preliminary to law, showed me his library. Besides his legal textbooks he had Voltaire, Rousseau, a number of saucy French novels in paper covers, Shakespeare's works, and Samuel Smiles' *Self Help*. When he asked my advice about his career, I suggested a European university – a literary degree at Cairo would be worth little, unless he wanted to take up politics.

I had not realized before just how much the British controlled Egypt. Egypt ranked as an independent kingdom, but it seemed that I owed my principal allegiance not to King Fuad, who had given me my appointment and paid my salary, but to the High Commissioner, whose infantry, cavalry, and air squadrons were a constant reminder of his power. British officials could not understand the Egyptians' desire for independence, considering them most ungrateful for all the beneficent labour and skill applied to their country since the eighties – raising it from bankruptcy to riches. There was no Egyptian nation, I was assured. The Greeks, Turks, Syrians, and Armenians who called themselves Egyptians had no more right there than the British. Before the British occupation the Pashas used to bleed the fellaheen white; and it was not the fellaheen, the only true Egyptians, who now called for freedom. Nationalism, a creed derived from the new smatterings of Western education we were giving the upper classes, should be disregarded as merely a symptom of the country's growing wealth. The reduction of the British official class in the last few years was viewed with disgust. 'We did all the hard work, and when we go everything will run down; it's running down already. And they'll have to call us back, or if not, the dagoes; and we don't see why *they* should benefit.' None of them realized how much the vanity of the Egyptians – probably the vainest people in world – was hurt by the constant sight of British uniform. On the other hand, I could not suppose that the morale of the Egyptian soldier would be very high in time of war; having seen one of their officers, incensed by the negligence of a sentry, pull open the man's mouth and spit into it.

Egypt had come to consider itself a European nation, but at the same time attempted to supplant Turkey as the leading power of Islam. This led to many anomalies. On the same day that my students staged their protest against the Professor of Arabic's irreligious views, the students of El Azhar, the great Cairo theological college, refused to wear the prescribed Arab dress of kaftan and silk head-dress and appeared in European clothes and tarbouche. The tarbouche was the national hat which even British officials wore. I myself owned one. It would have been difficult to find a hat more unsuitable for the climate. Being red, it attracted the heat of the sun, got very stuffy inside, and had no brim to protect the neck against sunstroke.

My brother Dick behaved beautifully to me, as he has always done; and so did my romantic sister Mollie, who is a water-diviner and, by my advice, always wears a beauty-patch on her right cheek-bone. Her adoring husband, Judge Preston of the Mixed Courts, found himself greatly embarrassed at the Turf Club – which I refused to join for fear of involving Nancy in social calls from the wives of British officials – when she claimed that her son Martin (who closely resembled him in features) was a parthenogenous birth. One day, Mollie asked me about my confirmation; I told her that the Bishop of Zululand performed the ceremony, and she gave me a rapturous hug. 'Darling,' she said, 'I *knew* we had lots in common! *I* was confirmed by the Bishop of Zanzibar!'

32

I DID two useful pieces of educational work in Egypt. I ordered a consignment of standard text-books of English Literature for the Faculty Library at the University, and I acted as examiner to the diploma class of the Higher Training College which provided English teachers for the primary and secondary schools. I have kept three diploma essays as a memento – the first by one Mahmoud Mohammed Mahmoud:

Environment as a Factor in Evolution

This is the story of evolutions. Once it was thought that the earth's crust was caused by catastrophes, but when Darwin came into the world and had a good deal of philosophy, he said: 'All different kinds of species differ gradually as we go backwards and there is no catastrophes, and if we apply the fact upon previous predecessors we reach simpler and simpler predecessors, until we reach the Nature.' Man, also, is under the evolutions. None can deny this if he could deny the sun in daylight. A child from the beginning of his birthday possesses instincts like to suckle his food from the mamel of his mother and many others. But he is free of habits and he is weak as anything. Then he is introduced into a house and usually finds himself among parents, and his body is either cleansed or left to the dirts. This shows his environment. Superficial thinkers are apt to look on environment as (at best) a trifle motive in bringing up, but learned men believe that a child born in the presence of some women who say a bad word, this word, as believed by them, remains in the brain of the child until it ejects.

Environment quickly supplies modification. The life of mountainous goats leads them to train themselves on jumping. The camel is flat-footed with hoofs for the sand. Some kind of cattle were wild in the past but lived in plain lands and changed into gentle sheep. The frog when young has her tail and nostrils like a fish, suitable for life at sea, but changing her environment, the tail decreased. The sea is broad and changeable, so those who live at sea are changeable and mysterious. Put a cow in a dirty damp place and she will become more and more slender until she die. Also horses; horse had five fingers on his legs but now one only from running for water in the draught. Climate also affects bodily habits of the dear Europeans who live in Egypt. They who were smart and patient and strong with a skin worth the name of weather-proof became also fatigable and fond of leisure . . . From the theory we learn that human beings should be improved like the beasts by creating healthy youngs and by good Freubel education.

The next essay is one written by Mohammed Mahmoud Mohammed:

The Character of Lady Macbeth

Sir, to write shortly, Lady Macbeth was brave and venturesome; but she had no tact. She says to Macbeth: 'Now the opportunity creates itself, lose it not. Where is your manlihood in these suitable circumstances? I have children and I know the love of a mother's heart. But you must know I would dash the child's head and drive away the boneless teeth which are milking me rather than to give a promise and then leave it.'

Macbeth says: 'But we may fail.'

'Fail?' says L.M. 'But stick to the point and we will not fail. Leave the rest to me. I shall put drugs in the grooms' drink and we shall ascuse them.'

Macbeth says: 'You are fit to lay men-children only.'

The impression on the reader becomes very great and feels with anger.

The last essay is by one Mahmoud Mahmoud Mohammed:

The Best Use of Leisure Time

Leisure time is a variety to tireful affairs. God Almighty created the Universe in six days and took a rest in the seventh. He wished to teach us the necessity of leisure time. Man soon discovered by experience that 'All work and no play makes Jack a dull boy'. But this leisure time may be dangerous and ill-used if the mind will not take its handle and move it wisely to different directions. Many people love idleness. It is a great prodigality which leads to ruin. Many Egyptians spend their times in cafés longing for women and tracking them with their eyes, which corrupts and pollutes manners. They are perplexed and annoyed by the length of daytime. Others try to rest through gumbling, which is the scourge of society and individual. But let *us* rather enjoy external nature, the beautiful leavy trees, the flourishing fields, and the vast lawns of green grass starred with myriad of flowers of greater or small size. There the birds sing and build their nests, the meandering canals flow with fresh water, and the happy peasants, toiling afar from the multitude of town life, purify the human wishes from personal stain. Also museums are instructive. It is quite wrong to keep to usual work and fatigable studies, but quite right to free our minds from the web of worldly affairs in which they are entangled.

Yes, let us with the lark leave our beds to enjoy the cool breeze before sunrise. Let us when the lasy or luxurious are snoring or sunk in their debaucheries sit under the shady trees and meditate. We can think of God, the river and the moon, and enjoy the reading of Gray's *Elegy* to perfection. We shall brush the dues on the lawn at sunrise, for,

> *A country life is sweat*
> *In moderate cold and heat.*

Or we may read the Best Companions, books full of honourable passions, wise moral and good pathos; reading maketh a full man, nobody will deny Bacon. Or we may easily get a musical instrument at little price, 'Every schoolboy knows' that music is a moral law which gives a soul to the universe. Criminals can be cured by the sweet power of music. The whale came up from the dark depths of the sea to carry the Greek musician because it was affected by the sweet harmonies which hold a mirror up to nature. Are we not better than the whale? Also gymnastic clubs are spread everywhere. Why do a youth not pass his leisure time in widdening his chest? Because a sound mind is in a sound body. Yet it is a physiological fact that the blacksmith cannot spend his leisure time in striking iron or the soldier in military exercises. The blacksmith may go to see the Egyptian Exhibition and the soldier may go to the sea to practise swimming or to the mountains to know its caves in order that he may take shelter from a fierce enemy in time of war.

Milton knew the best uses of leisure time. He used to sit to his books reading, and to his music playing, and so put his name among the immortals. That was the case of Byron, Napoleon, Addison, and Palmerstone. And if a man is unhappy, says an ancient philosopher, it is his own fault. He *can* be happy if his leisure time brings profit and not disgrace.

I decided to resign. So did the Professor of Latin, my only English colleague. And the one-legged Professor of French Literature, who was an honest man. The others stayed on.

The Egyptians treated me hospitably. I attended one heavy banquet at the Semiramis Hotel, given by the Ministry of Education. Tall

Sudanese waiters dressed in red robes served a succession of the most magnificent dishes I had seen anywhere, even on the films. They included a great model of the Cairo Citadel in ice, its doors and windows filled with caviare – we used a golden Moorish spoon to scoop this out. Someone told me recently that this banquet, which must have cost thousands, has not yet been paid for. I found little to do in Egypt (not having Lawrence's appetite for desert travel) but eat coffee-ices at Groppi's, visit the open-air cinemas, and sit at home in our flat at Heliopolis and get on with writing. Mollie, who lived near, continued sisterly. During the season of the Khamsin, a hot wind that sent the temperature up on one occasion to 113 degrees in the shade, I put the finishing touches to a small book called *Lars Porsena, or The Future of Swearing and Improper Language*.

The best thing I saw in Egypt was the noble face of old Pharaoh Seti the Good, unwrapped of its mummy-cloths at the Cairo Museum. The funniest thing was a French bedroom-farce at a native theatre played in Arabic by Syrian actors. The men and women of the cast had, for religious reasons, to keep on opposite sides of the stage; they sang French songs (in translation), varying the tunes with the quarter-tones and shrieks and trills of their own music. The audience talked all the time and ate peanuts, oranges, sunflower-seeds, and heads of lettuces.

I went to call on Lord Lloyd at the end of May, just before the close of the academic year. Soon after, he invited me to dine at the Residency. I won twenty piastres off him at bridge and was told: 'Collect it from my A.D.C.'; but felt that a loser should decently dip into his own trouser pocket to pay card-debts, so let the money go. Lloyd believed in his job more than I did in mine. When he asked me how I found Egypt, I answered: 'All right,' with an intonation that made him catch me up quickly. 'Only all right?' Nothing more passed between us. He used to drive through Cairo, at about sixty miles an hour, in a powerful car with a Union Jack flying from it, and motor-cyclist outriders to clear the way; for Sir Lee Stack, the Sirdar, had been killed in the previous year while driving through the city, and a traffic jam had materially helped his assassins. One day a student showed me the spot near the Ministry of Education where it happened. At first I took the crowd gathered there for a party of political sight-seers, but the attraction proved to be a stark naked woman lying on the pavement, laughing wildly and waving her arms – one of the hashish dope-cases then very common in Egypt. The crowd was jeering at her; a policeman standing a few yards off paid no heed.

I attended a levée at the Abdin Palace, King Fuad's Cairo residence. It began at nine o'clock in the morning. The King gave honourable precedence to the University staff; we came in soon after the diplomatic corps and the Ministers of the Crown and some time before the army. While still in England, I had bought suitable clothes – a morning coat and trousers – for this occasion. To be really correct, my coat should have been faced with green silk, the national colour of Egypt, but I was told that this would not be insisted upon. Opinions differed greatly as to what constituted correct Court-dress. Most of the French professors arrived in full evening dress, with swallow-tail coats, white waistcoats, and opera hats; a few, ordinary dinner jackets. All wore decorations around their necks. They looked like stragglers from an all-night fancy-dress ball.

After signing my name in the two large hotel-registers, one belonging to the King and the other to the Queen, I drank a refreshing and horribly sweet rice-drink, by courtesy of the Queen, and mounted the noble marble staircase. On every second step stood an enormous Nubian soldier, royally uniformed, with a lance in his hand. My soldier's eye admired their physique, but deprecated their somewhat listless attitudes; still, no doubt, they pulled themselves smartly to attention as the Egyptian Army General Staff went past. My brother had warned me that, on meeting King Fuad, I must not be surprised at anything extraordinary I heard; a curious wheezing cry was apt to burst from his throat occasionally when he felt nervous. During his childhood, the family had been shot up by an assassin in the employ of interested relatives; but little Fuad took cover under a table and, though wounded, survived. We moved from room to room. At last, a quiet Turkish-looking gentleman of middle age, wearing regulation Court-dress, greeted us deferentially in French; I took him for the Grand Chamberlain. I bowed, said the same thing in French as the professor in front of me, and expected to be led along to the Throne Room. However, the next stage was the exit. I had already met King Fuad.

A few days later I attended a royal soirée – an Italian variety show. King Fuad had been educated in Italy, where he attained the rank of cavalry captain and learned a great regard for Italian culture. The performance belonged to the 1870s. A discreet blonde shepherdess did a hopping dance in ankle-length skirts, and a discreet tenor confined his passion to the top notes; and a well-behaved comedian made nice little jokes for the Queen. I clapped him, for having done his unsuccessful best to raise a laugh; but everybody glared round. An official whispered to me that, this being a command performance, the actors were entitled to no applause. Unless His Majesty professed himself amused, the turns must be greeted in silence. I wore Court-dress again but, not to be outdone by the Frenchmen, had put on my three campaigning medals – and regretted that I lost St Anne of the Third Class with the Crossed Swords. And those refreshments! I shall not attempt to describe the Arabian Nights buffet, so splendid that it has remained a mere blur in my memory. I pocketed some quite fantastic confections to bring home.

Our children had to drink boiled milk and boiled water, and be constantly watched in case they took off their solar topees and blue veils. Then they all got measles, so were carried off to an isolation hospital and fed on the things that we had been particular since their birth never to give them; and the native nurses stole their toys. They returned thin and wretched-looking – Sam, the baby, with per-manently scarred ear-drums – and we wondered if we should ever get them safely home to England. We booked our passages some time at the end of May, but even after selling the car had only just enough money left to go third-class on a small Italian boat with a cargo of onions. We disembarked at Venice and stopped a day. After Egypt, Venice seemed like Heaven. We ate European eggs there for breakfast. Egyptian eggs were about the size of a pigeon's egg and always tasted strongly of the garlic which seemed to form a large part of the Egyptian fowl's diet.

Egypt gave me plenty of caricature scenes to look back on. For instance: myself wearing a smart yellow gabardine suit and seated at a long, baize-covered table in the Faculty Conference Room. Before me a cup of Turkish coffee, a solar topee, and a badly typed French record of the minutes of the last meeting. I am talking angry bad French at my Belgian and French colleagues in support of the young Professor of Latin, who has just leaped to his feet, pale with hatred. He is declaring in worse French that he positively refuses to make a forced contribution of fifty piastres to a memorial wreath for one of the Frenchmen (who had just died), since he was never consulted. I am declaring that neither will I, and that, since the Dean has made a point of excluding us from the previous meetings where he took decisions affecting our lectures, all dead French Professors can go bury themselves at their own expense. It is a lofty, elegant room, once a harem boudoir. A portrait of the Khedive, with a large rent in it, hangs crookedly at one end; at the other stands a large glass show-case, full of Egypto-Roman bronze coins, muddled together, their labels loose, and the glass cracked. Through the window, market-gardens, buffaloes, camels loaded with green fodder, country-women in black. Around the table my horrified, shrugging colleagues, turning to one another and saying: '*Inoui . . . Inoui . . .*' And outside the rebellious shouts of our students, working themselves up for another strike.

The rest makes no more than conversation – of the Government clerk who was so doubly unfortunate as to be run over by a racing-car, and then recognize the driver as the eldest son of the Minister of Justice; and of the rich girl in search of a husband, who went as paying guest at fifteen guineas a week to a senior British official's wife, agreeing to pay for all wines and cigars and extras when society came to dine but who, meeting only senior Government officials and their wives, complained that she did not get her money's worth; and of my night visit to the temple of a headless monkey-god, full of bats; and of the English cotton-manufacturer who defended conditions in his factory on the ground that the population of Egypt had been increasing far too rapidly under British rule, and that pulmonary consumption remained one of the few checks on it; and of the lame student's mother who, at the sports, said how much she regretted having put him on the mantelpiece when a baby and run off (being only twelve years old), to play with her dolls; and of 'The Limit', so named by Australian soldiers, who told my fortune accurately in moonlight, under the long shadow of the Cheops pyramid; and of my visit to Chawki Bey, the national poet of Egypt, in his Moorish mansion by the Nile, who was so like Thomas Hardy, and in whose presence his sons, like good Turks, sat dutifully silent; and of the beggar in the bazaar with too many toes; and of the British colonel who, during the war, on a dream of dearth, had played Joseph, dumping half the wheat of Australia in Egypt, where it found no buyers and was at last eaten by donkeys and camels; and of a visit to ancient dead Heliopolis, with its lovely landscape of green fields, its crooked palm trees, its water-wheels turned by oxen, and its single obelisk; and of our life in the other Heliopolis, a brand-new dead town on the desert's edge, built by a Belgian company, complete with race-course and Luna Park, where the R.A.F. planes flew low at night among the houses, and where the bored wives of resentful officials wrote novels which they never finished, and painted a little in water colours; and of the little garden of our flat, where I went walking on the first day, among the fruit trees and flowering shrubs, but came upon no less than eight lean and mangy cats dozing in the beds, and never walked there again ...

So back to Islip; much to the disappointment of my parents, who hoped that I had at last seen reason and settled down in a position which equally suited my needs and my talents; and to the undisguised relief of my sister-in-law.

The remainder of this story, from 1926 until today, is dramatic but unpublishable. Health and money both improved, marriage wore thin. New characters appeared on the stage. Nancy and I said unforgivable things to each other. We parted on May 6th, 1929. She, of course, insisted on keeping the children. So I went abroad, resolved never to make England my home again; which explains the 'Goodbye to All That' of this title.

EPILOGUE

THOUGH often asked to publish a continuation of this autobiography, which I wrote in 1929 at the age of thirty-three, I am always glad to report that little of outstanding autobiographical interest has happened since. The proofs of *Goodbye to All That* reached me in Majorca, where I had gone to live as soon as I finished the writing, and which is still my home.

The one serious set-back to my quiet life here came with the Spanish Civil War in 1936, when all British subjects were advised to leave, by warship. I wandered around Europe and the United States for three years; and spent the Second World War in England, because three of my children had joined the Armed Forces – the fourth, Sam, being prevented by deafness from doing the same.

Jenny became a W.A.A.F. war-correspondent, entering Paris with General Le Clerc's tanks, and Brussels with General Adair's; and nearly getting killed at Arnhem. Catherine, a W.A.A.F. radio-operator, married Squadron-Leader Clifford Dalton, now Engineer-in-Chief to the Australian Atomic Energy Commission. David joined the First Royal Welch, who had lost very heavily during the defence of Calais, assisted at their famous reunion with the Second Battalion in Madagascar, and then went on with them to India and Burma. He was killed on the Arakan peninsula in March 1943, after going up with a sergeant and one man to bomb the Japanese out of three strong-points, which had held up the battalion's advance. They captured the first strong-point, and when his companions were wounded, David rushed the second single-handed; but was shot through the head trying to take the third. The War Office turned down his recommendation for a posthumous Victoria Cross on the ground that the attack had failed – an Indian battalion retired, the Japanese infiltrated, and what remained of the Royal Welch were forced to cut their way back.

I volunteered for infantry service as soon as war broke out, but when informed that His Majesty could not employ me except in a sedentary appointment, I returned to work – on a book about Sergeant Roger Lamb, who fought with the First Battalion in the American War of 1776–83; and on another about John Milton's behaviour in the English Civil Wars. To avoid getting bombed unnecessarily, I settled in South Devon. Half-way through the war, someone invited me to join the special constabulary, but our village policeman declined to forward my application. His reasons, as I found out by discreet inquiry, were that my German second name made him suspicious; that I had been heard talking a foreign language to two disreputable foreigners – Spanish refugee friends, as it happened, one a major, the other a staff-colonel; and that the words HEIL HITLER! had been found scratched on a vegetable marrow in my garden. So I continued merely as an Air Raid Warden, but took a stern line a few days later when my age-group got called up for medical examination and the policeman brought me a third-class railway-warrant, together with an order to appear before a medical board at Exeter. As an officer on the pensioned list, I refused to travel except first class, a privilege to which my rank entitled me – he and I might find ourselves in the same compartment, and it would never do for us two to mix socially. So far as I was concerned, the Red Lamp (to put it that way) still burned red, and the Blue Lamp still true blue.

Nancy and I eventually got divorced. I married again, have had four more children, enjoy good health, travel as little as possible, and continue to write books. What else can I say, unless that my best friend is still the waste-paper basket?

Though Charterhouse certainly has a very good name nowadays, and is even suggested as a worthy school for Prince Charles to attend, I do not send my boys there; on principle. The other day, however, I met 'Uncle Ralph' Vaughan-Williams, O.M., for the first time since 1912, and as we talked fondly of Max Beerbohm (who had been in the same form as Uncle Ralph at Charterhouse) we suddenly found ourselves singing the *Carmen Carthusianum* in unison, to the surprise of a crowded Palma restaurant. I felt a little surprised, too. And it certainly is strange to think that the best British caricaturist and essayist, and the best musician of my day, have also been products of that most Philistine school.

Goodbye to All That reads as ripe ancient history now, and I have so far passed the age when policemen begin to seem very young, that police-inspectors, generals, and admirals do the same. Many of the familiar names that swim up from the past have acquired novel senses. For instance, mischievous young Corporal Mike Pearson, whom I recommended for a commission from the Oxford Cadet Battalion in 1917, has become Mr Lester Pearson, Canada's most famous citizen. And, by the way, Malcolm Muggeridge, until recently editor of *Punch*, who succeeded me at Cairo University, tells me that Colonel Nasser was one of my pupils there. I should not be surprised.

Rural Majorca, too, with its five very moderate hotels, is now billed as Europe's most favourite holiday place: it boasts of ninety tourist planes flying in daily throughout the summer and a new first-class hotel completed every week. I can't pretend that I am pleased; and my children, the youngest of whom is four years old, look oddly at me when I tell them that I was born in the reign of Prince Charles's great-great-great-grandmother, before aeroplanes flew, when it was wicked for women to wear trousers or use lipstick, when practically nobody had electric light, and when a man with a red flag was required by law to walk in front of every motor-car. Yet I do not seem to have changed much, mentally or physically, since I came to live here, though I can no longer read a newspaper without glasses, or run upstairs three steps at a time, and have to watch my weight. And if condemned to relive those lost years I should probably behave again in very much the same way; a conditioning in the Protestant morality of the English governing classes, though qualified by mixed blood, a rebellious nature, and an overriding poetic obsession, is not easily outgrown.

READ MORE IN PENGUIN

In every corner of the world, on every subject under the sun, Penguin represents quality and variety – the very best in publishing today.

For complete information about books available from Penguin – including Puffins, Penguin Classics and Arkana – and how to order them, write to us at the appropriate address below. Please note that for copyright reasons the selection of books varies from country to country.

In the United Kingdom: Please write to *Dept. EP, Penguin Books Ltd, Bath Road, Harmondsworth, West Drayton, Middlesex UB7 0DA*

In the United States: Please write to *Consumer Sales, Penguin USA, P.O. Box 999, Dept. 17109, Bergenfield, New Jersey 07621-0120*. VISA and MasterCard holders call 1-800-253-6476 to order Penguin titles

In Canada: Please write to *Penguin Books Canada Ltd, 10 Alcorn Avenue, Suite 300, Toronto, Ontario M4V 3B2*

In Australia: Please write to *Penguin Books Australia Ltd, P.O. Box 257, Ringwood, Victoria 3134*

In New Zealand: Please write to *Penguin Books (NZ) Ltd, Private Bag 102902, North Shore Mail Centre, Auckland 10*

In India: Please write to *Penguin Books India Pvt Ltd, 706 Eros Apartments, 56 Nehru Place, New Delhi 110 019*

In the Netherlands: Please write to *Penguin Books Netherlands bv, Postbus 3507, NL-1001 AH Amsterdam*

In Germany: Please write to *Penguin Books Deutschland GmbH, Metzlerstrasse 26, 60594 Frankfurt am Main*

In Spain: Please write to *Penguin Books S. A., Bravo Murillo 19, 1° B, 28015 Madrid*

In Italy: Please write to *Penguin Italia s.r.l., Via Felice Casati 20, I–20124 Milano*

In France: Please write to *Penguin France S. A., 17 rue Lejeune, F–31000 Toulouse*

In Japan: Please write to *Penguin Books Japan, Ishikiribashi Building, 2–5–4, Suido, Bunkyo-ku, Tokyo 112*

In Greece: Please write to *Penguin Hellas Ltd, Dimocritou 3, GR–106 71 Athens*

In South Africa: Please write to *Longman Penguin Southern Africa (Pty) Ltd, Private Bag X08, Bertsham 2013*

BY THE SAME AUTHOR

Wife to Mr Milton

She was sixteen and doomed to a life-long passion for a Royalist captain. He was thirty-four, a poet and Puritan, obsessed by her long golden hair. Marie Powell married John Milton in payment of a debt. It was a mismatching of bitter ineptitude, for in temperament and convictions they were worlds apart. Their marriage is the focus of this superb novel.

Count Belisarius

The sixth century was not a peaceful one for the Roman Empire. Invaders threatened on all frontiers. But they grew to fear and respect the name of Belisarius, horseman, archer, swordsman and military commander of incredible skill and daring. Belisarius led the Imperial armies wherever the Emperor Justinian sent him; to the Eastern Frontier on the Euphrates, across the Mediterranean to Carthage, and to Rome.

In his palace at Constantinople, Justinian plotted and intrigued, dominated by his wife Theodora, whose spies were everywhere. Justinian hated Belisarius for his success, his nobility and his universal popularity. But Belisarius was the one man who could save the Empire . . .

Collected Short Stories

'My story is true . . . every word of it. Or when I say that my story is "true", I mean at least I am telling it in a new way . . .'

So begins 'The Shout', the tale of a man possessed by a lethal magic, perhaps Robert Graves's most famous story. This collection spans 1924–62; it takes in the worlds of love and war, history and myth, and settings as various as England, Ancient Rome and Majorca. In so far as its author asserts the truth of his stories, they can be read as episodes of autobiography, this collection forming an essential companion to *Goodbye to All That*.

BY THE SAME AUTHOR

I, Claudius

Robert Graves's magnificent reconstruction of the grandeur and folly and vileness of early Imperial Rome is one of the most distinguished historical novels of this generation. Its setting varies from a Roman palace to a desert in Tripoli, a dark German forest, a garden at Pompeii, a camp in the Balkans, the Sibyl's cavern at Cumae, and a cliff-top on the island of Rhodes. The action is strange, tragic, and ludicrous, for Rome knows herself under a long-standing curse – the curse of the gods with whom she broke faith when she destroyed Carthage – and lost all moral self-control. Treachery, incest, black magic, and unnatural vice flourish. Insane cruelties are committed. And through it all moves the strange, lovable figure of Claudius himself, despised, neglected, and apparently ineffective, but destined in the end to become Emperor against his will.

Claudius the God

The hairy fifth to enslave the State,
Shall be that idiot whom all despised.

So ran the Sibylline prophecy which Claudius found among the private papers of Augustus, and he could not fail to recognize in this description of the last great Caesar but one, himself, the paralytic idiot 'Clau-Clau-Claudius', as he was derisively nicknamed. In this book he continues his historical memoirs, bringing the story from his own acclamation as Emperor at the death of his terrible nephew, Caligula, to his assassination in the year 54. Like its forerunner, *Claudius the God* presents an astonishing picture of the grandeur and degeneracy of first-century Rome. But Claudius himself, quite as much as his age, comes to life in these pages – Claudius, who survived the violent reigns of four earlier Caesars, who remained Emperor for fourteen years, and who yet was thought by his contemporaries to be a fool.

BY THE SAME AUTHOR

Selected Poems

The power of Robert Graves's poetry lies in the tension – almost a contradiction – between the 'practical impossibility' and the transcendent 'miracle' of absolute love continuing between a man and a woman.

Surrounding this central theme is a rich mythology in which the White Goddess (the Muse who inspires the poet when in love) plays an essential role. So also do fear, fantasy, the supernatural and the grotesque. This brilliant alchemy of inspiration, realism and truth established Graves as one of the finest love poets of the century. In this poetry of personal relationships Graves is an undisputed master. This collection of poems was compiled by Paul O'Prey with the author's approval.

'A great and notably independent lyric poet' – Philip Toynbee in the *Observer*

The Greek Myths
(*in two volumes*)

The first modern dictionary of Greek Mythology, Robert Graves's *Greek Myths* covers in two volumes and nearly two hundred sections the Creation myths, the legends of the birth and lives of the great Olympians, the Theseus, Oedipus, and Heracles cycles, the Argonaut voyage, the tale of Troy, and much else.

All the scattered elements of each myth have been assembled into a harmonious narrative, and many variants are recorded which may help to determine its ritual or historical meaning. Full references to the classical sources, and copious indexes, make the book as valuable to the scholar as to the general reader; and a full commentary to each myth explains and interprets the classical version in the light of today's archaeological and anthropological knowledge.